Architectural Alchemy

AI's Role in Enterprise Architecture

Benjamin Ketcherside

Published in The Woodlands, Texas by Paradisiacal Architecture Press

First edition

ISBN: 979-8-218-37784-7 (eBook) ISBN: 979-8-218-37780-9 (Paperback)

Library of Congress Control Number: 2024903891

To the figures of influence and inspiration in the field of enterprise architecture—the comrades, mentors, Laurent and Jerry: You have collectively enriched my mind and refined my thoughts. Your influences have seeped into the foundation of my understanding, forming an integral part of the intellectual mosaic I now possess.

To my extraordinary team at Microsoft: You have ignited the spark of innovation and challenged the boundaries of excellence within me. Each discussion, brainstorm, and challenge overcome with you have added to the scaffolding of my thought process, reinforcing my comprehension, and broadening my horizons.

And lastly, to my family: You are the rock upon which I build my strength and the wellspring from which I draw my resilience. Your belief in my potential and unwavering support have been the cornerstone of my endeavors, emboldening my spirit and nurturing my mind.

Without your invaluable contributions, I would not be who I am today and for that, I remain eternally grateful.

Contents

Introduction

Howdy, regarding this book it is important to firstly establish the overall purpose and expected key readership to provide context right from the start. This book aims to bridge the gap between the highly technical world of Artificial Intelligence, (AI), and the structured strategic planning of The Open Group Architecture Framework (TOGAF). It brings these two disciplines together for business leaders and enterprise architects who want to leverage AI to transform their organizations.

The core focus will be on educating readers on the integration of AI components into practical architecture development. Key areas covered will include: assessing suitability of AI applications; following ethical AI design practices; mapping AI capabilities to business motivators; incorporating AI into logical and physical architecture layers; and applying iterative agile planning for AI solutions. The intended outcome is equipping readers with knowledge, best practices, and methodologies to effectively evaluate, design, and implement transformative AI-based on TOGAF principles.

As the author of this book, my passion for this topic stems from over a decade of experience spanning across software development research, product management, and enterprise architecture. I have witnessed first-hand the powerful impact AI can bring to organizations when cultivated responsibly and tied closely to business objectives. However, I have also seen many empty promises around AI from technology vendors that don't understand company motivators. This fueled my interest in TOGAF and its outside-in approach beginning from business strategy.

My journey has evolved from focusing strictly on software development to appreciating the broader ecosystem required for AI success. I have increasingly spent more time collaborating with enterprise architects to ensure solutions I help craft are architected holistically—spanning data, software, infrastructure, and most importantly, people. The convergence of my hands-on software development background with TOGAF's comprehensive architectural view ultimately led me to write this book to enable more practitioners to build organizationally-optimized AI.

I aim to leverage both my technical and business architectural perspectives to provide readers an enriched viewpoint on intelligently leveraging AI technology, matched to enterprise needs and priorities. The book will distill out complex concepts into relatable guidance, share creative application examples, and help set organizations on a path to assimilate AI with reduced risk and amplified rewards. Please enjoy the journey!

Chapter One

A New Dawn in Enterprise Architecture

T he advent of artificial intelligence technologies has fundamentally transformed Enterprise Architecture, (EA), over the past decade. Enterprise architecture refers to the organizational blueprint that aligns information technology solutions and business vision. AI is revolutionizing enterprise architecture by infusing autonomous decision-making, predictive insights, process automation, conversational interfaces, and other intelligent capabilities into the core systems and workflows of organizations.

The integration of AI into enterprise architecture has steadily progressed in alignment with major advances in machine learning and other AI technologies. One landmark development was the emergence of machine learning algorithms that could rapidly analyze big data sets to produce valuable insights and patterns. This allowed enterprise architecture to leverage predictive analytics and data-driven decision making in a scalable way for the first time. Another breakthrough was the creation of chatbots and virtual assistants powered by natural language processing, enabling conversational AI agents to handle customer and employee inquiries previously addressed by humans.

Today, AI influences enterprise architecture via augmented analytics, intelligent workflows, Robotic Process Automation (RPA), knowledge graphs, and other innovations that are being embedded into how systems, data, and processes are designed and interconnected. Specific AI technologies having high impact include: machine learning, speech recognition, computer vision, predictive modeling, decision management systems, conversational platforms, and RPA. Enterprise architecture teams must architect the organization in a way that maximizes the business value of AI tools for functions like forecasting, personalization, anomaly detection, automation, and more.

The success of AI integration is measured through metrics related to efficiency, accuracy, cost reduction, risk mitigation, and revenue growth. Return on Investment, (ROI), is evaluated by comparing the costs of development, training, and maintenance of AI systems with their impact—such as percentage improvements in critical process metrics. Additional metrics analyze how much human effort and labor is eliminated through automation, and how much new insights are uncovered through advanced analytics powered by AI. Tracking these vital signs over time is crucial for enterprise architecture teams to maintain, govern, and enhance AI integrations across the organization.

Introduction to AI in Enterprise Architecture

Enterprise architecture refers to the organizational blueprints that align information technology solutions and systems with business processes and objectives. As artificial intelligence capabilities have matured in recent years, interest has grown rapidly in integrating AI into enterprise architecture frameworks and practices. But what exactly constitutes AI in this business context?

At its core, artificial intelligence refers to computer systems or software that can perform tasks that have historically required human cognition and decision-making abilities. This includes capabilities such as visual perception, speech recognition, language translation, data analytics, predictive modeling, automated planning and scheduling, machine learning, and more. The integration of these AI functionalities into enterprise architecture enables organizations to automate, enhance, and scale a vast array of business operations, analytics, and optimizations.

Exploring this further, architecting AI solutions demands careful coordination from initial strategy development to system deployment. Enterprise architects must align AI projects with clearly defined business goals, infrastructure requirements, data pipelines, governance protocols, and more, while collaborating across multiple teams. And as integrated AI systems become more prevalent, architectural frameworks must evolve to support crucial activities like monitoring data drift in machine learning models and retraining systems in response to changing real-world conditions.

In essence, enterprise architects are positioned at the intersection of business needs and AI technologies, responsible for bridging functional gaps and delivering high-value AI capabilities that accord with overarching enterprise architecture principles. Realizing the full promise of AI requires architectural thinking and planning at both the project implementation level as well as the broader, more strategic, organization-wide level. With a thoughtful, holistic approach, architects can enable seamless integration of artificial intelligence that drives automation, insight, efficiency, and competitive differentiation over both the short-term and the long run.

How AI Can Help Enterprise Architecture

Enterprise architecture frameworks provide a structured approach to designing and implementing an organization's overall information systems architecture. They establish principles, models, and standards to optimize business processes, data flows, system integrations, and technology implementations across the enterprise. Integrating AI into these frameworks enables organizations to inject intelligence, automation, and analytics into their architectures.

One valuable application is using AI for advanced analysis and visualization of enterprise architectures. AI algorithms can process architectural data to detect patterns, surface insights, model future state scenarios, highlight potential issues and risks, and provide visual dashboards to view dependencies and relationships across business capabilities, processes, applications, data, and infrastructure. Rather than rely solely on manual analysis, AI augments and enhances architectural analytics.

Another key capability AI facilitates is increased automation of routine governance, compliance, and documentation tasks within architecture frameworks. This includes automating policy and standard recommendations, compliance checks and audits, architectural documentation and reporting, and monitoring architecture configurations and changes. Automating these repetitive, low-value tasks enables architects to focus their efforts on high-value architecture optimization rather than administrative upkeep.

Additionally, AI opens up more intelligent architecture design decision-making. AI can conduct real-time assessments of architecture decisions using predictive modeling and recommendations tuned to the organization's specific objectives and constraints. This allows organizations to rigorously simulate architecture scenarios to determine optimal pathways and roadmaps. Rather than just intuition, rigorous AI analysis better informs architectural decisions and trade-offs.

Finally, integrating AI within architecture frameworks creates opportunities to realize self-optimizing, self-healing qualities that respond to changing business landscapes. Continuously applying AI to monitor, analyze, and adapt architectures enables more agile, resilient enterprise systems capable of optimizing themselves. This represents the ultimate vision for AI-powered enterprise architectures.

AI infusion in enterprise architecture spans enhanced analytics and modeling, increased automation, optimized decision-making, and self-optimizing architectures. As organizations advance their architectural maturity, integrating AI unlocks immense potential for more intelligent business systems.

For better understanding, we will explain some of the important use-cases that AI is going to revolutionize in enterprise architecture in the next section.

Data Management

The sheer volume of structured and unstructured data generated in modern enterprises is enormous. Everything from customer transactions, manufacturing sensor logs, market trends, climate readings, genomic databases, and more, create endless streams of digital information. Organizations that find ways to harness insights from these vast data sources can gain significant competitive advantages.

Fortunately, recent breakthroughs in artificial intelligence provide sophisticated techniques to process these swelling data volumes in manageable, actionable ways. Machine learning algorithms, in particular, can help automate the otherwise impossible task of analyzing such huge datasets, saving humans from this overwhelming burden.

Deep learning and neural networks are forms of advanced AI that can systematically mine through myriads of data types by detecting hidden patterns and correlations that would be impossible for people to manually perceive. These AI systems recognize signals within the noise at a very large scale. This enables data-driven projections, recommendations, and predictive modeling to enhance business decision making with facts instead of intuition alone across the enterprise.

For example, an AI-powered sales forecasting system can ingest e-commerce order feeds, inventory datasets, and external market growth data to optimize upcoming quarterly revenue projections company-wide. Or a predictive maintenance suite can monitor production equipment in factories using IoT, (Internet of Things), sensors and computer vision. It then prescribes tailored maintenance schedules for each machine to minimize disruptive downtime events.

When thoughtfully integrated, artificial intelligence has the power to transform organizations into highly data-driven operations, where information flows freely between systems to enhance every business function. Further, AI itself improves legacy data infrastructure behind the scenes by optimizing database maintenance, cloud migration planning, cost reduction, and backup resilience. This keeps data readily available for AI applications.

Rather than drowning under endless swathes of data, the savvy application of AI allows enterprises to properly harness these assets and surf towards higher profitability. What used to bury organizations can now buoy them to new heights.

Process Automation

Leveraging artificial intelligence to automate high-volume, repetitive, clerical and operational tasks can be a game-changer for enterprises today. By deploying software robots and machine learning tools to handle routines once done manually, organizations free up human employees to shift their efforts towards more meaningful, creative, and strategic work.

Automating repetitive workflows allows knowledgeable workers across departments to focus less on data-entry, analyzing purchases or sales figures, reviewing contracts and documents, compiling customer retention offers, and other tedious responsibilities that software can handle quickly and accurately. Instead, they can dedicate more mental energy to envisioning future product innovations that truly delight users, mentoring employees more holistically, or developing customer relationships more profoundly.

Enriching traditional roles by removing the most mundane aspects also directly improves employee satisfaction and retention. Staff equipped with automated workflows and intuitive data dashboards can prioritize higher-value analysis of customer needs, idealizing improvements, or guiding young talent. Rather than scripting piecemeal bots, advanced process automation suites continually monitor for friction points on the digital assembly line, identifying workflow inefficiencies in real-time for constant optimization.

With reliable AI powering more seamless operations behind the scenes, the overall organization functions smarter and faster. Both workers directly interfacing with automation and those focused on more creative efforts gain compounding productivity improvements and cost savings over time. By thoughtfully integrating human ingenuity and diligent AI together throughout an enterprise's activities, businesses can thrive amidst digital transformation.

Partnering human creativity with AI's tireless ability to handle high-volume tasks intelligently, via automation, enables work forces to become more inspired, empowered and fulfilled. Organizations can then achieve unprecedented digital agility and efficiency.

Decision Support

AI-driven data analytics, predictive modeling, and prescriptive recommendations are empowering real-time, tailored, decision-making across organizational operations. By continuously processing the latest quantitative inputs and qualitative patterns from diverse sources across an enterprise, AI systems can account for many complex, rapidly-changing variables in an instant. This allows leaders to leverage AI guidance to take well-informed actions quickly, outpacing competitors still relying solely on human intuition.

For example, an AI-enabled supply chain management platform can persistently track purchasing trends, pricing data, weather forecasts, regional transportation costs, production line capacities, and more, across global facilities. As new orders arrive, the system can suggest optimal sourcing, inventory allotments, shipping routes, and other parameters to fulfill orders profitably and efficiently. Supply chain managers can review the logic behind each AI-generated allocation scenario as well, enabling transparency and trust in its recommendations.

In talent recruitment, AI platforms help hiring managers evaluate applicant resumes, demonstrated skills, video interviews, and other attributes to determine best fits for open roles based on key performance indicators and success profiles. The algorithms learn over time to prioritize and rank the leadership qualities sought across the organization for consistent hiring. Providing tailored shortlists with explanatory rankings assists managers in making final people decisions.

With intuitive data visualizations accompanying its dynamic guidance, enterprise-level AI decision tools feel like trusted assistants rather than inscrutable black boxes. They earn confidence by continually learning on the job. Much like an experienced advisor counseling executives on long-term strategy, embedded AI decision support becomes a persistent guide for leaders seeking to act faster and smarter at each turn. The wisdom accrues with returns as the business matures. Ultimately, data-fluent AI provides the impartial second opinion needed to thrive in complexity and uncertainty.

Customer Experience

At the core of AI's ability to transform customer experiences is its capacity to apply sophisticated machine learning algorithms to large volumes of customer data. This includes analyzing account histories, purchase patterns, web activity, satisfaction ratings, and other engagement data points collected across channels over time. The insights derived from this analysis allow businesses to develop comprehensive, information-rich profiles of each individual customer.

Equipped with these granular customer profiles, companies can leverage AI to power real-time automation that is tailored to align with individual preferences and expectations. For example, AI can create customized product recommendations for email campaigns, website visits, and mobile apps that feel relevant to where that particular customer is in their buyer's journey. Chatbots can also reference individual records to handle common inquiries conversationally, like order status or guiding users through profile updates. By moving past the constraints of one-size-fits-all approaches, these kinds of tailored recommendations and services feel more helpful and satisfying to consumers.

Sophisticated customer data platforms enabled by AI also optimize key capabilities like customer segmentation, cross-channel campaign management, and multi-channel coordination. Ensuring consumers receive an intriguing offer via email that complements a coinciding SMS campaign, focused on their frequent purchase category, demonstrates the workflow mastery happening behind-the-scenes thanks to AI. And with appropriate consumer consent, this kind of tactical AI orchestration can deliver consistent omni-channel experiences that avoid excessive messaging fatigue.

The longer-term advantage of enterprise AI lies in its ability to continuously analyze customer interactions across channels over time to identify emerging needs and preferences. Instead of reacting to life changes, proactively reaching out to schedule HVAC system maintenance as summer heats up, or recommending bundled mobile, TV, and WiFi plans amid household shifts, demonstrates the valuable foresight possible. Such thoughtful, valuable touches build durable rapport by making customers feel genuinely cared for and understood at an individual level thanks to enterprise AI capabilities.

Innovation

Staying competitive in today's fast-changing business world requires companies to continually innovate and bring new ideas to market. Artificial intelligence, when focused on amplifying human capabilities, can become a key driver for ongoing innovation across entire product life cycles.

Even before product launch, AI analytics help by assessing market trends, buyer personas, and browsing habits to conceptualize new product ideas most likely to gain adoption and meet rising customer expectations. Algorithms can also scan patent databases or academic papers to uncover promising new material science breakthroughs, evaluating technical feasibility for engineering teams to refine further. In some cases, AI may even proactively suggest new features by analyzing what functionality has gone viral among user segments in the past.

Post-launch, sensors embedded in goods can feed user interaction data back to the company in real-time via internet connectivity. AI assessment of this qualitative feedback during beta testing and post-purchase helps iterate designs, personalization options, and educational materials to onboard customers and increase satisfaction. AI-enabled uptime monitoring can also continuously enhance functionality and reliability.

By continuously surveying the competitive landscape for emerging substitution threats and analyzing the voice of the customer through lifecycle data, AI gives organizations the external awareness and internal coordination essential to allocate R&D resources wisely. Intelligent automation also grants extra cycles for developers and researchers to brainstorm creatively, leading to AI-inspired innovation that balances data with human imagination and judgment.

In the end, leveraging AI's creative abilities in step with human needs drives faster innovation cycles, allowing companies to keep pace with accelerating technology shifts and demands for sustainability. The combination of data-driven AI and human-centered design sustains progress.

What Next?

Successfully incorporating artificial intelligence capabilities into the complex digital infrastructure of an enterprise requires substantial commitment and a thoughtful, strategic approach from organizational leadership. Rather than just chasing AI trends, management needs to clearly define goals, honestly assess current capabilities, and make decisions on AI integration based on what will best achieve the target outcomes.

Therefore, enterprise architects aiming to adopt AI have an immense responsibility to deeply educate themselves on the rapid advances and latest innovations within the AI field. Architects must become fluent in how promising technologies like machine learning, neural networks, and natural language processing can be carefully woven into legacy systems and data flows to optimize processes versus drastically disrupting operations. The architect serves as the master integrator—bridging the gap between IT infrastructure and business goals.

This is no small feat in such a complex, evolving landscape. It takes considerable resources and dedication. This book provides enterprise architects a guiding light. Through insightful expert perspectives, real-world examples, and looking at missteps to avoid, architects can feel empowered in leading AI adoption. Each progressive chapter delves deeper into the components of AI, from foundational models to leading practices on integrating AI enterprise-wide.

Architects completing this book discover a wealth of pragmatic knowledge in enterprise AI application, along with proven frameworks to align initiatives to organizational maturity and objectives. Rather than getting lost in abstract AI concepts or the engineering details, readers gain the big picture understanding and actionable blueprint required to actively support through every step of the AI journey. Equipped with this knowledge, architects minimize disruption and feel confident in unlocking AI's immense opportunities.

The Evolution of Enterprise Architecture With AI

Realizing the profound benefits of artificial intelligence requires patience and a commitment to adoption over a time frame of years rather than just months. AI pioneers across various major industries who take an adaptive long-term view are seeing enormous rewards compounding in areas like efficiency improvements, accurate forecasts and predictions, and hyper-personalization capabilities.

By closely examining long-term real-world use case trajectories at leading enterprises, clear patterns emerge for embedding enduring and valuable machine learning. A decade ago, early retail AI applications had a narrow focus on optimizing bids for online website advertising based on visitor clicks. However, today's omni-channel fashion leaders like Zara deploy advanced computer vision algorithms that have been trained on millions of store images to automatically tag displayed products within new merchandise photographs. This in turn powers lightning-fast product searches encompassing millions of SKUs for online customers, while simultaneously boosting automation in warehouses.

The financial services sector shows a similar AI progression. Initially, AI simply scored customer credit risk probabilities at banks. However, forward-thinking institutions now leverage conversational chatbots, deep learning for fraud detection, and automated wealth advisory services to attract and protect client assets under management. Gradually expanding AI access to more internal datasets over successive projects has allowed AI talents to proliferate and personalize useful offerings.

And across healthcare systems, early AI pilots concentrated narrowly on classifying skin cancer using dermatology image data. But after proving meaningful accuracy and efficiency gains, scalable cloud infrastructure now enables hospital-wide AI adoption to drive gains in numerous domains—including optimizing surgery schedules with natural language processing and utilizing robotics to fill pharmacy orders. These virtuous cycles do take time to mature.

But early incremental AI successes build essential momentum and trust in demonstrating genuine enterprise value. With sustained data, talent, and integration investments compounding benefits over years, maturing AI capabilities can ultimately transform customer and employee experiences at vast new scales.

Let us take a look at two of the most popular companies that have used AI within their enterprise architecture to help their brand become more popular.

IBM Watson

IBM Watson first emerged in healthcare by aiding physician-diagnostic accuracy for cancer treatment plans. Watson could provide surface insights from vast arrays of medical journals that were beyond an individual practitioner's retention. Now, Watson's capabilities have greatly expanded through combining analysis of radiology images, genomics datasets, and even drug trial research papers. This allows Watson to uncover personalized therapies for precision medicine and new pharmaceutical discoveries.

In the financial services sector, Watson tools began by improving call center assistant abilities before progressing to more advanced applications like fraud surveillance. Watson now monitors millions of transactions via deep learning and also provides chatbot client advisors. Watson further aids finance through compliance, lending, and transparent AI model governance to promote financial inclusion.

Across all these sectors, IBM maintains stringent data privacy while still allowing Watson Healthcare to benefit from select data. Locally stored data can be masked and then securely shared to feed Watson's discoveries while global chief privacy officers govern standards and maintain patient privacy. This principled approach allows AI advancements to benefit society.

By developing Watson through open releases and collaborative partnerships focused on solving meaningful human challenges, IBM provides a case study in responsible scaling of enterprise AI. The approach balances people, technology, and continuous learning. Sustained engineering support for open-source AI modules allows skills transfer to train more talent holistically across domains. Prioritizing purpose-driven innovation in this way wins public trust.

Through expansive use cases in essential sectors like healthcare and finance over the past decade, IBM Watson proves artificial intelligence's rising influence throughout enterprise operations. Underlying it all is Watson's advanced natural language processing and machine learning which crunches vast data into recommendations and predictions. But IBM scales the technology responsibly through a principled approach centered on trust and transparency.

Deep Mind

Google's DeepMind subsidiary has pioneered groundbreaking artificial intelligence capabilities that showcase the tremendous potential AI has for optimizing critical enterprise functions like energy usage, search relevance, and healthcare treatment planning. A key milestone proving AI's proficiency for sophisticated strategy and complex problem solving was DeepMind's AlphaGo program defeating the world Go champion in 2017.

Powering AlphaGo's triumph was innovative reinforcement learning methodology that recursively improved the system's gameplay decision-making over months of training by competing against prior versions of itself. DeepMind then adapted similar self-directed learning principles to data center cooling infrastructure management, yielding striking 40% efficiency gains. The AI scheduling systems continuously refined dynamic temperature and power balancing to optimize workloads.

Applying machine learning directly now also upgrades Google web search continuously through an evaluation flow where user clicks first inform improvements that subsequent clicks then parse and confirm. Confirming the AI-generated suggestions assist people in finding information more easily, UX lift metrics validate the search relevance refinements. Healthcare AI research applies similar iterative learning to focus on assisting clinicians through enhanced diagnosis and treatment planning as well.

DeepMind Health responsibly shares select medical data insights broadly to scientific communities, promoting life saving discoveries through principled AI application. High privacy standards guide progress through governance committees overseeing the initiatives. By balancing strong technology capabilities with collaborative human partnerships and ethics, DeepMind drives cross-sector innovation using artificial intelligence as a versatile tool for shared gains.

Challenges and Misconceptions About AI in Enterprise Architecture

When exploring the use of AI capabilities to enhance enterprise architecture, leadership teams often encounter skepticism and misunderstandings about what can realistically be achieved. Some common misconceptions surround the accuracy of AI, how quickly it can be implemented, or the costs involved. These myths can sometimes create formidable challenges when introducing AI into long-standing legacy architectures.

One of the biggest challenges with enterprise AI adoption involves data complexity. Historically siloed data, stored across disconnected systems, can severely hamper developing enterprise-wide AI solutions. The immense data integration and preparation efforts required often get underestimated. Cleaning and labeling vast datasets to make them usable for reliable AI requires substantial engineering resources. Achieving accuracy and consistency can be difficult across decentralized data.

Integration with existing technology components also provides major challenges. AI solutions rely heavily on machine learning and statistical algorithms. Connecting these advanced analytical applications into legacy, on-premise systems can involve extensive upgrades to computational capabilities, cloud readiness, and network security protocols. The transformation costs to make AI accessible across enterprise stacks are often unexpected barriers.

How to Overcome These Challenges

When adopting AI, simplistic notions about seamless, out-of-the-box enterprise integration need to be dispelled upfront in order to set realistic leadership expectations. Like any other complex technology transformation, AI comes with inherent challenges around costs, timelines, capabilities, and integration with existing systems.

Rather than pursuing full-scale AI integration across the entire organization from the onset, a more pragmatic approach is to implement AI solutions for targeted applications at first. This allows enterprises to demonstrate valuable AI use cases, better understand integration requirements, account for adoption obstacles, and build critical knowledge—without taking on excessive risk exposure across critical systems.

Pursuing an incremental rollout strategy for AI implementations is also advised over a big-bang approach. Methodically selecting high-value, high data-accessibility use cases first provides an easier pathway to getting started. Examples may include applications for predictive forecasting, inventory optimization, customer call routing, and other capabilities that leverage clean, consistent data from sources like ERP or CRM systems.

As expertise and confidence build with these initial AI application integrations, enterprises can then progress to more complex, data-intensive development with longer timelines across areas like R&D, next-best action marketing, predictive maintenance, and other use cases.

Setting pragmatic expectations up front on costs, timelines, capabilities, and integration needs for the full AI journey, enables enterprises to navigate typical challenges. Employing proven strategies centered around use case prioritization, iterative integrations, and building internal skills reinforces realistic, executive perspectives. This helps enterprises reap benefits from AI digitization, without being derailed by common hurdles other impatient organizations face.

Visual Timeline

In the 1980s and into the 90s, artificial intelligence capabilities were relatively limited and AI adoption in business settings was minimal. This time period saw early AI experiments mainly focused on expert systems and machine learning algorithms that could encode human knowledge and rules to provide basic recommendations and decision support. Challenges existed around computational power and data availability. While innovative, AI lacked integration into wider enterprise infrastructure and daily operations.

The 2000s saw greater AI advancements from improved statistical and mathematical models for machine learning, and wider availability of system integration methods. This enabled more enterprises to experiment with AI in targeted functions like supply chain optimizations, predictive analytics, automated customer service chatbots, and personalized algorithms for recommendations. However, most applications remained narrow in scope. AI adoption was siloed rather than organization-wide, holding back its larger potential impact.

Present day, AI utilization has become more pervasive, strategic, and transformative for enterprises. The exponential growth in data volume, computational processing power, cloud computing, open source algorithms, and rapid development frameworks now allow enterprises to embed AI across organization-wide architectures. AI is becoming integrated directly into core business processes, decisions, and customer experiences versus operating in isolation.

Looking ahead, Gartner and other analysts predict this trend will continue in the 2020s with AI playing an even more pivotal role as a key building block woven into the fabric of enterprise infrastructure, operations, and innovations. Continued evolution in machine learning, and conversational AI in particular, will enable a more seamless human-AI collaboration and amplify business results. Investments in building internal AI talent and management practices are also expected to grow exponentially in the coming decade.

While early AI adoption in past decades was limited, recent convergence of advanced algorithms, data networks, and intelligent applications along with recognized business benefits is driving widespread integration of AI throughout end-to-end enterprise architectures. This will transform AI from an isolated tool into an essential core component empowering nearly all aspects of enterprise innovations and capabilities.

Chapter Two

Decoding AI—Basics for the Non-Geek

A rtificial intelligence refers to computer systems that are designed to perform tasks that would otherwise require human intelligence. At a basic level, AI systems are able to learn from data and experiences, adapt to new inputs, and carry out human-like tasks. The key goal of AI is to create intelligent machines that function and react like humans.

Some of the most common and impactful AI technologies today include machine learning, natural language processing, robotics, and computer vision. Machine learning allows systems to learn and improve from experience without being explicitly programmed. Natural language processing focuses on enabling human-like speech and text understanding. Robotics involves creating intelligent machines that can interact with the physical world. Computer vision equips systems to comprehend digital images and videos.

AI is already deeply integrated into many familiar consumer technologies, powering functionality like personalized recommendations, voice assistants, product tagging in social media, facial recognition, and much more. On the business side, AI is enhancing major enterprise applications from cloud computing services, to supply chain platforms, to business intelligence tools. AI allows modern technologies to automatically learn, reason, and improve without ongoing human intervention.

As for the future, AI disciplines like deep learning, reinforcement learning, and neural networks hold tremendous promise, but remain in nascent stages as of today. Deep learning employs advanced statistical techniques to enable more complex learning capabilities. Reinforcement learning allows systems to determine ideal behaviors within specific environments to maximize a defined reward. Neural networks are computing systems modeled after the human brain's biological neural networks.

All these emerging AI approaches have wide-ranging future applicability for enterprise architecture. As businesses embrace AI transformation, it will be critical for technology leaders to closely track innovations in the AI field and evaluate how new AI capabilities may be integrated into their technology stacks and infrastructure, to generate greater efficiency, insights, and competitive advantages. Adopting flexible, modular enterprise architecture with cloud-based deployment models can prepare businesses to rapidly adopt and benefit from advancing AI technologies as they mature.

Fundamental Concepts of AI

Artificial intelligence refers to computer software or systems that have been designed and programmed to perform functions and tasks that would otherwise require human intelligence and perception. A major objective in the continuing development of artificial intelligence is to create AI systems and machine learning algorithms that can increasingly operate dynamically and flexibly, much in the same way that the human brain functions with conscious thought and response.

This means developing AI computer systems that can carry out various forms of intelligent behaviors that come naturally to human beings, but can be quite complex to replicate artificially. Examples of these behaviors that AI seeks to mimic and perform at the machine level include capabilities such as visual perception and image recognition, speech recognition and natural language processing, logical reasoning and predictive analysis, discovering and applying knowledge, problem-solving across domains, displaying social intelligence, planning complex tasks, and providing an intuitive, personalized customer experience.

For artificial intelligence systems to exhibit these types of intelligent behaviors in the real world rather than just theoretically, AI algorithms and models must be trained on large volumes of high quality, domain-specific data. This allows the AI to become progressively smarter and more capable at handling complex tasks. From playing games better than the most skilled human players, to powering the recommendation engines shoppers interact with daily, to helping doctors interpret medical images and make better diagnostic decisions—artificial intelligence is aimed at conducting all of these complex cognitive functions seamlessly and accurately much like a human, but at speeds and scales beyond human capability. The end goal is for AI to increasingly take on more of the tasks humans currently perform using their own intellectual capacity and free up more time for people to focus their energy on more meaningful, creative work.

A Bit More on Machine Learning

Machine learning is a specific subset within the broader scope of artificial intelligence. What distinguishes machine learning is the ability of computer algorithms to iteratively enhance their performance and accurately make predictions related to certain tasks—all without needing explicit programming for that specific function each time.

The core capability that enables this is by digesting and gaining "experience" from exposure to substantial volumes of data that then informs the machine learning models. As more data is fed through the algorithms, the models can analyze the numerous data points to identify patterns, correlations, insights, and other nonlinear relationships that would not be apparent to humans reviewing the raw data.

These learned data patterns then become codified within carefully tuned parameters in the algorithm models. The models can then apply those patterns to make educated guesses or predictions about future data inputs. As machine learning models process even more subsequent data, they have the ability to assess the accuracy of their predictions and refine their internal parameters through continuous feedback loops and mathematical optimization techniques—thereby constantly evolving and improving over time.

Some of the most ubiquitous types of machine learning algorithms and models include supervised learning, unsupervised learning, reinforcement learning, and deep learning networks. Supervised learning models are trained on extensive sets of labeled example data to predict outcomes on unseen data. In contrast, unsupervised learning finds hidden patterns in unlabeled data without any example outcomes to guide the process. Reinforcement learning optimizes decision-making via continuous trial-and-error interactions with a dynamic environment. Deep learning utilizes neural networks with multiple layers to extract higher-level features and patterns from extremely large data volumes.

Overpowering the Limits of AI With Neural Networks

Neural networks are a specialized type of machine learning algorithm that is inspired by the network of neurons within the human brain. Just as the brain's neurons transmit signals between one another, neural nets contain layers made up of interconnected nodes that can transmit signaling data.

The structure of a neural net resembles neurons arranged in a web of layers, with each layer fully connected to the layers on either side. The input layer receives the data, the hidden layers process and analyze the data, and the output layer generates a prediction or classification. As new data flows through the neural net, the signaling connections between these nodes, known as weights, adjust based on the insights derived.

This adjustment process for optimizing the weights between nodes is at the core of how neural nets actually learn. As more labeled data is fed through the network, the back propagation algorithm measures how close the prediction is to the actual label. It then works backwards to tweak the weights between each node in the network to try and improve accuracy. This repetitive feed forward and back propagation process allows neural nets to learn highly complex patterns and relationships within large volumes of data.

The more data that a neural net processes through this learning cycle, the more accurately it can classify data or make predictions about new data by inferring patterns buried deep in the information. Across industries ranging from finance to healthcare and beyond, neural nets offer tremendous capabilities to analyze immense datasets and perform tasks like image recognition, language processing, risk assessment, complex pattern detection, and other artificial intelligence applications. Their brain-like ability to learn gives neural nets immense flexibility and predictive power from the raw data they review.

Adding Eyes to AI With Computer Vision

Computer vision is a specialized field within the domain of artificial intelligence that focuses specifically on enabling computer systems and applications to "see" and process visual data at scale. The core goal is to train computer algorithms to be able to accurately identify, categorize, and analyze digital images and videos to make sense of the vast amounts of visual data in the world.

Unlike humans who can intuitively interpret visual inputs effortlessly, computer vision seeks to teach computers this highly complex capability using innovative machine learning algorithms and neural networks. The most common set of techniques leveraged today are known as convolutional neural networks (CNNs), which are inspired by the biological vision processes in human and animal visual cortices.

CNNs work by breaking down digital visual inputs into various features through a series of mathematical convolutions and then using these learned features to identify patterns and classify images based on prior training. This enables the computer vision algorithms to detect and segment objects, scenes, faces, text, colors, and much more in both images and videos.

Some of the most valuable real-world applications of computer vision span across industries like autonomous vehicles using vision systems to "see" and navigate, medical imaging and diagnostics for improved clinical insights, surveillance and security systems for enhanced monitoring, photo organizing and searching for consumer applications, augmented reality experiences in mobile apps and games, and many more.

The exponential growth of visual data being generated globally also means that computer vision systems have an immense scope for unlocking value across sectors. As algorithms get more sophisticated, the level of visual understanding and intelligence demonstrated by computer vision is rapidly beginning to emulate and even surpass human-level performance in targeted use cases. Fueled by active research and innovation, computer vision continues to be one of the most promising subsets within the future of artificial intelligence.

The New Revolution With NLP

Natural language processing, (NLP), represents an area of artificial intelligence aimed at empowering computer systems to comprehend, interpret, and derive meaning from human languages. Unlike programs that can only process specific, structured data, NLP techniques allow systems to analyze and extract information from unstructured text or voice data.

At its core, NLP applies advanced computational linguistics and semantic modeling to read and decipher written or spoken human languages in their natural form. This capability enables NLP systems to recognize speech; tokenize and parse sentences grammatically; analyze the context and meaning of words or phrases; and determine the emotional sentiment or intent behind natural language.

To achieve understanding of human languages, NLP incorporates powerful techniques like speech recognition to transcribe spoken audio; syntactic analysis to study sentence construction; semantic analysis to interpret meaning; discourse analysis to assess relationships between language units; and pragmatics analysis to apply real-world context.

These NLP techniques have unlocked a wide range of valuable applications for both text-based and voice-based interactions. For example, chatbots and virtual assistants rely on NLP to engage in informative dialogues. Intelligent search engines process natural language queries to discern user intent. Sentiment analysis tools extract emotional tone and opinions from social media, reviews, and discussions. Document summation systems employ NLP to distill key facts and themes. Automatic language translation harnesses NLP to instantly translate materials into different tongues.

As NLP research continues to advance the linguistic capabilities of machines, even more human-like communication and understanding will become possible between people and computer systems. NLP will drive improvements in areas from information retrieval to business intelligence to human-computer interaction—achieving deeper insights from language data while enhancing decision-making across many domains.

AI's Role and Impact in Modern Technology

Artificial intelligence has become deeply integrated into many technology systems and platforms that are driving innovation and emerging trends across a wide range of sectors. Through machine learning, neural networks, computer vision, natural language processing, and other AI techniques, today's technologies are becoming more intelligent and capable than ever before.

Here are some key areas where AI's influence is particularly noticeable:

Automation and Robotics

Industrial sectors like manufacturing and supply chain management are being radically improved through the implementation of intelligent automation technologies and robotics. Robots endowed with computer vision, machine learning capabilities, and dexterous mechanical skills can handle a wide range of manual tasks with tireless precision.

In smart factories of the future, production lines will be staffed by adaptive robots overseen by AI control software that can orchestrate manufacturing from start to finish. These systems self-calibrate to account for variability in components, and self-tune in real-time to optimize assembly timing, sequencing, and quality control checks. With such reliability, speed, and output, AI-powered automation promises consistently higher throughput and part quality compared to human workers alone, especially for repetitive jobs. By handling rote tasks in fabrication and quality assurance, manufacturing automation increases production consistency, efficiency, and safety.

Similar AI and autonomy advances are revolutionizing supply chain coordination from inventory management inside warehouses to final mile delivery. Inside fulfillment centers, AI guides robots to adeptly pick, pack, and sort items for shipment with optimization algorithms balancing speed, storage space, and fragile product handling. Autonomous trucking, drones, and delivery rovers can then transport these orders on-demand with route planning and hazard avoidance capabilities that improve over time through machine learning. Such innovations enable round-the-clock processing of customer orders with lower operational costs.

By automating dangerous, tedious, and time-sensitive responsibilities across production and logistics, AI-powered technologies augment human capabilities for less burdensome, more rewarding work. Intelligent automation powered by artificial intelligence is transforming sectors dependent on complex physical tasks by enabling precise, tireless, around-the-clock services.

Data Analysis

Artificial intelligence represents a breakthrough that is fundamentally transforming how organizations in every industry go about gaining meaningful insights from data. Through advanced machine learning algorithms and models, AI systems now have the capability to rapidly process massive datasets on a scale and with a level of sophistication that exceeds the capacity of even the largest teams of human data scientists. Tasks that used to require months of effort can now be accomplished by AI in merely hours or minutes. This tremendous increase in speed and scale is revolutionizing data-driven decision making and strategic planning.

By continuously ingesting vast volumes of data, whether structured or unstructured in nature, AI models can conduct pattern recognition and complex analysis to uncover relationships and insights that would previously have remained hidden. And by iteratively learning from the results, continuously crunching the numbers, and refining their models, these AI systems are able to convert raw data into prescriptive and actionable recommendations to optimize critical areas like risks, innovations, customer experiences, and profits.

Across the financial industry, AI powers everything from risk exposure analysis based on parsing legal contracts using natural language processing to predicting fraudulent transactions, stock market shifts, and most profitable trades through deep neural networks. In marketing, AI is revolutionizing customer engagement and experience by allowing for real-time, personalized offers, content and channel strategies tailored to delight each individual customer based on analysis of their engagement patterns across channels. Healthcare AI is mining medical records, research databases, and genomic datasets to substantially improve diagnosis, treatment planning, and new therapy discoveries.

The exponential growth of data from transactions, IoT sensors, user behaviors, business applications and more demands such pattern recognition capabilities that only AI can enable. By providing a real-time, panoramic view of operations based on this sophisticated data analysis, AI allows leading organizations to tame information overload and uncover insights that drive significantly wiser strategies and decision making, tackling both commercial goals as well humanitarian challenges which were previously obscured by data complexity. The result is accelerating progress and innovation across domains.

Smart Assistants and Chatbots

Virtual assistants like Apple's Siri, Amazon's Alexa, Google's Assistant, and an expanding variety of conversational chatbots are pioneering new, more natural and contextual digital interactions for people. This has been enabled by the rapid development of artificial intelligence and machine learning, especially in advanced neural networks that can now interpret and respond to spoken and written language with increasing sophistication.

These AI systems are trained on massive datasets to analyze requests in context, hold progressively more human-like dialogs, and even mirror distinct personalities. For example, if you ask a question about the weather, they can understand you are inquiring about meteorological conditions, not making small talk, and provide back the local weather forecast. Or if you say you are hungry, they understand this implies you want recommendations for nearby restaurants. The assistants multitask seamlessly as well, so they can adjust connected thermostats, room lighting and other internet of things devices automatically based on conversational commands.

Intelligent chatbots integrated into messaging apps can efficiently look up account specifics, summarize recent transactions, provide order status updates and more for users. They utilize complex dialog trees so people can have rewarding, practical exchanges by text chat or voice without the typical frustrations of mechanical conversations. Some assistants even relate better long-term by exhibiting empathy, humor and specific hobbies they discuss as they build rapport with individuals.

In addition, virtual bilingual assistants now allow fluid communications across languages that were once barriers to understanding between people. Voice-based interfaces also increase access for those with disabilities. The increasing convenience and democratization of AI assistance through smart bots promises to make them ubiquitous aides that proactively monitor and meet user needs in the background across devices and interactions. Once laborious tasks are becoming automated and hands-free thanks to the power of artificial intelligence.

Entertainment

Artificial intelligence has become deeply integrated into the world of entertainment by powering highly personalized recommendations and even automating creative media production in some emerging cases. Mainstream services like Netflix, Spotify, and YouTube now extensively utilize

AI algorithms to suggest movies, television shows, songs and video content that is uniquely catered to each user's individual taste. These suggestions are based on analyzing the consumer's historical viewing and listening patterns. This allows audiences to efficiently discover new favorites from within expansive media catalogs that once felt overwhelming in their scope.

As the AI recommendation engines learn more about consumer preferences through increased data points over time, media platforms are getting smarter at selecting suggestions that are likely to specifically delight a given individual. The machines can serve up custom playlists to match your current mood or recommend the next binge-worthy sci-fi series filled with all the twisty plots and intrigue you love. Beyond predictive recommendations, AI is also enabling new forms of interactive film-making and storytelling. Services like Netflix now offer choose-your-own-adventure style stories that empower audiences to shape the actual narrative journey by making choices for the characters.

On the creative production side, AI tools are also helping to automate key tasks across animation, computer graphics, video game design, music composition and even visual art generation. Bot-created works that mimic or blend existing styles in novel ways are gaining attention in these industries for their unexpected creativity. Looking ahead, AI could one day enhance human creativity in the arts by handling rote tasks and sparking new ideas through unusual connections that humans would be unlikely to think of on their own.

By better understanding individuals and both predicting and shaping their desires, artificial intelligence promises to unlock more engaging, meaningful and inspiring entertainment experiences. Media enhanced by algorithms and automated production may soon enable interactive stories, games and art that speak to audiences like never before.

Internet of Things (IoT)

The Internet of Things has led to an explosion of connected smart devices and sensors in homes, offices, factories, and cities that are capable of capturing immense amounts of data. AI analytics technologies are now being integrated with these extensive IoT infrastructures to derive deeper insights from the rich data streams. The application of AI mechanisms such as machine learning, neural networks, and natural language processing allows the dumb endpoints within distributed IoT networks to become smarter and more efficient.

In consumer IoT segments such as smart homes, AI learning algorithms analyze usage patterns for thermostats, lights, appliances, and security systems to predict needs, automatically adjust settings, and save energy. For instance, AI can monitor home occupancy and travel patterns of homeowners to cleverly calibrate heating, cooling, and lighting without manual intervention. Intelligent voice assistants leverage AI to respond to natural language commands for home device control. Appliance sensors also feed maintenance history, usage data, and performance telemetry to AI algorithms that schedule predictive upkeep and part replacements before failures occur. This maximizes the lifetime value of appliances.

Similarly in industrial IoT implementations, AI examines real-time sensor, visual inspection and operations data from production line equipment to optimize machining accuracy, prescribe predictive maintenance and fulfill surging customer orders. By monitoring vibration, temperature, oil degradation, throughput yields and other metrics, AI becomes the central nervous system driving automation and resilience across factories with minimal downtime. It enhances the feedback loop between industrial IoT devices and back end intelligent systems.

Essentially AI augments IoT infrastructures across consumer and industrial application sectors by infusing distributed networks of dumb endpoints with intelligence for more informed and automated decision making. It transforms raw data into actionable insights for greater efficiency.

The fusion of AI and IoT unlocks new potential that would be impossible to achieve otherwise by either technology alone.

Real-World Implications of AI in Technology

The real-world implications of AI in technology span across various sectors, transforming industries, reshaping economies, and altering the fabric of society.

Here are some key areas where AI has had significant impacts

Healthcare

Artificial intelligence is ushering in a revolution in medical diagnostics and imaging. Algorithms can swiftly analyze MRI scans, X-rays, and CT scans—spotting abnormalities and detecting issues with accuracy rivaling or exceeding human radiologists. By surfacing potential problems much faster, AI enables earlier intervention which directly improves patient outcomes in diseases like cancer. Studies have already shown AI matching and sometimes surpassing doctors in identifying diagnosis from medical images. This allows treatment to begin sooner when it has the highest probability of success.

AI is also accelerating pharmaceutical innovation and research. Sophisticated computational models can predict how certain molecular compounds will interact with biological targets in the human body. This simulation of biochemistry allows AI systems to emulate years of physical lab work in just minutes. Researchers can then focus their time and resources pursuing only the most promising candidates for new therapies. AI drug discovery has already aided in developing major new medicines that are getting to market faster and saving lives.

The direct patient experience is also being enhanced by AI in multiple ways. "Virtual nurse" chatbots are providing companionship and emotional support for more isolated groups like elderly patients while also monitoring their health data around the clock for signs of trouble. Robot assistant devices are able to safely lift and transport patients, reducing risk and freeing up nursing staff to spend more quality care time with people. And medication management smartphone apps can remind patients when to take their drugs, manage refill schedules, and help avoid dangerous complications.

Looking ahead, as computing power and health data volumes grow exponentially more robust, the accuracy and ubiquity of healthcare AI will rapidly expand. While skilled doctors and nurses will always be irreplaceable, their capabilities will be greatly augmented by artificial intelligence working alongside them—understanding patients, diagnosing conditions, discovering new cures, and delivering compassion. The future of medicine will be defined by an ever-closer human-AI partnership aimed at making the system more efficient, more effective and more caring for all.

Finance

Algorithmic trading systems powered by machine learning are parsing enormous volumes of market data to detect subtle patterns and make quantitative market forecasts. This allows automated trading algorithms to enter and exit trades at optimal times and capture price moves a human trader would likely miss. By removing emotional influences and reacting faster, algorithmic trading systems with embedded AI aim to capitalize on short-term opportunities while mitigating everyday risks. Experts suggest well-designed algorithms can compound returns over long time horizons.

AI is also proving remarkably adept at detecting all forms of financial crimes and misrepresentation. Neural networks trained on past fraud examples are now able to pinpoint subtle signs of deception in credit card charges, insurance claims, mortgage applications and banking activity. By rapidly alerting investigators to suspicious cases for further examination, this application of AI is saving costs associated with fraud and building greater public trust in financial institutions.

Customer-facing AI tools are making personal finances easier to manage for the average banking customer. Chatbots now capably handle routine queries, while personalized virtual assistants provide tips and recommendations on spending, savings, and investing tailored to individual financial profiles and goals. More banks are also offering AI-powered tools for automated expense/budget tracking, cash flow forecasts, and other tasks to help customers better understand and improve their financial health.

By simultaneously boosting security, convenience, and outcomes, the adoption of AI in finance creates value for both institutions and customers in a customer-centrist way. Leaders will continue developing ethical, transparent and accountable AI systems that expand access to financial services. With proper governance, AI in finance promotes inclusivity and optimal economic participation across wider society.

Retail and E-Commerce

Personalization through AI is revolutionizing the shopping experience for consumers. Retailers are now using sophisticated algorithms to analyze individual customer data including browsing and purchasing history to determine product preferences and interests. This allows retailers to tailor product recommendations, marketing offers, promotions, and even the overall user journey on e-commerce sites for each shopper. The AI works in the background to deliver a customized, hyper-relevant shopping experience centered around what the specific customer is most likely to purchase. By feeling catered to directly, consumers appreciate the personal touch. AI-powered personalization makes customers feel truly valued. The tailored product suggestions increase conversion rates and sales as recommendations resonate so much stronger. The AI is constantly optimizing and learning using the data to refine its ability to match products perfectly for the customer.

On the inventory management side, AI is giving retailers an incredible advantage in demand planning and forecasting. Predictive analytics tools enabled by machine learning algorithms analyze past sales data, market and industry trends, seasonal impacts, and a myriad of other factors to forecast product demand far into the future. This provides immense visibility into optimal stock levels for each item, while minimizing waste and costs. Retailers can ensure popular products are consistently well-stocked to meet customer needs while slowly moving products are purchased more conservatively. The AI becomes continually smarter in its ability to predict fluctuations in demand for maximizing inventory efficiency. This level of insight eliminates much of the previous guesswork in inventory planning. The AI-powered platforms lead to leaner, yet sufficiently stocked inventory, critical for meeting customer demand and saving costs.

To drive excellent customer service, conversational AI chatbots are being leveraged to resolve routine customer inquiries with speed and consistency, allowing human customer service agents to focus on complex issues. For common questions like order status, product availability, delivery scheduling, and returns, the smart bots are capable of providing prompt resolution. The AI-powered conversations feel natural using natural language interactions while offering 24/7 automated support. This enables remarkably efficient service scalability. The combination of the AI chatbots and human representatives caters to both simple and intricate customer service needs through retail organizations. This allows them to manage customer issues across channels with maximum responsiveness.

Common AI Myths Debunked

One major myth is that AI will rapidly evolve to surpass and eventually displace human intelligence in the near future. In reality, most current

AI systems are narrow in scope: designed to perform specific, well-defined tasks. Despite impressive capabilities within their specialized area, the majority of AI lacks generalized intelligence and remains incapable of replicating the complexity and adaptability of the human mind. While advanced AI continues to evolve, the likelihood of it uniformly exceeding all facets of human cognition simultaneously remains low in the near term.

Another common misconception is that AI systems can independently teach themselves and learn without substantial human supervision. In fact, contemporary AI depends heavily on training datasets that are meticulously cleaned, labeled, and structured by teams of human experts to learn effectively. It requires extensive guidance and monitoring from developers and engineers throughout its learning phases. Unmanaged, self-supervised learning can result in biased, unsafe, or unusable AI systems. Ongoing human involvement is critical for developing beneficial and generalized AI.

There is also a myth that AI can only excel in the fields of math and science. In reality, AI innovations and applications now span a vast range of disciplines from healthcare, art, agriculture, transportation, customer service, and well beyond fields with quantitative foundations. With proper data inputs and training, AI can be molded to enhance and elevate nearly any industry requiring prediction, personalization, optimization, or automation. The versatility of AI across both technical and creative domains continues to expand.

Additionally, there is a misconception that AI systems always provide completely objective and rational decisions. AI systems, however, fundamentally originate from and reflect the data and design choices of their human creators. As a result, they risk inheriting or amplifying issues like biases, ethical blind spots, flawed logic, or limited knowledge existing in the original modeling and data. Maintaining responsible and ethical AI requires proactive efforts to ensure fair, transparent, and auditable AI decision making.

Debunking these and other misguided myths can help develop a more accurate public understanding of present-day AI capabilities, limitations, dependencies, and risks. This allows for setting realistic expectations, priorities, policies, and safeguards regarding the responsible development and deployment of AI moving forward.

Chapter Three

TOGAF Demystified—A Quick Guide for the AI Era

Introduced in 1995, The Open Group Architecture Framework has become an influential structure for architecting and governing enterprise information systems, serving the discipline of enterprise architecture methodology needs for over two decades. TOGAF defines clear processes for helping align IT investments with overarching business objectives. By synthesizing insights from both previous descriptive frameworks like Zachman alongside proven information engineering best practices, TOGAF strives for an optimized approach.

At its core, TOGAF offers organizations a robust architecture development method for collaboratively planning optimal future-state technology landscapes, while pragmatically migrating away from present-day legacy constraints. With sustainability in mind beyond single projects, TOGAF orients architectural efforts toward establishing ongoing governance that upholds data, integration, and vendor interoperability standards over long time horizons. These framework guardrails help to steer continual alignment of IT with strategic business goals.

For enterprise architects tasked with managing ever-evolving technical complexities across infrastructure, security, emerging innovations, and more, adherence to TOGAF boosts operational coordination by formalizing ecosystem relationships into reference models that promote shared understanding. From initial capability assessments to multi-phase implementation blueprints, TOGAF activities remain focused on achieving critical goals like improved agility, lower risks, and increased efficiency, with technology firmly supporting user needs.

This chapter will focus on helping you understand the significance of TOGAF with respect to enterprise architecture and how leveraging this structured framework can help companies align their information technology practices to overarching business priorities both now and in the future as environments and challenges evolve. Adopting TOGAF delivers value by fostering IT governance, planning, and sustainability while managing the intricacies of complex modern IT landscapes.

What Is TOGAF and Its Main Concepts?

The Open Group Architecture Framework, commonly referred to as TOGAF, provides organizations with a comprehensive, yet adaptable, methodology for designing, implementing, and governing enterprise architecture aligned to specific business goals and priorities. At its core, TOGAF offers a structured, iterative, four-phase cycle called the Architecture Development Method, (ADM), to help integrate infrastructure, application, data, and technological capabilities with what the organization is aiming to achieve across operations, products, and services.

The ADM cycle initiates with the Vision Phase, which focuses on framing the scope and strategic objectives for the architecture engagement. Strong communication and stakeholder participation across leadership and technical teams is crucial in this phase to define the high-level business strategies, needs, challenges, and desired outcomes that will drive the architecture work.

The next Define Phase has architects develop the specific requirements, specifications, components, and models aimed to create the solutions envisioned in the first phase. Activities in this phase include assessing the current organizational landscape and any capability gaps that may inhibit the implementation of target architecture states.

Following this, the Realization Phase plans for the actual construction and testing of the solutions defined. This translates requirements into usable architecture like infrastructure, integration capabilities, security protocols, data migration tools, etc. that can achieve the intended vision.

Finally, the Governance Phase sustains alignment of the architecture outcomes and principles with the original business strategic goals, direction, and decisions that launched the architecture engagement. This phase manages change implementation and ensures solutions continue enabling the organization as markets and priorities evolve.

A key aspect is that following this end-to-end Architecture Development Method cycle is intended to be practical, rather than dogmatic, for organizations. TOGAF is designed to guide rather than prescribe, allowing organizations to customize how ADM activities are applied based on internal constraints and contexts. The iterative nature also promotes continuity between business and IT to sustainably build agile, aligned technical fabrics that leverage processes, data, and personnel. With TOGAF at the helm, organizations can effectively weave an IT ecosystem that serves both immediate and long-term organizational goals.

Architecture Development Method

The practical centerpiece guiding enterprise architecture efforts in TOGAF is the Architecture Development Method. This systematic method contains eight iterative phases balancing critical business drivers and technical realities to progress architecture planning, design, and evolution. Rather than follow a strictly sequential flow, architects employ ADM iteratively—adapting along the way as learned lessons emerge and priorities shift. Still, the logical flow enables envisioning future solution states, analyzing gaps thoroughly, detailing designs carefully, and governing implementation effectively.

Initially in the Preliminary Phase, architects frame foundational architecture effort elements including defining the scope, key constraints, and assessing organizational readiness across people, process, and technology dimensions realistically. Next, the Visioning Phase articulates high-level target solutions directly addressing identified strategic business drivers and goals. Detailed Business, Information Systems, and Technology architectures are then developed enumerating logical and functional component requirements in each area respectively.

With needs fully enumerated, the Opportunities and Solutions Phases formulate executable project plans for high-priority initiatives. This planning phase focuses on pragmatically reconciling priorities, budgets, and resources to determine transition sequencing. After planning, comes formalizing the all-important Migration Planning Phase. Here, architects establish transition states and timeline roadmaps practically bridging the current and future blueprint states. Finally, establishing proactive architecture governance confirms that ongoing technology lifecycle and standards decisions align back to the original vision and principles stated.

Blending both art and science across domains, executing these ADM activities methodically transitions strategic visions into tactical outcomes sustainably over time. The method's comprehensive end-to-end process allows organizations to adapt frameworks like TOGAF in customized ways. This enables pragmatically optimizing architectures for an organization's unique enterprise context, culture, objectives, and priorities.

TOGAF's Relevance in the AI-Driven World

The Open Group Architecture Framework has sustained its applicability as a comprehensive enterprise architecture methodology, even as emerging technologies like artificial intelligence transform organizational landscapes. This continued relevance stems from TOGAF's core foundational principles that provide an adaptable, iterative approach to architecting for business needs both current and future.

At the heart of TOGAF is the Architecture Development Method, which serves as a structured but flexible guideline for developing, maintaining, and governing enterprise architecture. The ADM outlines an iterative cycle of key phases—from framing the architectural vision and business priorities, to delivering solutions and components. This step-by-step approach enables architects to determine where AI solutions may deliver value, integrate them seamlessly into architecture, and continuously refine as needs shift.

The adaptability of TOGAF's ADM to integrate new innovations like AI is central to the framework's staying power. As enterprises digitally transform themselves, TOGAF provides a path to embed AI where most impactful while ensuring holistic alignment of business goals through architecture. The methodology's circular nature means organizations assess, re-evaluate, and pivot their architectures continually—enabling nimble adoption of AI for evolving demands.

Additionally, TOGAF's technology-agnostic perspective emphasizes business outcomes over specific technological solutions. This principle affords enterprises the latitude to integrate AI capabilities most appropriate for their needs—while ensuring technologies serve to advance business strategy and priorities guided by architecture.

AI technologies can be integrated within this lifecycle at various stages.

Stage 1: Preliminary Phase and Requirements Management

The preliminary phase focuses on identifying if artificial intelligence could provide value to the organization and where its application would be most impactful. This involves closely evaluating each business area and core processes that rely on data-driven decision making. Assessing large volumes of data, patterns in customer behavior, efficiency of operations, and current methods for projecting future needs are areas ripe for AI augmentation.

Once a promising business case is identified, the task of assessing requirements examines the goals that need to be accomplished and details the key inputs, outputs, and desired functionality expected from the AI application across software, hardware, and integrations with existing systems. These requirements take into account dependencies on data accessibility, infrastructure readiness, employee skill sets, and cybersecurity protections.

Additionally, the requirements phase carefully considers the various stakeholders within the organization and marketplace that will be impacted by the AI integration. This encompasses everyone from executive leadership setting strategic priorities, to customer experiences, to front-line workers interfacing with new automated processes. Input from stakeholders and subject matter experts ensures a full spectrum of user needs is built into the AI application requirements.

With clearly defined business objectives, functional requirements, and stakeholder impacts established upfront, organizations can build an AI solution that aligns to organizational goals and user workflows, and delivers clear value to the business and customers alike. The preliminary planning and requirements provide the necessary guardrails for AI developers to work within as they architect the models, algorithms, interfaces, and analytics capabilities needed for a tailored, high-functioning AI application. Defining these foundations early allows the subsequent development phases to progress smoothly.

Stage 2: Architecture Vision

Defining architecture vision is a critical second stage when incorporating artificial intelligence capabilities strategically across an enterprise. This phase involves taking the established business vision and strategy and delineating specifically how AI technology will technically support and realize those higher objectives.

It entails extensive analysis by cross-functional leadership teams to identify and prioritize exactly which areas AI could have the biggest impact in accomplishing the organization's mission and strategic pillars. Whether enhancing customer experiences, optimizing complex operations, accelerating research and development, or driving higher revenues—the architectural vision maps out where and how AI can be decisively deployed.

For improving customer interactions, detailed plans would be developed around deploying conversational AI interfaces to provide personalized recommendations to each client. Machine learning algorithms would be embedded within engagement channels to predict customer needs more accurately and promote the most relevant products automatically. Data capture and analytics functionality would also be built using AI to discern subtle shifts in consumer behavior and realign engagement strategies accordingly.

If optimizing supply chain operations, the AI architecture vision may focus on using computer vision, IoT sensors, and predictive analytics in coordination across inventory, logistics, and distribution channels. This would allow for continuous process improvements, dynamic resource allocation, and mitigating operational risks in a complex global network. AI would enable creating a model of the end-to-end system to spot inefficiencies and simulate changes for maximum optimization.

The critical element in Stage 2 is having technical leaders, business strategists, and other key stakeholders co-create the architecture vision for where, how, and to what extent embedding AI capabilities can best support the overarching corporate strategy. This provides an AI transformational map tailored towards the organization's greatest priorities and objectives.

Stage 3: Business Architecture

The business architecture stage focuses on defining an organization's key business capabilities—the abilities that a business needs to meet its objectives. When considering adopting AI, companies need to conduct an in-depth analysis of how AI can reshape business processes and functions that underpin those high-level capabilities.

This starts by mapping out existing business capabilities and the intricate processes and activities that enable them. For example, a core capability like "supply chain management" has multiple processes tied to planning, procurement, warehousing, transportation, and more. The analysis examines each sub-process to identify areas where AI could automate tasks, gain efficiencies, or enhance decision-making.

Questions to explore include—What manual effort or bottlenecks exist in capabilities and processes that AI could optimize? What decisions depend on human judgment that could be augmented with AI? What data limitations restrain performance that AI could help unlock new patterns and insights? The end goal is determining where injecting predictive analytics, machine learning, conversational AI, and other technologies can have the biggest business impact.

The business architecture analysis also estimates the scope of organizational change required to integrate AI into processes, data architecture, and even corporate culture. This assessment reveals where workflows and roles will need to be redesigned, new data pipelines created, staff re-skilled, and change management applied to gain adoption. Understanding these implications allows for more accurate planning and cost-benefit evaluation when determining where and how to pilot AI capabilities.

The deeper business architecture analysis, as opposed to just a surface assessment, enables companies to fully re-imagine how AI can enhance all facets of key business capabilities. This ultimately helps tie AI adoption directly back to strategic objectives around improving customer experiences, increasing operational efficiency, reducing risk exposure, strengthening competitive positioning, and positively impacting the bottom line. The business architecture stage is core to later realizing the full transformational promise of AI across the enterprise.

Stage 4: The Advanced Architecture Implementation

Artificial intelligence has significant impacts on data strategy that business leaders must consider due to the data-intensive nature of many AI applications. Building an effective data architecture to support enterprise-wide AI initiatives involves defining consistent data management practices across departments, setting policies for data access and security, and creating integrated data pipelines that connect siloed datasets. The goal is to develop a scalable, flexible data foundation capable of feeding accurate, quality-controlled data to AI systems under varying conditions.

This requires auditing current data infrastructure to identify duplication, gaps, inconsistencies and outdated legacy systems. Data silos need to be dismantled through corporate data sharing policies so that data can be centralized in an enterprise data repository. Setting up automated data pipelines creates unified channels for routing real-time data from diverse operating environments directly into AI applications. Tracking data provenance end-to-end preserves data integrity while also documenting any data transformation or enrichment completed to improve AI model performance. Establishing clear data governance standards helps secure sensitive customer data and maintain compliance with regulations. The optimal data architecture reduces latency in data transfers, minimizes manual data manipulation, and serves data at the right frequency, format and granularity to power different AI use cases.

When integrating AI components into applications architecture, organizations must start by identifying high-level business objectives and desired outcomes from the user perspective. This shapes the types of predictive insights, recommendations, or automation capabilities needed from the AI application. The supporting system architecture is then designed by mapping out the core AI systems such as machine learning, natural language processing, computer vision, etc. required to enable the necessary intelligent functionalities. Application architecture must have the frameworks in place to train, evaluate, and regularly retrain AI models on new data, as well as integrate model predictions and prescriptions into business workflows. Ensuring flexibility within architecture allows for swapping out AI components as improved technologies emerge. By aligning applications architecture to both overarching business goals and evolving AI best practices, organizations can build intelligent systems with long-term value.

Stage 5: Technology Architecture

A robust technology architecture is crucial for ensuring AI solutions have the computational power, scalability, and seamless integration required to drive value across an organization. Careful planning of the technical infrastructure should align to the scope, objectives, and use cases identified in the initial stages of an AI strategy.

The foundation is provisioning adequate computational resources and data storage capabilities for powering AI models, applications, and services. This entails determining appropriate hardware infrastructure like high-powered GPUs servers for machine learning and leveraging cloud computing services to enable dynamic resource allocation aligned to evolving needs. Particularly for large organizations, a hybrid model combining on-premise servers with scalable cloud infrastructure may provide the right balance of control, customization, and agility.

Another key aspect is building capabilities to ingest, consolidate, clean, and process large volumes of structured and unstructured from across the organization's ecosystem. This data pipeline architecture should account for the initial use cases, while also being adaptable for future data sources and AI needs. Establishing robust data governance, security, and privacy controls are also necessary to manage risks.

Equally important is ensuring new AI solutions can properly integrate with, and augment existing, business systems and processes. This requires defining APIs and interfaces for connecting AI modules built internally or by third-parties into the broader technology landscape including databases, CRM, and ERP platforms. Loose coupling and containerization techniques allow blending AI into workflows without disrupting other critical software systems.

The Evolution of TOGAF in Response to AI Advances

TOGAF has served as a comprehensive framework and common industry method for enterprise architecture, enabling organizations to design, plan, implement, and govern integrated architectures to meet their business needs. As artificial intelligence technologies have rapidly advanced over the past decade, transforming businesses and entire industries, TOGAF has had to evolve in turn to help architects effectively leverage AI capabilities.

One of the most impactful developments came in 2018 with the release of the TOGAF 9.2 standard. It incorporated new guidance and practices focused specifically on supporting AI solutions, data and analytics, establishing operating models to sustain AI, and mitigating risks inherent with machine learning. This was the first time TOGAF formally addressed harnessing emerging technologies like AI, laying the foundations for further enhancements.

The forthcoming TOGAF 10 standard releasing in 2025 represents the next leap, with AI serving as a central theme. Expanded tactics on designing, governing, and deploying trustworthy AI solutions appear throughout the framework. New AI architecture viewpoints, catalogs, and techniques also aim to make AI implementation more effective, resilient, and ethical. Furthermore, reference architectures that provide best practice blueprints for common AI use cases will likely bolster adoption.

Looking ahead, TOGAF will need to continue evolving to keep pace with AI innovations in areas like augmented intelligence, causal machine learning models, and embedded AI applications. Some predictions indicate TOGAF eventually moving from static standard releases to a more flexible model with continuous updates. It may also shift from purely advising on best practices to providing active design support for architectures inclusive of AI. With AI advancement showing no signs of slowing, further enhancements to TOGAF will be critical for enterprise architects to harness the full potential of these transformative technologies.

Case Studies: Successful TOGAF and AI Integration

Enterprise architecture frameworks like TOGAF provide a structured approach for designing and governing an organization's overall technology landscape. Integrating emerging technologies like AI can bring tremendous value in areas like improved customer experiences, higher efficiency, and data-driven decision making. However, effectively blending these technologies requires careful planning and execution.

Real-world examples highlight best practices that organizations can apply.

Case Study 1: AI-Driven Financial Service Experience

A financial services organization established an overarching architecture vision, focused on enhancing customer experiences, driving greater operational efficiency, and achieving competitive differentiation enabled by AI technologies. With this vision guiding efforts, the company followed the structured approach outlined in TOGAF's Architecture Development Method to develop, validate, and approve priority capabilities and use cases for AI across the enterprise.

Utilizing the initial phases of the ADM, key stakeholders across technology, business, operations, compliance, and other areas were aligned on objectives for an AI strategy. An architecture board with executive leadership oversight was also created to govern the process for ideation, validation, and approval of AI solutions. Working groups were then chartered to identify current capability gaps inhibiting the achievement of the AI vision, while also brainstorming future AI use cases mapped to business value drivers around customer service, cost reduction, revenue growth, risk management, and differentiation.

The architecture board called for these use cases to be evaluated and prioritized based on clearly defined assessment criteria focused on Return of Investment (ROI), estimation, implementation complexity, and potential value delivered to stakeholders. An initial list of nearly 20 AI use cases flowed through this evaluation framework. Significant analysis and discussion occurred to align stakeholders on the top AI opportunities.

Ultimately, consensus was reached on three high-priority AI projects expected to yield strong ROI and progress the enterprise towards its AI vision. Personalized wealth management solutions to boost advisor productivity and customer experiences were approved first, followed by an automated financial advice engine for self-directed investing clients, and then an AI-enabled anti-fraud system to detect illegal financial transactions.

By leveraging TOGAF's ADM, this financial services company could effectively align a diverse set of stakeholders while also employing a robust, structured process to identify and govern AI investments on behalf of the enterprise. The approach enabled balanced outcomes meeting both business objectives and technical requirements at the outset of the organization's AI journey.

Case Study 2: AI-Driven Customer Experience Platform

A large, global healthcare provider undertook a multi-year modernization initiative to embed artificial intelligence capabilities across their systems and processes. As they embarked on this technology transformation journey, they leveraged The Open Group Architecture Framework to develop an enterprise architecture that aligned to their responsible AI principles from the outset.

The healthcare organization defined "responsible AI" as a key architecture principle within TOGAF to proactively address potential issues around ethics, transparency, and earning patient trust in applying AI to guide clinical decisions. Combining this principle with TOGAF's Technical Reference Model, they were able to shortlist critical technology components needed to actualize responsible AI such as trustworthy data pipelines for collecting and processing patient health data; AI lifecycle management tools to govern the development and monitoring of AI models; MLops stacks for providing model explainability and transparency into model performance; and a comprehensive model risk management framework to continually evaluate their AI systems for potential patient safety risks or biases.

With TOGAF, its architecture vision, and principles providing ongoing guidance, the global healthcare provider was able to methodically develop secure, sustainable AI systems that effectively augmented clinical decisions across areas like diagnostic imaging, treatment recommendations, and chronic disease management, without compromising patient well-being and safety standards—a major success factor given public skepticism surrounding healthcare AI. The architecture practice ensured modernization activities remained aligned to responsible AI standards which increased patient trust while also delivering clinical and operational improvements—a balance that has positioned the healthcare organization as an innovative leader pioneering ethical AI in the industry.

TOGAF Experts

TOGAF has become the globally recognized standard for enterprise architecture, providing organizations with a comprehensive yet flexible framework for designing, planning, implementing, and governing technology infrastructure and business processes. As AI capabilities continue advancing at a remarkable pace, integrating AI solutions into this architecture has become a strategic priority.

Leading industry professionals predict AI will be embedded into every layer of the technology stack that supports enterprise solutions. From data management systems enhancing analytics to machine learning algorithms improving decision engines, AI is poised to transform legacy architectures. TOGAF's component-based structure and adaptable design principles make it well-suited as an underlying framework to support AI integration initiatives across customer-facing systems, production workflows, and other operational areas.

Experts advise that organizations leverage TOGAF's iterative transformation cycle when introducing AI so changes can be made incrementally, measured for effectiveness, and scaled based on outcomes and user feedback. TOGAF provides established governance protocols to deploy new technologies methodically while managing risks. Using these built-in best practices will ensure AI projects achieve key milestones across capability increments and generate desired business value.

Additionally, experts highlight that as intelligent algorithms take on more processes, roles and responsibilities will need to be reassessed. TOGAF's people-focused, stakeholder-driven approach can enable skill development and facilitate change management to maximize user adoption. With AI penetrating deeper across operations, TOGAF offers an architectural backbone to align emerging technologies with evolving individual capabilities and organizational priorities.

The consensus viewpoint shared by industry professionals is that TOGAF's versatility and robust structure uniquely positions it as an integral framework for harnessing AI's full potential while navigating the complex transformations AI will continue driving for the enterprise.

Chapter Four

AI Impact on TOGAF Domains—A Comprehensive Analysis

A I is profoundly transforming architectural practices across key domains in the TOGAF framework. In the business architecture domain, AI is enabling organizations to gain deeper insights into customer behaviors, competitive forces, market dynamics, risk scenarios, and internal operational issues. Architects need to design business processes, strategies, and models that leverage AI to enhance decision-making, personalization, predictive analytics, and automation. This requires them to envision how AI can drive revenue growth, cost optimization, and differentiation.

The data architecture domain is experiencing explosive growth in volumes and sources of data to fuel AI algorithms. Architects now need to architect specialized data pipelines, advanced analytics platforms, and unified data lakes to manage the influx of structured and unstructured data.

Additional skills in data modeling, metadata management, and data ops are crucial to governing and integrating new data sources while ensuring quality, privacy and lineage tracking.

In technology architecture, AI is leading a shift towards cloud-based processing and intelligent self-optimizing systems. Architects need to plan for scalability, flexibility, and resilience to underpin AI and ML model development, training, and inference integration. Emerging skills in cloud native architectures, MLOps, and adaptive cybersecurity are vital to create robust, automated technology environments aligned to constantly evolving AI.

Across these domains, enterprise architects are now taking on more advisory roles in orchestrating AI strategy, ethics, governance, and enabling synergistic integration of AI use cases across the business. Soft skills in change management, collaboration, and communication are also becoming imperative to coordinate the numerous moving parts and address risks holistically when weaving AI into the enterprise fabric. Ultimately, architects are the custodians ensuring AI realizes benefits today, while sustainably transforming the organizational foundations for the future.

This chapter focuses on expounding how AI is impacting these domains in detail.

AI in Business Architecture

Business architecture refers to the high-level framework that guides an organization's objectives, governance, business processes, infrastructure, and key policies and initiatives. It establishes the foundation for how a business operates. AI is progressively altering many aspects of traditional business architecture models across various industries.

Exploration of where and how AI can drive the most impact is crucial. Organizations need to analyze the current overarching business architecture and determine priority areas where infusing AI has the highest potential value—whether boosting efficiency of manufacturing lines, increasing personalization of customer experiences, or optimizing major back-office functions. Assessment of AI capabilities in analytics, machine learning, natural language processing, and more can match the technology solutions to key business needs.

Proactively realigning organizational business architecture using AI influences competitive positioning. The technology can become a central driver of new revenue models, commercialization pathways, customer engagement processes, and workforce optimization. It enables data-driven decisions at scale and automation of resource-intensive tasks. AI can reshape activities ranging from supply chain to sales operations. However, to maximize results, businesses must holistically transform their architecture around AI, not just bolt it onto existing ways of working.

The impacts on business strategy and operations are multi-dimensional. AI can achieve key strategic priorities—delivering personalized customer experiences, accelerating innovation cycles, and opening new markets. It also transforms operations—optimizing manufacturing plant schedules, predicting equipment maintenance needs, and managing inventory. AI should be integrated across departments to upgrade quality and speed of existing processes, while enabling new capabilities. Business leaders must continually assess AI opportunities across these dimensions.

How Will AI Impact Business Architecture in the Future?

Artificial intelligence is proving to not just be another technology fad, but a truly disruptive force that is radically redefining how businesses across all industries architect their organizations, craft strategic plans, and conduct day-to-day operations. The promise and potential of AI is so immense that those organizations who recognize its capabilities early and take swift, decisive actions to bake AI into the very DNA of their business models will likely outperform peers financially, operationally, and competitively over the long-term.

However, integrating AI solutions capable of optimizing processes, predicting outcomes, automating tasks, and continually learning cannot be done in a fragmented, siloed manner. To become an "AI-first" enterprise requires vision, investment, and commitment from executive leadership and stakeholders across the organization to holistically transform the business architecture, strategy, and operations.

From the business architecture perspective, the organizational structure itself may need to drastically evolve. New executive leadership roles like Chief AI Officer and dedicated AI strategy teams are becoming more common to drive the AI vision. Reconfiguring reporting structures where workflows and tasks can be augmented by AI is critical as well. The underlying technology architecture must also be entirely rebuilt to collect, store, process and analyze vast volumes of data from all corners of the organization. So AI readiness must be planned for and funded at the highest levels.

Leadership also needs to re-craft long-term strategic plans where AI is embedded into core objectives, initiatives, and budgetary decisions rather than applied randomly in siloed use cases. Every aspect of the business strategy must be filtered through the lens of AI transformation—from R&D and new product development to marketing operations and sales enablement. Bold investments should target high-ROI AI implementations first.

Operationally, workflows and roles will inevitably evolve as jobs are redefined and reconfigured. The biggest mistake would be not proactively retraining the workforce to attain new AI-related skills. The businesses who can foster a culture of digital literacy and provide learning opportunities are far more likely to successfully integrate AI operationally.

AI in Data Architecture

AI is increasingly being integrated directly into the architecture of software applications in order to make them more intuitive, intelligent, and autonomous. As organizations look to add capabilities like advanced analytics, machine learning, conversation interfaces, cognitive services, robotics, and more into their apps, architects need to examine how best to incorporate AI components into the overall application structure.

On the front-end, this includes evaluating how users will interface with the AI features in the application's client layer. Architects need to determine the best channels and interaction mechanisms through which the AI agent or virtual assistant can communicate with end users. Whether via text, voice, camera inputs, or a combination, the client-side architecture must enable transparent AI conversations and experiences.

Business logic architecture is affected as traditional hard-coded software rules and processes become augmented or replaced by dynamic AI algorithms and models. Architects must design supporting components and cloud infrastructure that can serve and execute the models that underlie the intelligent behaviors and predictive capabilities embedded into the application. This may require analyzing how the architecture can leverage AI model management systems and lifecycle management tools.

At the data level, architects need to incorporate AI data pipelines, catalogs, and stores into the architecture to prepare, manage and analyze the volumes of data that AI models require for training and execution. This includes planning for real-time and batch data flows that allow the models to consume information that enables intelligent outputs.

Across all layers of the application, architects have to evaluate overall performance, scalability and reliability factors—as poorly designed AI components can bottleneck processes or fail unexpectedly in sub-optimal architecture environments. Adhering to best practices in AI software architecture helps ensure robust, production-grade applications.

By proactively examining these architectural considerations, organizations can best leverage AI's capabilities in their custom applications to create optimal solutions for their specific business challenges and technical environments. The role of the architect is key to unlocking AI's full potential.

Tip: Analyzing AI-Powered Innovations From Different Viewpoints

As artificial intelligence continues advancing, AI-powered innovations in software applications are unlocking new capabilities and use cases across industries. To properly evaluate the impact of an AI-driven application innovation, organizations need to conduct in-depth analyses across several key dimensions.

On the technical side, it is important to assess metrics related to the accuracy, efficiency, and reliability of the AI technology powering the innovation. Evaluating elements like data precision, model robustness, transparency, and scalability can illustrate the overall maturity and production-readiness of the underlying AI. Cross-validating performance results on representative data samples can further validate effectiveness.

Additionally, the assessment should examine how seamlessly and securely the AI innovation integrates within existing technology environments. Factors like ease of API integration, compliance with security protocols, and flexibility across cloud and on-premise systems can demonstrate true adaptability. Analyzing interoperability and data governance considerations can highlight downstream technology risks as well.

From a business application standpoint, evaluating the specific use cases unlocked by the AI innovation is critical. Determining the breadth of problems the AI applications can solve as well as their potential impact on business metrics like revenue, costs, efficiency, accuracy, and customer experience allows quantification of application value. Comparison benchmarks measuring expected enhancements versus traditional non-AI approaches further highlights the differentiated value-add.

Finally, analyzing end-user experiences and feedback is equally important. Usability, intuitiveness, and learning curves for users interacting with AI applications reveal adoption readiness. And user satisfaction surveys can capture acceptance, pain points, and new ideas from those leveraging the AI innovations day-to-day. Incorporating these user perspectives allows refinement and helps ensure utilization at scale.

AI in Application Architecture

AI is playing an increasingly pivotal role across the entire application development lifecycle. From conceptualization to maintenance, AI capabilities like machine learning, natural language processing, and neural networks are being leveraged to make applications more intelligent, efficient and innovative.

1. Conceptualization

During the conceptualization phase, AI can analyze market and customer data to detect patterns and insights that better inform application design decisions. AI can determine what features users want, forecast adoption and consumption patterns, and highlight untapped opportunities.

1. Design

In the design phase, AI can review past user experiences and behavior to architect more intuitive, user-friendly interfaces. Designs may also leverage capabilities like computer vision and conversational AI to enable advanced modes of engagement.

1. **Augmentation**

AI augmentation during coding boosts developer productivity by automatically generating code based on specifications in natural language. AI can also detect vulnerabilities and flaws in code, enabling predictive maintenance.

1. **Testing**

For testing, machine learning models can be trained on previous test data to autonomously generate optimized test cases. This allows more rigorous and efficient testing. AI can also monitor systems in production to identify anomalies.

1. **Continuous Analysis**

Through continuous analysis of performance data, AI informs decisions on resource provisioning, scaling, and configuration tuning both before and after deployment. This ensures optimal efficiency, availability and cost-effectiveness.

1. **Maintenance**

Finally, forward-looking AI predictive models forecast maintenance needs. This allows issues to be addressed proactively, minimizing downtime.

Infusing AI throughout application development amplifies innovation, efficiency, and resilience while future-proofing systems to remain adaptive and robust. The integration of AI marks the evolution to more autonomous applications.

Analysis of AI-Driven Application Innovations

One key area where AI is driving innovation in apps is by powering more personalized and tailored experiences for each end user. By incorporating algorithms that learn and model individual preferences, habits, and behaviors over time, applications can essentially adapt specifically to each user. This enables content, product recommendations, notifications, and even visual layouts and themes to be customized to the interests and needs of the person using the application. As users interact more, the AI continues to refine and optimize this personalization, leading to stronger engagement.

AI is also innovating architecture by dramatically improving efficiency for developers. By taking over automating tasks like code testing, debugging, analytics configuration, and certain build and deployment processes that previously required extensive manual work, AI frees up developer time and brainpower. This empowers them to channel their energies into more complex programming challenges, creative feature development, user experience optimizations, and innovation. It also speeds up development cycles. The productivity gains unlock innovation potential across application teams.

The scalability of applications is further expanding with the help of AI capabilities. By more intelligently allocating cloud resources to match real-time usage demands, AI prevents over or under provisioning. It also removes the need for manual monitoring and adjustments in resource levels. This elasticity enables applications to scale up or down fluidly to accommodate spikes and lulls in traffic. This is crucial for innovation as developers can focus less on capacity limitations and more on enhancements.

Lastly, AI is enabling applications to innovate through more intuitive and smart interfaces. Integrating capabilities like natural language processing, computer vision and image recognition allows apps to understand inputs like voice commands, free-form text and images. This makes interactions more flexible, accessible and aligned with how humans communicate. With these cognitive services, applications can innovate to be more conversational and contextual.

AI in Technology Architecture

AI has become integral to how organizations construct both information technology, (IT), and operational technology, (OT), architectures in order to make them more intelligent, efficient, and responsive. AI is requiring companies to transform legacy architectures by integrating AI models and tools into data pipelines, application stacks, IoT platforms, and cloud-based infrastructures.

Specifically, AI is demanding more dynamic, high-performance data storage and movement capabilities for unstructured data sets used to train machine learning models. This includes object storage on cloud platforms as well as purpose-built high-speed data lakes. The data infrastructure needs to rapidly synthesize real-time and batch data from IoT sensors, edge devices, databases, and other sources to power AI. Flexible, scalable cloud services are also being woven into architectures to handle AI/ML model building, deployment, and management.

Additionally, AI chips and hardware acceleration are increasingly being built into servers, appliances, and devices to run intensive AI-driven workloads faster and more efficiently on-premise. This includes GPUs, FPGAs, and ASICs that cater to AI processing requirements. Embedded AI capabilities in endpoints across networks—like cameras, robots, and vehicles—are also demanding enhanced connectivity and intelligence within edge architectures.

Looking ahead, continuing advances in AI will make technology architectures even more dynamic and responsive. Organizations are expected to deploy more AI software and services from cloud marketplaces, leverage AI-optimized chips and hardware for faster on-site processing, and construct more mesh-like architectures that seamlessly integrate cloud, edge devices, and end-user environments.

Architectures will also become more customizable depending on AI workload types, providing flexible resources to power different requirements for machine learning, computer vision, language processing, planning, robotics, and more. The ability to optimize and secure these AI-powered architectures will be critical for organizational success.

Strategies and Methodologies for AI Integration

The Open Group Architecture Framework provides a comprehensive structure for designing, planning, implementing, and governing enterprise information technology architecture. To effectively integrate AI capabilities into TOGAF, organizations can employ targeted strategies across key TOGAF domains.

In the Architecture Vision domain, outline a vision focused on how leveraging AI will specifically transform business goals, objectives, and use cases to drive greater innovation, efficiency, and competitive advantage. This guides the integration approach across other downstream domains. In the Business Architecture domain, conduct workshops with leadership to align on AI ethics, evaluate business processes and functions prime for AI augmentation, and set goals around boosting decision support.

When formulating the Data Architecture, perform audit analytics to determine where AI techniques like machine learning and deep learning can be applied within data environments to automate classification, analysis, and optimization. Assess existing information architecture and systems for relevance and quality of data that can train AI models. Develop a roadmap to address gaps through consolidating data repositories, improving capture procedures and data pipelines.

Within the Application Architecture domain, map out a phased deployment of AI technologies aligned to use case priorities, dividing between AI-focused initiatives and augmenting existing solutions with AI. Take stock of technological resources required, including specialized AI tool-sets and large-scale processing infrastructure like high-performance computing capabilities.

Finally, for the Technology Architecture domain, plan out the nuts and bolts of underlying infrastructures to support the unique demands of AI solutions which require vast data storage, immense computational power, and high-throughput data transfer. Develop an integration blueprint to enable rapid scaling while adhering to architectural governance, security, compliance, and administration policies.

Executing these steps by domain, while collaborating across domains, helps pave a path for successfully embedding AI capabilities into TOGAF's comprehensive architectural practice. The methodologies underscore cohesively identifying the business imperatives for AI, while properly mapping out technical foundations for its real-world implementation.

Challenges and Solutions in AI Integration

The integration of AI capabilities within large enterprise IT landscapes built on The Open Group Architecture Framework principles poses some unique challenges. Primary among them is architectural misalignment between existing TOGAF domains and components and the rapid iteration and data feedback loops utilized in AI development. This can create disconnected systems and processes that prevent organizations from leveraging AI to its fullest potential.

Another major challenge is the extremely data-intensive nature of AI algorithms, requiring vast structured and unstructured datasets that strain current data infrastructure. Cleaning and preparing heterogeneous data at scale for AI consumption can be highly complex and time-consuming using traditional extract, transform, and load (ETL) and data warehousing architectures common in TOGAF models. Additionally, many current

TOGAF application portfolios were not developed with open AI integration in mind, necessitating API expansion and increased interoperability.

On the human side, lack of organizational fluency in both AI best practices and TOGAF principles can make it difficult for enterprise architects and AI developers to collaborate effectively. Existing IT governance procedures may also need to be updated to account for AI experimentation, testing, and deployment at the speed required for AI success.

To overcome these challenges, organizations can take an agile, iterative approach that introduces AI capabilities in a modular fashion within TOGAF components rather than force-fitting monolithic AI systems into existing architecture. Using TOGAF's Architecture Development Method to incorporate AI as new capability increments aligned to business priorities is also recommended.

Updating data management architecture to support AI's data requirements is also crucial. Introducing an enterprise data mesh with self-service access, AI model-specific data pipelines, and scalable cloud data infrastructure can help overcome technical barriers. Expanding APIs and loose coupling applications can aid integration efforts. Education programs that bridge knowledge gaps around AI and enterprise architecture can enable execution by skilled cross-functional teams.

With the right architectural strategy, technical foundations, and governance evolution focused on AI experimentation and operationalizing, organizations can overcome integration hurdles to infuse AI capabilities into TOGAF environments to serve critical business needs.

Future Prospects: AI's Potential in Emerging TOGAF Domains

The Open Group Architecture Framework provides a comprehensive structure for designing, planning, implementing, and governing enterprise information technology architecture. As AI capabilities continue advancing rapidly, TOGAF domains will evolve to leverage AI more extensively.

Within the TOGAF Architecture Development Method, AI is expected to play an increasing role in various phases. During preliminary phase activities such as defining architecture principles and identifying frameworks for specific verticals or horizontals, AI can analyze massive amounts of data to provide insightful recommendations. The detailed design process for models and views can be augmented by AI through automatically generating components, accelerating prototyping, and reducing errors. Even in later implementation and migration planning stages, AI can optimize timelines and resources.

The TOGAF Technical Reference Model will also integrate with AI more substantially. AI applications for intelligent data management will emerge to automate functions across data classification, quality, governance, and sharing between architecture building blocks. Likewise, AI capabilities around intelligent automation, predictive analytics, and self-learning will transform application and technology services. The Technical Reference Model will need to incorporate AI as a fundamental technology component moving forward.

Lastly, the overarching TOGAF framework will need to address AI's increasing ubiquity. Ensuring ethical usage of AI and adherence to safety, transparency, accountability, and control requirements will be paramount across architecture domains. Standards for effectively managing AI's integration into enterprise architecture will feature more prominently in TOGAF. Additionally, best practices and guidelines for leveraging AI to enhance architecture development and governance processes will likely be released.

AI injection into TOGAF domains will accelerate considerably in the coming years. AI promises to not only transform underlying architecture capabilities but also the way architectures themselves are envisioned and created within organizations. Tracking AI's evolution and aligning architecture frameworks accordingly will be key.

Chapter Five

AI and TOGAF— Enhancing EA Artifacts

A I has the potential to significantly improve the development of foundational EA artifacts like reference architectures, technology standards, and solution architectures. By analyzing vast volumes of data about existing architectural assets and current technology trends, AI systems can provide informed recommendations and guidelines for creating robust artifacts optimized for an organization. This enhances quality through ensuring best practices and future-proofing.

There are already success stories of companies leveraging machine learning techniques to develop reference architectures that embody preferred designs, integration patterns, and technology capabilities tailored to their business needs. By processing organizational data on budgets, capabilities, and requirements, AI can assist architects in modeling the optimal state architecture and associated transitional roadmaps. This enhances utility by creating customizable artifacts for re-use across portfolios.

Another key way AI boosts the value of artifacts is by enabling rapid, automated viable prototypes and reference implementations that bring architecture vision to life. As soon as reference architectures and solution architectures are designed, AI solutions can immediately produce working code implementations that reflect shared intent. This allows organizations to test ideas faster and provide tangible examples to stakeholders on how architectures manifest in real executable solutions.

Looking ahead, an area AI is poised to disrupt is allowing enterprise architecture itself to become more dynamic and responsive. As business conditions and technology landscapes shift, AI will permit real-time updates to artifacts by analyzing trends, assessing impact on architecture, and recommending modifications—all with or without human intervention. This self-learning and adaptation capability will allow EA to organically evolve in sync with factors inside and outside the organization.

The implications are increased consistency, relevancy, and accuracy of critical EA assets over time. AI automation also alleviates some of the overhead in manually creating and updating architectures. However, as with all emerging technologies, governance and human oversight is vital to ensure ethics, control, and security remain top priorities as AI permeates EA artifacts. With the proper guardrails and vision, AI can make enterprise architecture a thriving ecosystem that continuously transforms itself beyond static documentation to an intelligent decision system.

This chapter is designed to help you understand this use-case of enterprise architecture with the help of AI in detail.

AI's Role in Enhancing EA Artifacts

Enterprise architecture serves as a critical strategic function within organizations, providing a comprehensive blueprint that aligns business capabilities and technical infrastructure. The numerous EA artifacts produced, including architectural diagrams, relationship matrices, application portfolios, and extensive documentation, serve as the foundation for communicating architectural strategies and standards across the enterprise.

The integration of artificial intelligence technologies into enterprise architecture disciplines holds remarkable potential to transform the nature and quality of these EA artifacts. By automating manual processes, AI can accelerate EA artifact creation and enhance consistency, accuracy, and precision within diagrams, catalogs, and models. This includes leveraging machine learning techniques to rapidly analyze large volumes of technology and business data to identify insights and patterns that can inform architectural decisions and artifacts.

Additionally, AI offers more dynamic EA artifacts through continuous updates. Instead of static diagrams and documentation that quickly become outdated, AI allows architectures to reflect real-time changes within the technical, application, and business layers at an enterprise scale. This enables greater agility and responsiveness from EA practices.

Augmented intelligence that combines AI along with human architecture skills can also drastically improve the utility of EA artifacts for strategic leaders and other business stakeholders. As AI handles time-consuming tasks like data consolidation, experienced architects can focus on high-value work to create artifacts that better communicate insights, track progress toward goals, and link architecture to measurable business outcomes. This human-machine collaboration amplifies the value delivered by enterprise architecture efforts.

AI applications can bolster these artifacts in different ways and some of these are explained for your understanding on the topic.

Automated Pattern Recognition

Enterprise architectures often comprise large sets of detailed diagrams, documents, models, code, and other artifacts that describe the structure of organizational systems, processes, and technologies. Manually evaluating all these intricate EA artifacts for insights is typically unfeasible. This is where leveraging AI and machine learning algorithms can be tremendously valuable.

AI has the capability to computationally examine massive amounts of EA artifacts including architectural diagrams, reference models, interface specifications, infrastructure descriptions, engineering drawings, and even source code. By statistically analyzing these artifacts, AI can detect both commonalities and anomalies among the components and patterns within an organization's EA.

For example, AI can identify frequently used architectures, designs, coding styles, infrastructure configurations, and other standard elements present across multiple EA artifacts. This allows the identification of de facto standards and best practices within the current EA. Additionally, the AI can also flag unusual, atypical, and uncommon components that deviate from these organization-wide patterns and established practices.

Recognizing these EA patterns and anomalies provides extremely useful insights. Firstly, it highlights areas where more standardization would be beneficial across the enterprise architecture. This allows organizations to enforce consistent EA policies, simplify integration between systems, and streamline operations. Secondly, the identification of anomalies allows unusual elements that pose potential risks, inefficiencies, or technical debt to be addressed and remediated early on.

The computational pattern recognition and analytical capabilities of AI can dramatically augment an organization's understanding of its own enterprise architecture. The AI provides a valuable diagnostic perspective by revealing insights around standardization opportunities and areas of concern across a complex, multifaceted EA. This ultimately supports improved decision making, planning, and execution driven by data-based intelligence.

Intelligent Recommendation Systems

One of the key emerging roles for artificial intelligence in the enterprise architecture domain is serving as a sophisticated recommendation engine for improving EA models, documents, and artifacts. Because AI systems can rapidly analyze vast volumes of data and architectural knowledge, they can essentially leverage that repository of information to simulate subject matter experts and provide intelligent suggestions to enterprise architects and planners.

For example, consider a business process model that a team of enterprise architects just designed laying out critical workflows for an organization. This meticulous diagram represents the ideal future state according to the architects' expert perspectives. However, no one group of people, even skilled enterprise architects, have full visibility into all the latest technological advancements and innovations that could optimize those workflows.

This is where the power of AI comes into play. The AI system can ingest and synthesize architectural design patterns, technology trends, and examples of process innovations at a scale no human can match. It can then meticulously analyze the architects' proposed business process model and explore millions of combinations to discover optimization opportunities. The AI may uncover alternative workflows enabled by robotic process automation, augmented reality, blockchain, or other emerging capabilities that align well to the process objectives but the architects did not consider originally.

Similarly, the AI recommendation engine can examine integration points across architecture diagrams spanning business, data, application, and technology architectures. It can suggest new API connections, data pipelines, micro-service implementations, or other integration approaches to better link systems. The AI has no preconceived notions or biases that might limit exploration of unconventional integration opportunities.

The key overall value is that AI systems become a virtual brain trust that enterprise architects can leverage. It brings an exponential level of institutional knowledge plus analytical precision that uncovers enhancements human minds may never discern on their own given the immense solution possibilities. With AI as an enhancement engine, enterprise architecture artifacts evolve to their most innovative forms.

Real-Time Artifact Refinement

Enterprise architecture, models and artifacts provide a structural blueprint that outlines policies, systems, organizational structures, processes, data formats, technologies, and more that collectively make up the current operations of an enterprise. However, keeping these EA diagrams, documents, inventories, and dictionaries continuously updated has proven challenging. The static representations often reflect how things should operate in theory rather than the real-world practical state.

This is where artificial intelligence closes the gap. By ingesting real-time operational data through an array of inputs across back end databases, applications logs, API feeds, business transactions, system performance metrics, network traffic patterns, and more, the AI accumulates an accurate snapshot of how enterprise components are functioning and interacting at any given moment.

Equipped with advanced pattern recognition, predictive analytics, and machine learning capabilities, the AI engine can compare its aggregated real-time operational awareness with the existing EA artifacts. Any discrepancies, conflicts, redundancies, or performance issues get flagged. The AI can then dynamically update the EA diagrams, documentation, blueprints, and dictionaries to assign the appropriate taxonomies/classifications, connectivities, data flows, and technical specifications that reflect the real-world state of the enterprise currently.

This enables EA artifacts to remain living representations that automatically stay relevant to how systems and processes are actually operating right now based on the AI analysis rather than manual updates trying to match outdated theoretical documentation. Access to accurate and current EA documentation also aids executives, business leaders, IT teams, and system architects when making better informed decisions backed by real-time intelligence regarding changes, risks, migration planning, and more. The AI-powered continuous updates ensure context is always current.

Natural Language Processing for Artifact Generation

Enterprise architecture models and documents contain large amounts of textual descriptions that explain various aspects of an organization's business operations, technology landscape, data flows, application interfaces, and future strategic plans. Manually producing all of these descriptive artifacts can become tedious and time consuming for EA teams. This is where AI capabilities around natural language processing can help streamline the process.

By leveraging NLP algorithms, systems can ingest and comprehend technical documentation, system designs, business requirements, transcriptions of stakeholder interviews, or other textual data sources relevant to an organization's enterprise architecture. The NLP models can interpret the context and meaning within these documents through semantic analysis to automatically extract key descriptive details.

These extracted details are structured and organized by the AI system to then auto-generate full descriptive paragraphs and content that would otherwise need to be manually written by enterprise architects and related documentation specialists. NLP can identify relevant trends, patterns, insights, and recommendations from the source text and transform those findings into supplemental descriptive narratives for the various EA blue-prints, models, flowcharts, and inventory spreadsheets.

By having the NLP algorithm handle the heavy lifting of consuming volumes of source documentation and stakeholder conversations, it can relieve architects of the burden around producing descriptive write-ups while ensuring those critical details are still captured in the EA artifacts. The AI-generated content is customized and dynamic based on the specific technical environments, business contexts, and strategic needs outlined in the ingested source materials.

Over time, the NLP system can continue to iterate on and expand the auto-generated descriptive elements of the EA inventory as new documentation and stakeholder feedback is made available. This creates a scalable approach to keeping textual records up to date by leveraging AI instead of manual processes. The efficiencies gained ultimately help accelerate EA delivery and provide more meaningful artifacts to business leaders and technology teams guiding enterprise evolution.

Practical Examples and Case Studies

Let us take a look at some of the case studies to help you understand how AI can help EA artifacts.

Case Study 1: AI-Powered Demand Forecasting in Retail

A large multinational retail chain undertook an initiative to incorporate artificial intelligence capabilities into its demand forecasting processes. This entailed building an AI-based platform that could analyze immense volumes of historical sales data, as well as evolving consumer behavior patterns, to predict future demand with a heightened degree of accuracy.

Prior to implementation, the enterprise integrated the AI demand fore-casting system with existing technology artifacts the organization had developed as part of its broader enterprise architecture. Specifically, the AI solution was mapped to key elements within the business capabilities model such as inventory visibility, supply chain optimization, and customer analytics. Additionally, the forecasting algorithms and data inputs were aligned with components of the retail chain's information systems architecture including its point-of-sale systems, inventory databases, and enterprise data warehouse.

The impact of augmenting their demand forecasting with AI was measured across several key aspects. First, the efficiency of inventory and supply chain operations showed marked improvements. By leveraging the predictive capabilities of the AI algorithms, the retail chain could ensure optimal stock levels at each store location, significantly reducing both overstock situations as well as stock-outs. This enabled more precise inventory planning and purchasing cycles.

Second, embedding AI-generated forecasts and insights directly into business decision-making processes around supply chain and inventory management made those decisions more agile and responsive. The availability of real-time data and demand signals powered data-driven decisions and optimized planning cycles to react to shifts in consumer trends.

Finally, from a cost perspective, the reductions in overstock and product waste coupled with improved cash flow management attributed to better demand visibility delivered measurable cost savings. Specifically, warehousing expenses associated with excess inventory were minimized due to more accurate demand forecasts.

The AI implementation enhanced demand forecasting effectiveness in retail by increasing efficiency, augmenting complex decision-making, and reducing business costs.

Case Study 2: AI in Healthcare for Personalized Patient Care

A healthcare provider aimed to improve patient outcomes through the introduction of an innovative AI platform that leveraged the power of machine learning to process and analyze large volumes of patient data, including medical histories and prior treatment plans. The platform was designed to operate seamlessly with the organization's existing service-oriented architecture and integrate smoothly with the data reference models that were a core component of its enterprise architecture framework.

By ingesting and processing substantial amounts of patient data from dispersed sources, the intelligent AI system was able to identify patterns and meaningful insights that enabled much more accurate predictions of patient health risks. These enhanced predictive capabilities allowed the platform to further recommend highly personalized treatment options for each individual patient based on their unique profile and characteristics.

The impact of this AI implementation was measurable improvements across three crucial areas. First, patient health outcomes were improved through this predictive, personalized approach to care. Recovery rates accelerated as more tailored treatment plans could be enacted right from the start rather than relying on trial-and-error or one-size-fits-all options.

Second, the automation of time-intensive data analysis via AI meant healthcare professionals could dedicate more of their precious time towards direct patient interactions and care rather than data processing duties. This drove marked gains in operational efficiency across the organization.

Finally, the ability to extract deeper data-driven insights from the analysis of substantial patient datasets allowed for continuous improvement of healthcare delivery over the long-term. By determining which treatment plans yielded the best outcomes for different patient profiles, the organization could continuously refine and optimize their care models.

Leveraging AI to drive personalized patient care at scale led to recovery, efficiency, and delivery gains that created significant strategic and competitive advantages for this healthcare provider. The AI technology integration with existing architecture also ensured rapid returns on investment in the platform.

Future Trends in EA Artifacts Driven by AI

As artificial intelligence capabilities continue to advance, we can expect to see a convergence of these technologies with established enterprise architecture methodologies. This integration of AI into core EA artifacts and practices can evolve enterprise architecture in very impactful ways across multiple dimensions.

One area primed for enhancement is the automation of EA documentation. Given AI's capabilities with data processing and pattern recognition, algorithms can be developed to assist in generating and updating architecture diagrams, reference models, matrices, and other documentation in near real-time. Rather than manual updates by architects and analysts, these critical EA views into the enterprise can remain dynamic and current with minimal effort. This automation can greatly reduce the typically cumbersome overhead of documentation while providing more valuable insights.

In addition to automating reporting and visualization, predictive analytics will become an integral part of EA decision-making. By digesting volumes of historical data and identifying trends, AI models can forecast future system states across parameters like scalability, performance, and maintenance. Architects can leverage these AI-powered predictions to evaluate tradeoffs and make more informed decisions on EA evolution. This has the potential to increase accuracy when planning for the scalability and longevity of architecture investments.

AI will also lend its capabilities to enhancing the overall quality of EA artifacts. As algorithms learn from organizational data and human-driven EA practices over time, they can highlight inefficiencies, redundancies, and inconsistencies that may not be apparent to architects. The continually running analysis can identify issues and refinement opportunities in an automated fashion to keep the EA aligned with business goals. This will both optimize existing artifacts and better inform new contributions.

Core EA tools will likely adopt embedded AI capabilities as well to introduce more automation, intelligence, and sophistication into EA practices. Examples include AI-driven recommendations for architecture improvements, context-aware help systems for architects, and automated policy and compliance checking capabilities. Rather than passive repositories, these tools can turn EA content into proactive advisors on optimizing architecture.

Finally, AI promises to make EA content more collaborative, accessible, dynamic and adaptive over time. Chatbots and virtual assistants can enable stakeholders to more easily query and understand EA artifacts. Natural language processing breaks down barriers for non-technical audiences. And rather than static snapshots, AI allows EA representations to dynamically adjust to changes in business drivers, technology landscapes, and new innovations emerging within the organization. This can break down silos and help enterprise architecture become a more agile asset that is aligned with the pace of digital transformation.

Case Studies of Failed AI Implementations

Examining cases where organizations have unsuccessfully integrated AI capabilities into core enterprise architecture models, processes, and systems can reveal valuable insights into pitfalls to avoid. Common integration failures often arise when AI solutions are embedded without thoroughly mapping out dependencies and linkages across business capabilities, application portfolios, information flows, and technical infrastructures.

For example, one major retailer pursued an AI strategy to personalize promotions to customers based on purchase data and behaviors. However, the data inputs, processing rules, and outputs between their AI platform and existing loyalty systems were not adequately mapped out prior to integration. This caused downstream issues where customized promotions were out of sync with actual account statuses and purchase eligibility. The root causes traced back to disjointed data schemas, unmapped business rules, and broken integration points that should have been addressed proactively in EA planning artifacts.

Lessons learned from such experiences highlight the importance of cross-walking AI conceptual architectures with current-state EA landscapes early on to fully expose connectivity gaps and prerequisites. Diagramming information flows, data relationships, system interactions, and business process hand-offs is imperative to identifying integration touch points between AI and existing core systems. Analyzing these connection maps then allows architects to formulate integration strategies and highlight prerequisites that must be fulfilled before embedding new AI capabilities.

Proactively addressing these core integration points in EA transition roadmaps can prevent disconnected AI solutions that fail to generate desired business value. This may involve schema reconciliation, establishing data pipelines across systems, API expansion to enable inter-connectivity, or even adjustments to policies, processes, and reporting structures to truly unify AI with existing programs and systems.

Applying these lessons around meticulous integration analysis, mapping prerequisites, and cross-walking architectures enables organizations to circumvent major pitfalls from previous unsuccessful AI integration attempts within EA environments.

Chapter Six

AI–Driven Architecture Development Method

TOGAF's ADM provides a robust and structured process for developing, maintaining, and governing enterprise architectures. Integrating AI capabilities into the ADM can enhance and even transform many of the traditional architectural processes to make them more intelligent, responsive, and adaptive.

Some best practices for incorporation include using AI to automate the development of baseline and target architectures, using machine learning to develop patterns and standard components for reuse across architectures, and leveraging natural language processing to turn architectural description documents into machine-readable artifacts. AI can also be used to assess architecture options and make recommendations to accelerate decision making.

An AI-driven ADM introduces more dynamism into architecture development. It enables real-time analysis of change requests, automated updates to architectures based on new requirements, continuous monitoring of technology and business trends to prompt architectural revisions, and simulation of architecture variations to determine optimal state transitions. This contrasts with traditional document-centered methods focused on periodic and manual updates.

AI can specifically assist in key ADM processes such as business architecture development; requirements gathering and management; architecture creation and documentation; transition planning; and implementation governance. AI can generate draft artifacts; identify interconnections and dependencies; highlight inconsistencies or issues; and accelerate analysis—allowing architects to focus their efforts on high-value tasks.

However, effectively integrating AI into ADM also poses challenges around change management, trust in AI recommendations, transparency in AI decision making, and access to high-quality architecture data. Maintaining human oversight and governance over AI-driven architecture processes will remain critical.

Overall though, injecting AI capabilities to enhance and accelerate TOGAF's ADM methodology can enable enterprises to achieve more agile, responsive, and intelligent architectural frameworks tuned to business priorities. This integration of AI and ADM will be key to creating truly adaptive enterprises.

This chapter focuses on explaining enterprise architects how to effectively make the transition and provide some fundamental details about the strategy.

Integrating AI Into TOGAF's ADM

To effectively integrate AI into TOGAF's ADM, organizations should consider the following strategies.

Identify Areas Where AI Can Add Value

The preliminary visioning phase is a critical part of ADM where the as-is state of the enterprise architecture is analyzed. AI-powered analytics and assessments can greatly accelerate and optimize the evaluation of the current architecture. AI models can rapidly process volumes of data to provide invaluable insights. Determining the to-be architecture specifications also benefits from intelligent automation surveying the latest technological innovations referenced in the technology architecture.

AI further boosts ADM during the transition planning phase by automatically generating multiple scenarios that simulate various tradeoffs between the different enterprise objectives and requirements. The AI system can rapidly formulate and test many roadmap combinations to reveal the optimal transition paths.

Additionally, AI delivers immense value during ADM implementation. Test case prioritization and validation is a hugely tedious process that AI can optimize by intelligently determining the integration testing sequences to maximize coverage and defect discovery while minimizing execution time. AI analytics also provide continuous recommendations for improving architecture scalability, resiliency, and other operational attributes.

Forward-leaning organizations worldwide recognize AI's broad potential, but architecture development represents an especially promising area because it involves synthesizing multi-domain data into strategic blueprints. ADM's structured methodology integrates well with AI augmentation at multiple points across its phases. Each new ethically implemented AI capability further secures the enterprise architecture's data integrity while producing yet another competitive advantage.

By thoughtfully layering AI's advanced analytics onto ADM's empirically sound framework, organizations can efficiently construct durable foundations. Upon these robust bases they can derive extensive lasting benefits from AI-enhanced architecture development capabilities for many years.

Develop AI-Driven Tools and Techniques

Artificial intelligence unlocks tremendous potential across organizations by enhancing human capabilities through specially designed tools and techniques. Developing or adopting customized AI-powered data processing, analytics and decision support systems that align with strategic goals enables measurable performance gains. However, quality implementation requires meticulous planning centered on ethical priorities from the start.

Success begins by closely evaluating current pain points and limitations that are amenable to AI-based solutions, such as inefficient processes, inconsistent outputs or limited insights. Cross-functional leadership then assesses high-potential application areas based on organizational needs, available data, and use case maturity. Concurrently, champions must foster understanding of AI capabilities and constraints at all personnel levels to smooth adoption.

Technical teams design tailored systems by harnessing proven AI approaches including machine learning, neural networks and natural language processing. During development, they proactively tackle challenges around explainability, transparency, and bias mitigation to build trust in AI. Ongoing monitoring also ensures models stay accurate and relevant despite new inputs. Integration with existing architectures may be necessary for optimal human-AI synthesis.

Applied thoughtfully, such solutions promise enhanced productivity, quality and analytics. However, implementation is not a one-time event, but an ongoing partnership between users and developers. Leadership needs to actively nurture understanding and provide governance for safe, ethical AI deployment.

The fruits of this coordinated strategy are multifaceted. Systems that can analyze massive data to uncover key trends, risks and opportunities lead to better-informed planning. Predictive capabilities empower more proactive operations and resource allocation. Automating repetitive tasks enables workers to instead focus on creative, analytical and interpersonal activities. AI thereby bridges natural human limitations to boost both organizational performance and human potential.

Train and Educate Stakeholders

We must take a thoughtful, holistic approach as we build artificial intelligence literacy across all levels of an organization. Comprehensive education and training will empower a diverse coalition of stakeholders to participate in and guide AI progress responsibly. This strategy delivers manifold returns by optimizing development, implementation and oversight.

Curriculum and modalities should be tailored to suit each group's learning needs and styles. Technical teams require hands-on up-skilling in AI techniques like machine learning and NLP to facilitate practical application. Workshops led by internal experts and self-paced online modules teach the latest tools and best practices. Leadership and non-technical roles benefit from grounding in ethical frameworks, bias mitigation methodologies, and change management strategies. Case studies showcase AI development protocols firsthand. Periodic refreshers maintain universal fluency with innovations.

Broad competency minimizes usage gaps and builds enterprise-wide transparency and trust in AI systems. Employees across functions gain the acumen to harness data and algorithms for enhanced recommendations. Common understanding springs from a shared language around capabilities, limitations and responsible oversight. AI application permeates the collective skill set.

The well-informed, empowered community can then actualize AI's immense promise. Surface-level automation of repetitive tasks allows workers to focus on creative, analytical, and interpersonal activities. Predictive insights lead to better-informed planning and decision-making. Proactive operations and resource allocation derive from systems spotting key trends.

The ultimate fruits are multifaceted as AI capabilities compound when underpinned by a knowledgeable coalition positioned to amplify possibilities. With stakeholder literacy as its foundation, an organization's AI-powered transformation flourishes through progress guided by informed advocacy. Comprehensive education brings this enlightened strategy to life.

Establish Governance and Monitoring

Using AI technology in a responsible way requires companies to create ongoing supervision to promote fair outcomes as situations change. By carefully evaluating AI systems using structured criteria, organizations can find and reduce risks early while still improving quickly. Having consistent monitoring and accountable leaders is key to safely adding AI to systems.

Company leaders are ultimately responsible for how AI is used and how it impacts people, based on the priorities they set for oversight. Cross-functional teams should develop policies, thresholds and processes that balance innovation goals with transparency commitments. Important performance measures should include both technical metrics around accuracy and efficiency as well as ethical measures like fairness, interpretability, and user trust.

Assessments should happen on multiple schedules to catch opportunities and issues on different timescales. Real-time dashboards track system processing to flag processing failures or unusual data for fast intervention. Regular audits by independent internal teams check for emerging bias, performance drift, and result repeatability that require fixing before causing downstream impacts. External reviews on a regular basis provide outside analysis on evolving best practices for accountable AI management per current legal expectations.

Insights from assessments across all schedules feed improvement initiatives prioritized based on their match to organizational values. By putting in place structured AI monitoring paired with a supportive culture encouraging scrutiny and accountability, technology leaders can build stakeholder trust in AI systems, getting partners for realizing AI's huge potential.

The fruits of this responsible oversight approach are wide-ranging. Technical issues are detected early before greatly impacting operations. Bias and other ethical concerns are found through transparency enabling swift correction. And steady progress toward responsible AI best practices gives strategic advantage in a complex regulatory climate. With diligent governance, organizations can apply very powerful AI capabilities rooted in human-centered priorities for everyone's benefit.

Benefits of AI-Driven ADM

There are a lot of benefits associated with ADM that are designed to be driven by AI technologies. Let us take a look at some of the expected benefits in detail.

Improved Efficiency

Implementing artificial intelligence and machine learning techniques into technology systems and processes can drive exponential efficiency gains through increased automation, improved output quality, and optimized team productivity. By systematizing repetitive and rules-based tasks that previously required extensive manual effort, organizations free up significant bandwidth among their human talent. With algorithms reliably handling the most tedious and time-consuming responsibilities, personnel availability surges to take on more creative, analytical challenges that can unlock innovation.

Some of the most mundane yet meticulous technology architecture activities are ideal for applying AI optimization. For example, evaluating infrastructure networks involves assessing vast and complex configurations for potential enhancements. Machines can easily parse through endless technical specifications and run simulations to surface beneficial tweaks that architects may miss given finite time and human limitations. Similarly, AI accelerates code testing by rapidly validating modules against predefined requirements to speed up defect discovery.

By implementing reliable analytics-based tools to handle mundane planning, implementation, and governance tasks, technology teams multiply their capacity to pursue high-value strategic initiatives. Architects gain more opportunities to envision bolder innovations and transformations knowing that extensive analysis is augmented by predictive models and algorithms. Developers can expand solution experimentation recognizing that recommendation engines can rapidly optimize configurations. Business liaisons take on more impactful cross-domain process improvements as AI continually handles the daily operational tuning and administration.

Integrating AI across technology systems and processes enables more dynamic and creative architectural visions by delegating drudgery. Human staffers gain purpose over procedures and transformational outlooks over incremental admin. Leadership backing such AI implementations also fosters happier, more engaged teams by respecting human talents and promoting human-AI collaboration. The collective result is profound efficiency gains that drive increases in innovation, velocity, and employee satisfaction from AI elevating technology capabilities.

Enhanced Decision-Making

Artificial intelligence systems unlock powerful new decision support capabilities for enterprise architects by continuously analyzing massive datasets that exceed human processing capacity. Through combining learned pattern recognition across vast data volumes with simulations evaluating countless alternatives, AI-powered analytics fundamentally improve judgment quality. Rather than replacing architect expertise, AI serves to dramatically augment clarity and confidence during complex evaluations.

Consider the challenge of resource allocation tradeoffs, which requires balancing utilization, performance, cost and expected demand across locations, departments and currencies—a multidimensional puzzle. AI can readily process expansive data points far surpassing spreadsheet capacities. Machine learning algorithms detect usage trends while neural networks forecast budget adjustments and future needs. Simulations assess the financial, operational and risk impacts of thousands of allocation scenarios in seconds.

Presented with optimal scenarios based on architect-defined constraints, executives gain a comprehensive perspective that would otherwise require weeks of fragmented analysis. Bolstered by both detailed and strategic visibility, leadership can rapidly shift allocations to minimize expenses and risk while optimizing user experience. And by continuously monitoring outcomes, AI algorithms progressively refine decision logic delivering increasingly accurate support over time.

AI empowers architects with superhuman capabilities—able to parse immense details while concurrently weighing complex tradeoffs beyond natural mental bandwidth. Thought leaders describe this concept as augmented intelligence, with human ingenuity elevated by machine capabilities in symbiosis. When implemented responsibly, architect decisions guided by AI promise unprecedented innovation previously only imaginable.

The key ideas are that AI allows processing of vast data to uncover patterns, makes predictions through simulations, surfaces optimized scenarios to leadership based on constraints, enables continuous improvement of decision making over time, and augments human intelligence through this decision support capability.

Increased Agility and Responsiveness

As business conditions, innovations, and user expectations continuously evolve, leading companies recognize the importance of having an adaptable technology architecture that can rapidly respond to these fluid changes. Platforms once considered state-of-the-art can quickly become outdated legacy systems in the face of market disruptions. Integrating artificial intelligence capabilities throughout the architecture development process can infuse critical sensing, analytics, and automation that enable organizations not just to survive, but thrive through relentless change.

Specifically, machine learning techniques like prediction and optimization allow companies to uncover and react to shifting customer preferences, supply signals, and macroeconomic forces faster than the competition. By analyzing usage patterns, companies can detect strategic needs taking shape and then make proactive adjustments to their technology roadmaps that align with these forthcoming realities. Additionally, systems powered by AI lower barriers to re-configuring infrastructure through automated provisioning, testing, and component upgrades.

Combined, the enhanced foresight from AI-analysis and the configuration of automated systems provide extraordinary adaptability. As market contexts evolve, organizations have the indicators needed to make preemptive pivots ahead of rivals still wedded to static business models. Architects can stress test transformation plans under multiple scenarios to build resilient designs. Furthermore, continuous tuned monitoring allows the rapid detection of deviations that trigger essential modifications in near real-time.

By infusing AI-driven data agility into architecture, companies can establish first-mover advantage. Leadership plays a key role in conveying the possibilities of AI and promoting responsible innovation. With comprehensive opportunity awareness and rapid response deployment enabled by AI's perpetual capabilities, technology architecture attains unparalleled dynamism to outmaneuver competitors.

Better Collaboration

Realizing the immense promise of artificial intelligence technology is profoundly dependent on effective collaboration between cross-functional teams and diverse experts across organizations. While modern technical systems and architectures are complex to build, their successful integration into business operations relies extensively on stakeholders and team members coordinating around shared goals. AI-powered platforms provide an invaluable intersection point to enable this critical teamwork.

Thoughtful user experience design in AI systems grants intuitive access to data visualization, communications channels, and productivity features that connect team members. Key stakeholders can come together through threaded conversations linked to specific projects, requirements, and other components. Alerts automatically notify appropriate experts of any updates related to their responsibilities so the right people are kept informed. Embedding user surveys allows stakeholders to share feedback for continuous enrichment of the AI system's performance.

Enabling ubiquitous access across the organization is key so that participation is not limited by domain or authority level. Architects gain holistic views of the enterprise with drill-down capability into details to empower informed tradeoff decisions. Engineers receive technical specifications along with historical context to advance designs most effectively. Support technicians can monitor overall system health and collaborate with others on remedies. Executives have access to summations and notifications for items needing their strategic input.

Under-girding these activities, machine learning capabilities mine interactions to uncover synergies between teams, extract action items from exchanges, and forecast resource needs. Natural language processing parses conversations to prompt clarifying questions or identify potential miscommunication early on when it is simpler to correct. Together, the integrated AI augments all stakeholders' abilities to execute ambitious architectures successfully.

AI-powered work spaces advance enterprise architectures through enhanced transparency, insight, and cross-functional coordination. However, technology alone cannot guarantee effectiveness. Positive outcomes rely ultimately on inclusive environments that empower contributors across the development lifecycle. With AI as an ally, leaders can foster a culture of communication and trust to pioneer transformative architectures previously unimaginable.

Challenges of AI in ADM

Integrating AI bears significant challenges that demand proactive planning to ensure responsible and ethical implementation that provides strong return on investment (ROI). Naively pursuing AI without acknowledging key hurdles risks poor outcomes including deficient ROI, skeptical stakeholders, eroded organizational trust due to ethical breaches, and more. However, by proactively addressing integration challenges, leaders can unlock AI's benefits responsibly.

Foremost, organizations must plan for a multi-year journey towards maturing AI capabilities, given complex dependencies on advancing talent strategies, data pipelines, and cultural readiness simultaneously. While deploying AI tools tactically can demonstrate narrow efficiencies quickly, permeating AI across governance and planning requires completely reorienting architectures over years. Leadership needs pragmatic expectations combined with sustained resourcing of platform improvement and skill development.

Resilient strategies transparently address stakeholder concerns directly with ethical guardrails that stress fairness, interpretation of AI models, plus bias mitigation as safeguards improving accountability and easing job redundancy anxiety. Communication campaigns clarifying that AI aims to augment and support workers through elevated creativity and judgment can overcome misconceptions of complete replacement.

Above all, successful AI integration relies on quality data foundations earning user trust in completeness and fueling integrity. Architects should assess existing data assets and pipelines for gaps, ensure governance practices withstand scrutiny, and listen to stakeholder concerns. Evaluating AI via ethical frameworks and nurturing good data establishes goodwill benefiting all groups.

Thoughtfully acknowledging hurdles transforms challenges into opportunities for mindful advancement. A pragmatic yet optimistic approach, tempered by vigilant ethical application of AI, allows integrating AI-enhanced architecture development in a manner that broadly empowers stakeholders.

Case Studies of AI-Driven ADM Successes and Failures

Let us take a look at some of the case studies where AI is used and how successful they are. Remember that some of the case studies may not be related to the tech industry but can still help you understand the AI limitations and the advantages they come with. While the ultimate goal of an enterprise architect is to innovate and utilize according to their needs it is still important to be realistic while working on their goals.

Case Study 1: Personalized Medicine

Personalized medicine powered by AI represents an encouraging advancement for healthcare. In a compelling example, an automated AI system was developed that analyzes an individual patient's genetics, lifestyle, and environment to create a tailored treatment plan for their specific needs. This accounts for the incredible variability in patients and allows for nuanced recommendations to improve health on a personal level.

The creators of this AI tool prioritized extensive testing on diverse patient data to ensure applicability for many demographics, enabling more inclusive and ethical technology. Additionally, they engineered feedback loops so the system progressively learns from real-world outcomes and refines its recommendations over time.

The end result is sophisticated technology thoughtfully applied to provide care customized to each unique patient in a profoundly humanistic way—using AI to empower both patients and providers. Systems like these demonstrate how ethically developed and conscientiously applied AI for automated decision making can enhance experiences related to health and well-being.

The expandable nature of thoughtfully designed AI hints at a future where transformational personalized care could be made accessible to all who need it. Overall there is tremendous optimism around AI and other advanced technologies gradually making quality healthcare more personalized, proactive and democratized globally, when implemented responsibly with due ethical considerations.

Case Study 2: Predictive Policing

Predictive policing technologies leverage sophisticated artificial intelligence systems that analyze historical crime data to discern patterns and forecast locations and times of likely future criminal activity. By processing volumes of information with advanced algorithms, this software provides police commanders an additional tool to strategize optimal resource allocation for enhanced crime prevention in their jurisdictions.

Multiple documented case studies exist of police departments successfully deploying these AI prediction programs and achieving measurable reductions in target crime rates compared to existing trends. However, this positive impact relied on developers building the systems responsibly from the start, including designing programs free from biases and transparent about limitations. It also required police leadership committing to ethical adoption by using AI forecasts as input rather than absolute directives, complemented by community feedback and front-line officer assessment of real-time conditions.

These early outcomes provide an optimistic example of AI and automation benefiting public safety when thoughtfully implemented in the public interest. Predictive algorithms grounded in unbiased data analysis—combined with a commitment to serving community needs—have empowered departments to more positively engage districts through targeted prevention. Still, opportunities remain to expand adoption and continue improving integration of emerging technologies with on-the-ground personnel and citizens.

Responsible optimization of such tools provides significant reason to hope for transitioning AI from an abstract concept to a concrete accountability-enhancing and trust-building reality across departments. With a foundation set for addressing institutional challenges, predictive policing seems poised to evolve from novelty into a proven standard fixture that synthesizes technology with ethical governance for better serving communities.

Case Study 3: Automated Approvals

Banks have developed underwriting solutions that utilize artificial intelligence to analyze applications for loans and credit cards. These systems apply approval rules and criteria that have been collaboratively created by both technology teams and human underwriters at the institutions. The criteria allow the AI to instantly approve applicants who meet certain predetermined thresholds based on their financial and credit details. Any applications that fall outside of these set parameters get forwarded on to human colleagues for additional review and evaluation.

This balanced AI and human collaboration approach has increased applicant satisfaction by significantly reducing wait times for many customers to receive near real-time application decisions or instant approvals. The process of having both data scientists and underwriting experts work together to configure the approval rules has been essential. It allows the AI's pattern recognition capabilities to be combined with human judgment and domain expertise within lending risk analysis. Ongoing monitoring also ensures the system's criteria stays aligned with general best practices in underwriting. Additionally, responsible reporting transparency enables both applicants and human reviewers to understand the rationale behind each decision made by the AI, creating explainability.

Early positive customer response and user experiences demonstrate the immense opportunity for AI and automation to increase trust and confidence in lending when applied appropriately by banks. Thoughtful implementation of this technology enables high-volume, straightforward use cases to become streamlined and efficient while allowing human collaborators to focus their personal expertise on more complex special situations and edge cases. The result is an overall increase in both productivity and personalization across the lending process. As algorithmic tools and AI capabilities continue rapidly improving year-over-year, the combination of artificial and emotional intelligence hints at even further gains in creating positive applicant experiences and broader financial inclusion. This promises a future where lending decisions can achieve an ideal balance of both speed and care while upholding legal, ethical, and transparency standards.

Case Study 4: Problematic Hiring Algorithm

Artificial intelligence presents promising opportunities to remove biases from hiring decisions. However, this can only happen if technology creators prioritize ethical considerations from the outset. Problematically, one hiring algorithm designed to score and rank job candidates was later found to systematically assign lower scores to applicants from traditionally marginalized ethnic groups. The impacted communities deserve transparent explanations for why this tool discounted qualified candidates.

In this case, the core flaws originate from the initial development process. The creators failed to proactively embed perspectives from diverse groups, assess diversity implications, or rigorously audit for discrimination prior to deployment. Additionally, insufficient controls meant biases persisted once reported instead of being swiftly addressed.

This challenging example spotlights why technology companies must urgently cooperate across industries to spearhead affirmative standards, auditing processes, and monitoring programs that consciously counteract preferences for majority demographics. Policy makers carry an equivalent responsibility to fund unbiased AI research and require equitable algorithmic impact reviews.

Proactive collaboration can transform this solemn lesson into optimism. Appropriate ethical guardrails can ensure technology provides historically excluded groups access to generational economic opportunities. However, this first necessitates platforms admitting shortcomings, embracing difficult conversations, and dedicating resources to rectify errors. Only a commitment to equitable participation can truly burnish AI's role as an empowering force multiplier.

While AI presents a promise to remove bias, inclusive ethics must be proactively centered from the beginning by creators. Impacted groups deserve transparency around flaws. Standards, audits, and oversight can counteract majority preferences and biases. Achieving AI's full potential requires platforms to have difficult conversations, admit mistakes, and dedicate resources to equitable participation.

Case Study 5: Sub-Optimal Medical Diagnoses

There is tremendous potential in leveraging artificial intelligence for medical diagnoses, but close cooperation between technology developers and health practitioners is imperative to ensure patient safety. One case involved an AI system designed to assess respiratory conditions that provided imprecise diagnostic suggestions, inappropriately guiding treatment in ways detrimental to health. Further analysis identified two main issues undermining this tool's reliability. Firstly, the diagnostic algorithms were built without adequate consultation of medical experts. Secondly, non-clinical developers made assumptions that lacked sufficient validation using real clinical data.

These gaps highlight why responsible medical AI necessitates diverse teams combining strong technical skills and medical expertise to align models with clinically validated insights. Ongoing review boards and rapid reporting procedures must provide channels to quickly identify deficiencies before harm occurs. Healthcare has unique life-impacting considerations beyond business or entertainment, so this example serves as a wake-up call for improved governance that ushers innovations safely from conception through to practice.

If technology inventors and health practitioners collectively embrace transparency, accountability, and ethical AI design, tremendous potential exists to augment clinicians' abilities and increase access to top-tier care for underserved communities. But fulfilling this promise requires a collective commitment across all stakeholders to patient well-being through open and equitable collaboration.

Analyzing case studies on failures and successes when applying AI for automated decision making can improve an enterprise architect's perception when looking to implement their own solutions for their organization's problems.

Contrasting AI-Driven ADM Processes With Traditional Approaches

When it comes to strategic organizational decisions, we used to rely entirely on the judgments of our trusted leaders and experts. Small groups would get together in boardrooms, discuss options and scenarios, leverage their wisdom and experience, and land on what they collectively felt was the best path forward. And for many years, this traditional decision making methodology served companies well.

But today, there is a powerful new approach that organizations can take—infusing their strategic decision processes with the insights and recommendations gleaned from artificial intelligence systems. By combining rich datasets, predictive modeling, machine learning, and neural networks, AI can digest volumes of information and provide highly customized decision recommendations in mere seconds.

And the differences between this modern, AI-driven approach, and the traditional, human-based methodology, are quite profound. AI allows decisions to be made with full transparency into the underlying data, removing much of the emotion, bias, and subjectivity that can cloud individual judgements. The decision logic can be audited, traced back, and constantly optimized over time. The option of testing dozens of scenarios to game out contingencies and model future uncertainties becomes much more feasible.

Of course, traditional wisdom and human intuition still play a key role. But rather than having a couple experts around a table guessing at the future, AI gives them supercharged, quantitative capabilities to deeply understand tradeoffs, risks, and opportunities. This allows strategic decisions to be made with more clarity and confidence than ever before. So, while the traditional approach served us well historically, augmenting it with modern AI now opens up new potential.

Chapter Seven

AI-Powered Decision Making—Upgrading the C-Suite

Increasingly, business leaders are leveraging AI-driven insights to enhance complex strategic planning and decision-making processes. The technology allows executives to process vast amounts of data, identify patterns and opportunities that humans alone may miss, and provide predictive analytics to model different growth scenarios and outcomes. Rather than replacing human intuition, AI serves to complement it—augmenting the creative, subjective evaluations leaders must make when charting their company's future direction.

Leading enterprises are implementing AI solutions specifically to empower senior leadership strategy development and planning. Dedicated AI strategy teams work closely with the C-suite to determine high-value application areas, conduct pilot projects, analyze results, refine the AI systems, and gradually scale their usage. This collaborative approach allows executives to become more comfortable applying AI-generated recommendations while the technology providers better understand the types of insights and dashboards that resonate most with strategic thinkers. Communication flows both ways—the AI informs strategy while human leaders inform AI refinement.

As an enterprise architect, there is a prime opportunity to act as a conduit—facilitating clear and productive information flows between the AI teams generating insights and the executives determining strategy. Architects can aid AI teams in understanding executive priorities, decision drivers, and planning needs while also helping demystify AI capabilities and value propositions for leadership. This enables both sides to align efforts for maximum strategic impact and return on AI investment.

Best practices that enable this integration include: extensive collaboration during AI solution design; hands-on executive involvement in piloting initiatives; processes that combine AI insights with human domain expertise before finalizing strategies; education for leadership on AI methodologies and reasoning; executive access to data scientists to resolve questions; and iteration of AI systems based on executive feedback and performance. By serving as a core link between AI teams and the C-suite, architects help unlock AI's immense potential in augmenting and enhancing enterprise strategic planning.

This chapter focuses on sowing the roots that will help you as an enterprise architect to utilize the power of AI while making decisions.

The Growing Role of AI in Strategic Decision-Making

Artificial intelligence has immense potential to revolutionize the way organizations develop strategy and make critical decisions. By gathering and evaluating massive datasets—from sales figures to supply chain signals, customer activity reports and HR analytics—advanced AI systems can identify subtle patterns and trends that would previously have gone unnoticed. Machine learning algorithms are immersed within these vast data pools, conducting predictive simulations and modeling, to bring to the surface insightful correlations and scenarios essential for informing strategic planning.

Where executives once relied heavily on past experience and intuitive judgments when shaping high-level strategy, they now have sophisticated AI tools and analytics at their disposal, providing them with an invaluable advantage. For example, AI systems can discern how minor pricing changes may ripple across the entire existing customer ecosystem based on advanced forecasting algorithms. They can also detect early signs of emerging market shifts by analyzing relevant leading indicators and public sentiment signals.

Automated AI-generated reports regarding risks, opportunities and potential strategic directions allow leadership teams to make bold moves aligned to data insights versus gut instincts alone. Executives save immense time otherwise required to manually compile relevant reports and data. Freed from information overload, and confident in the machine learning recommendations, leaders can devote greater strategic focus to creative thinking and scenario planning essential for competitive differentiation and growth.

The future role of the C-Suite will increasingly entail querying ever more advanced AI systems to inform strategy setting and decision making. Rather than replacing human judgment, AI will serve to enhance leadership by revealing connections, predictors and options that no individual could reasonably expect to pinpoint alone. This intelligence amplification unlocks entirely new avenues for innovation and sustainable advantage over industry rivals.

The Interplay Between AI-Driven Insights and Human Intuition

Leaders today have an invaluable ally in artificial intelligence systems. Far from displacing human judgment, AI serves to strengthen and expand the strategic decision-making capabilities of executives. AI excels at detecting subtle patterns in data, running simulations, and generating predictive models. However, it lacks creative imagination, emotional intelligence, wisdom gathered from experience, and other distinctly human strengths that remain essential to strategic leadership.

The most unbeatable partnership is formed when executives combine their vision, intuition, and insight with the empirical evidence and simulations powered by AI. For example, marketing teams leverage AI for customer sentiment analysis, gathering invaluable insights into perceptions across demographics and past campaigns. However, when conceiving future campaigns, creatives rely heavily on human strengths like imagination, emotion, and original thinking. Similarly, while AI provides finance executives with automated forecasts of currency and commodity price shifts, the CFO calls upon seasoned institutional knowledge when deciding on financial strategies and investments.

Savvy leaders understand AI-generated predictions provide thought-starting points rather than absolute truths. They honor the accuracy of algorithms but go beyond their outputs by querying assumptions, evaluating alternatives, and war-gaming strategies—channeling their innate human capacity for creative problem-solving and strategic foresight. Rather than over-reliance, they maintain accountability for choices supported by data-driven intelligence. This balance allows leaders to steer their organizations with vision and wisdom, aided by empirical insights, toward sustainable innovation and value.

The bottom line is that while narrow AI holds invaluable potential, human judgment remains irreplaceable for sound strategic leadership. Only by wisely integrating the quantitative insights from AI and the qualitative wisdom of experienced leaders can organizations reach heights unattainable by either alone. The future belongs to executives who embrace partnership between human strengths and artificial intelligence.

The Role of AI in Executive Decision-Making

Advanced AI systems available today can be an invaluable asset for leaders making complex strategic decisions. They work by continuously analyzing massive amounts of data from across the organization and external sources. Using powerful statistical learning techniques, the AI can model patterns and connections to generate useful insights and recommendations tailored to the specific problem at hand.

For instance, suppose a leadership team is exploring expanding into a new market. Rather than simply providing raw data, the AI assistant could simulate how revenues, costs and market share may be impacted given its understanding of competitive dynamics learned from past observations. The AI may highlight growth opportunities hidden in the noise that humans are likely to miss. Similarly, for adjusting pricing strategy, the system could estimate demand elasticity between product lines accounting for various interactions. Leaders can then evaluate these analytical recommendations when deciding on changes intended to optimize overall profitability.

The key advantage is that AI systems go beyond basic task automation. They provide personalized, actionable intelligence that is most relevant to leaders' strategic decision-making needs. This curation of empirical inputs saves executives the hassle of drowning in oceans of data themselves. Freed from information overload, leaders can instead dedicate their unique human strengths to higher-order work like exploring innovative ideas and multi-dimensional scenarios. With human insights and intuition working together with AI-generated analysis, data-driven organizations are empowered to achieve unprecedented performance.

Rather than replacing human judgment, appropriately designed AI solutions augment leadership decision-making through targeted, analytical decision support. Combining the complementary strengths of both can propel organizations to new heights.

Companies Implementing AI at the Strategic Level

Leading companies across industries are increasingly integrating artificial intelligence capabilities into their executive planning and strategic decision-making processes. Rather than narrowly applying AI to specific tactical tasks, these forward-thinking organizations are providing their leadership teams with enterprise-wide access to artificial intelligence tools and insights that can inform competitive positioning.

For example, major global financial institutions now commonly adopt predictive modeling techniques powered by AI to guide high-level investment allocations across different markets and regions. Additionally, consumer product manufacturers are embedding AI-driven logistics forecasting algorithms into their systems in order to optimize complex distribution networks by balancing costs, risks, and customer service levels. Some healthcare networks are utilizing AI to screen large patient populations and identify target candidates for clinical trials by matching genomic profiles with probability estimates for success.

Across business sectors, C-suite adoption of AI capabilities is accelerating, as executive teams increasingly leverage these technologies to shape overarching organizational policies and strategy directions. Finance departments are utilizing AI tools for financial planning purposes by running simulations to predict returns under different interest rate assumptions. Marketing teams are deploying customer lifetime value models powered by AI to inform spending allocation decisions across various potential acquisition channels. Operations departments are interfacing with predictive maintenance systems driven by AI to continually assess production systems stability in relation to output targets. Even strategy consulting firms are embedding industry analytics powered by artificial intelligence into their scenario planning processes to uncover key opportunities related to future trends not visible to human analysts alone.

Rather than simply reacting to market changes, leading companies are taking a proactive approach to strategy formulation and leveraging AI-generated signals to envision future industry trends and shifts earlier. As competitive pressures continue mounting across sectors, widespread enterprise-level adoption of artificial intelligence technologies for strategic planning and decision support is set to increasingly separate winners from losers. Organizations that are able to effectively democratize access to predictive, prescriptive, and other sophisticated AI capabilities amongst their leadership teams will be well-positioned to maintain dominance amidst turbulence and uncertainty.

Enterprise Architects Leveraging AI to Communicate Up and Down the Organization

Enterprise architects occupy a critical position between technical teams and business leadership. Their role involves translating complex infrastructure into strategic business value and converting high-level goals into technical requirements. With artificial intelligence now deeply integrated into organizations, architects have a major opportunity to harness AI to enhance decision-making at multiple levels.

On the technical side, architects can deploy monitoring and analytics AI across infrastructure components like servers, databases and networks. This AI provides utilization and reliability insights that transform reactive issues into predictive optimization aligned to application and user needs. For data teams, architects enable discovery and governance by cataloging exponentially growing datasets and models with metadata management AI.

Towards business aims, architects can simulate the performance of potential new features using customer usage predictive AI. This helps create product roadmaps that target user pain points. For executives, architects can prototype AI-powered dashboards synthesizing financials, operations, and market data to evaluate scenarios and planning.

With their broad vantage point, architects can coordinate decentralized AI across units to amplify communication, visibility, and agility organization-wide. Specialized AI tools inform processes both horizontally across teams and vertically from technical levels up to leadership. Architects who master this AI orchestration across domains vastly elevate their leadership mandate as transformational change agents.

In this way, enterprise architects shepherd embedded AI tools to continuously distill signals into actions through architectural oversight. Their unique position allows coordinating decentralized AI to multiply their standing as force multipliers enabling organizational transformation.

Enhancing Decision-Making Processes With AI

More and more these days, we see companies deploying AI tools in their executive suites to really change how they develop strategy and make big picture plans. These systems use some truly advanced machine learning capabilities to help leaders cut through the noise and complexity of today's fast-changing business landscape. The key here is that AI actually enhances and builds upon human judgment instead of replacing it.

For example, the analytics engines these AI assistants are equipped with can process mountains of data from sales, marketing, HR, finance—you name it. They spot interesting patterns and connections that even the smartest strategists might never notice on their own. Leaders can then query the AI, asking for recommendations personalized to their specific situation and goals. The AI serves up insights into options they probably hadn't considered, while also predicting risks and highlighting emerging opportunities early enough to act.

Now, this doesn't mean the AI is making the decisions. The leaders are still very much in charge and accountable. But it's like they gained a whole team of extra sharp analysts to help them see more angles and possibilities. It saves them time they would have spent buried in reports, too. This frees up mental bandwidth for creative problem solving and weighing potential moves from a cultural or ecosystem perspective—the complex stuff that's hardest to quantify.

The most effective leaders know when to balance the AI's impartial data-driven suggestions versus their own experience and intuition. By leveraging the strengths of both human and machine intelligence, executives can feel confident placing strategic bets even when the future looks murky. It's the ultimate collaboration where each side pushes the limits of the other, achieving more together than either could have alone. That's how companies can stay ahead of disruption.

Balancing AI Insights With Human Intuition

At the core of leveraging AI to augment strategic planning is recognizing that human intuition and judgment remain critical components that should interact with data-driven AI insights. Rather than just producing recommendations in a black box, effective AI systems serve to expand the empirical inputs available for human analysis before decisions are made.

For instance, when evaluating potential new market expansion, AI tools can rapidly process customer data across various psycho-infographic dimensions to estimate addressable demand if entry occurs. This provides a detailed demand projection for human executives to then weigh with additional considerations that AI cannot capture—like cultural brand perceptions, potential regulatory barriers, and alignment with corporate values.

So, while AI provides expansive analytical scale, human interpretation and scrutiny helps contextualize recommendations.

Critical to this collaboration is understanding the inherent limitations of AI predictive modeling. No algorithm can fully simplify the intricacies of human behavior and psychology into absolute projections. Leaders should avoid over-trusting AI outputs without deeper diligence through sound judgment and critical thinking. Combining external data literacy and wisdom around corporate priorities helps executives avoid potential pitfalls from acting solely on AI insights.

When balanced partnerships between AI and human strengths are fostered through responsible collaboration, organizations can realize an evolution toward augmented intelligence for strategic planning. Decision making transforms from intuitive guesswork toward more empirically-grounded analysis. Blending data-driven machine outputs and wisdom-driven human interpretation unlocks new potential for confident growth amidst turbulence.

To activate this potential at scale, realizing the full promise of trustworthy AI for strategy requires thoughtful integration of people, processes and technologies across the enterprise. Success begins with leadership defining and communicating a compelling vision for data-driven decision making, then mobilizing resources and culture to activate that vision through careful adoption.

Best Practices for Integrating AI Into Strategic Planning

Rather than taking a scattered, ad-hoc approach to analytics and AI projects, companies need to build enterprise-wide AI platforms with strong data governance. This allows them to strategically target high-value business areas where machine learning can drive insights.

To maximize value, companies should invest in roles that connect their AI engineers with business domains. For example, hiring Chief AI Officers and AI Ethicists that thoroughly understand company operations to translate relevant problems for the engineers to solve. Encouraging collaboration through reviews and feedback loops also helps refine the AI to meet cross-functional needs.

With foundational data management in place, companies can then focus on data literacy programs. This allows all employees to get comfortable accessing and interpreting recommendations from AI models versus relying on intuition. Leaders should promote a culture of healthy scrutiny that challenges model assumptions but also data-driven testing and acceptance.

Ongoing measurement frameworks allow both executive teams and AI developers to monitor adoption rates, efficiency gains, and improvements in decision-making performance. This connects AI accomplishments to core business objectives and return on innovation investment. It also demonstrates how machine learning unlocks creative human capacities that were previously untraded at such scale.

In this comprehensive way, integrating AI into strategic planning creates exponential flywheel effects. The AI assistants enhance human intelligence, while human oversight prevents model drift. This allows companies to transform from static organizations into continuously learning, optimizing, and adapting enterprises.

The key is architecting a thoughtful foundation to unify data, people and AI models—targeting the intersections that provide the most business value.

Specific Examples of AI's Impact in Executive-Level Decision Making

Leading companies across various industries are leveraging artificial intelligence to enhance and optimize executive decision-making. From supply chains to content creation to fraud prevention, AI systems are analyzing massive volumes of data in real-time, identifying patterns and generating insights that allow leaders to make reliable strategic decisions.

For example, at the global beverage company Coca-Cola, predictive analytics AI tracks tens of thousands of environmental, supply and demand signals at once. It then guides supply chain planning by directing dynamic delivery routes, inventory levels, and beverage production volumes to minimize waste and meet customer needs. Despite volatility, AI enables Coca-Cola's leaders to optimize their intricate, worldwide distribution network.

The media streaming platform Netflix employs AI algorithms that personalize film and television recommendations to hundreds of millions of subscribers based on predictive taste models. But, Netflix also uses AI demand analysis to inform content investment decisions on new Netflix Originals. By uncovering evolving consumer preferences, genres, and talent trends, AI insights fuel Netflix's decisions on which types of shows to produce and fund.

In financial services, credit card provider American Express developed a deep learning AI system that detects up to 80% of fraud weeks earlier than with previous fraud methods. By alerting leadership faster, this enables rapid protective measures for customers, prevents revenue losses, and informs new fraud prevention strategies.

Across these companies and industries, artificial intelligence has moved beyond narrow use cases into enterprise-wide adoption. AI synthesizes exponentially more signals and data points than humans can process. With appropriate learning and oversight, AI therefore has the potential to elevate strategic decision-making by exposing influential patterns that would otherwise remain hidden. Rather than replace human judgment, AI enhances insight, foresight, and oversight.

Analysis of Outcomes and the Role of AI in These Decisions

When we look at innovative companies today, the power of artificial intelligence to massively boost executive decision-making capabilities is clear. Just take Netflix as an example. Their leadership relies on advanced AI algorithms that learn viewers' preferences based on data about what content subscribers actually watch. These predictive models enable Netflix to make smart decisions on what new shows to invest in, which promotions to target different groups with, and how to tailor the browsing experience for each user. By continuously updating the AI to reflect evolving tastes, they have achieved an impressive personalized experience at scale for over 200 million global subscribers. Hits like House of Cards were green-lit based on AI insights into what types of shows had an audience.

Beyond entertainment, AI is revolutionizing supply chain operations that have enormous complexity. Look at Coca-Cola—with hundreds of bottling plants, tens of thousands of retail partners, over 500 brands... That's a lot to optimize logistically! Their AI systems analyze signals from sensors, weather data, inventory levels, predicted demand, and more in real-time. This allows them to guide decisions on production volumes, delivery routing, inventory planning, and prevent waste or stock-outs amid fluctuating demands. Coca-Cola has already reduced product waste by over 40% using these predictive AI capabilities.

In banking, American Express developed deep learning AI to detect new types of fraud much faster. By digesting volumes of transaction data, their algorithms identify suspicious activity weeks earlier than was possible. This informs fraud prevention policies that have stopped billions in losses and protected millions of customers. The enhanced risk intelligence allows American Express to make quick, data-driven decisions to safeguard accounts.

Across all these examples, maturing AI adoption has transformed reactive firefighting into confident, agile decision-making even amidst uncertainty. By detecting risks early and revealing key insights, AI empowers leaders to set reliable strategic courses into the future.

Insights From Top Executives on Incorporating AI Into Decision-Making

Visionary leaders like former IBM CEO Ginni Rometty are ushering in an era where AI will augment, not replace, human capabilities in executive decision-making. Rometty believes AI's true power lies in surfacing non-obvious insights from massive datasets, expanding the aperture of information for leaders to evaluate more scenarios and unlock innovation. However, she cautions against over-automation, stressing that AI should enhance, not eliminate, human judgment and discernment.

Alphabet CEO Sundar Pichai shares an optimistic vision for AI's potential to address humanity's greatest challenges. By informing critical choices—from climate change to personalized medicine—Pichai sees actionable data knowledge as a key enabler of human progress. Meanwhile, Microsoft CEO Satya Nadella focuses on developing trustworthy AI systems that align recommendations with transparency, accountability and ethics. Centering human values and oversight in AI adoption builds confidence for leaders to reliably leverage AI's outputs in decision-making.

According to AI pioneer Andrew Ng, realizing the promise of AI-enhanced decisions requires investing in robust data infrastructure and people. By democratizing access to machine learning through talent development and reusable models, organizations can securely apply AI to guide both operations and strategy. In this way, visionary business leaders are thoughtfully pioneering new AI-enhanced decision paradigms to drive progress, not displace human discernment.

The common theme is that while AI holds great promise, responsible adoption that centers ethics and augments human insight is key to realizing the full potential of this technology. Business leaders are thus focused on developing trustworthy AI systems that enhance data-informed decision making without eliminating the human element of judgment and values.

Challenges and Benefits as Observed by These Leaders

Implementing AI to assist with organizational decision-making comes with both immense opportunities and risks requiring thoughtful mitigation. Even technology leaders like IBM's CEO Ginni Rometty have highlighted that quality, governance, and context of data remains an obstacle to getting the most robust and unbiased predictions from AI. To unlock the potential value, companies need accurate and representative training data that has metadata documenting where it came from and what it represents. This allows the AI to learn properly and avoid problematic outputs.

Additionally, leaders like Microsoft's Satya Nadella have emphasized the ethical considerations that arise with AI's increasing capabilities. Establishing human guardrails through cross-functional review boards is wise to provide oversight that AI recommendations align with principles of fairness and accountability before reaching executive decision makers. Leaders should be able to examine the underlying data and modeling that is driving AI-generated strategies rather than just treating these advanced technologies as "black boxes" without transparency.

On the people side, Andrew Ng highlights the importance of up-skilling workforces to apply AI tools through understanding techniques, implications, and limitations. Rather than siloed specialist roles, the goal should be broad re-skilling that amplifies the capabilities of all functions through AI literacy—equipping analysts, marketers, and most roles to identify use cases while leaders can then confidently commission solutions.

While navigating the complexities of pioneering adoption, maturing AI capabilities promise transformative payoffs if responsibly managed. AI can automate repetitive jobs for focusing top talent on higher reasoning—envisioning scenarios, creative problem solving, and strategic innovation. The generated insights uncover novel opportunities while predictions enable proactive risk management over reactive firefighting. By openly yet carefully harnessing AI's extraordinary potential, it can become a keystone for intelligent, responsive, and ultimately more human organizations.

Overview of New AI Technologies Influencing Executive Decisions

Artificial intelligence is rapidly advancing and providing enterprise leaders with increasingly powerful decision-making aids. Natural language processing systems, for example, can now directly analyze decades worth of unstructured customer data—from support logs to employee feedback to news reports—to uncover non-intuitive insights. By decoding the intricate complexities of human expression, this technology brings transparency to the subtle signals that can inform enhanced decisions.

Reinforcement learning is also optimizing key business processes through trial-and-error experimentation at speeds impossible for humans alone. Supply chain systems, for instance, use environmental feedback to continuously fine-tune inventory policies based on cost, demand uncertainty, and customer service goals. This data-driven approach lets leaders improve outcomes amidst the complexity and constant change in today's markets.

Generative adversarial networks, meanwhile, catalyze innovation by artificially constructing believable scenarios that forecast the risks and returns of strategic options. Marketing executives can scrutinize simulated promotional campaigns tailored to represent diverse customer archetypes before selecting the optimal approach. Leaders gain confidence by stress testing decisions under representative models of possible futures.

Fundamentally, explainable AI brings interpretability to algorithmic recommendations so that leaders fully comprehend system behaviors before taking action. With model transparency and audit trails tracing data lineage, executives move beyond blind trust in black box outputs toward accountable and ethical adoption of analytical decision aids.

The key is that modern AI grants enterprise leaders systematically enhanced insight, foresight, and oversight to drive better-informed choices. As these capabilities continue to develop, decision-making is transformed from reliance on intuition to confidence in data-driven intelligence.

Predictions on Future Technologies and Their Potential Impacts

It's clear that artificial intelligence is advancing rapidly, and will likely be deeply integrated into business decisions in the future. Instead of just providing raw data, AI systems will analyze endless information from across the company and distill it down to the most relevant, personalized and actionable recommendations for leaders to act on. So rather than replacing human judgment, these AI assistants will enhance discernment with data-driven inputs while handling number-crunching tasks too complex and vast for humans.

At the same time, next-gen AI simulations will be able to construct highly realistic alternate scenarios—think different product launches, economic conditions, etc. Leaders can examine these controllable simulations to essentially stress test potential decisions before committing resources one way or another. And AI platforms will interconnect emerging technologies like internet-connected sensors, blockchain ledgers, and interactive visualizations for multi-layered decision analysis.

But with the promise comes some peril too. As AI becomes entwined with key decisions, establishing trust and transparency in these systems grows crucial. Extensive audits will need to trace data flows across systems, while independent algorithms double check things for fairness, accountability and safety. Standards bodies will likely expand existing frameworks for responsible AI development so these don't become inscrutable black boxes. Savvy leaders should champion ethical AI that earns confidence by explaining how it works and prioritizing integrity.

By shaping these systems proactively, pioneering executives can transcend human cognitive constraints and drive growth in these disruptive times. The future of AI promises to elevate rather than replace human ingenuity—priming organizations to reach new heights responsibly.

Analyzing Data and Results From AI Implementations in Strategic Decisions

To truly determine the value AI contributes when integrated into executive decisions, organizations need continuous measurement across critical areas—before and after implementation. By comparing specific metrics and key performance indicators pre- and post-AI integration, companies can quantify the tangible benefits delivered in clear business terms. This visibility enables securing ongoing investments and resources to support AI at scale.

For example, revenue forecasts powered by machine learning algorithms should demonstrate reduced deviation from actual results compared to previous manual forecasting or basic modeling approaches. Customer retention AI solutions should prove superior at predicting individual churn risk over historic customer attrition averages.

Additionally, leaders must track how augmented intelligence changes the strategic decision process itself—not just outcomes. Comparing the speed at which predictive insights are adapted into new pricing policies measures adoption velocity. Monitoring the expanding variety of use cases across different functions provides visibility into scope creep indicating organic integration. Conducting surveys to capture executives' self-reported confidence levels and analytical comprehension gives the qualitative lift in decision quality and visibility indicating whether relationships between AI systems and strategic thinkers are truly gelling.

Broader performance indicators can also assess how AI amplification transfers into competitive positioning and advantage. Reduced headcount costs can quantify efficiency gains from automation, while faster product iteration measures innovation velocity powered by intelligence automation. First mover advantages in new markets revealed through AI scenario planning and forecasts underscore strategic potential that overshadows simple cost savings.

With continuous feedback loops that connect AI adoption and usage to strategic value creation, leaders both provide hard ROIs justifying ongoing investment and reveal gaps needing enhancement. Organizations' mature augmented intelligence cultures are rooted in responsibility, human enablement, and a relentless focus on achieving positive impacts through blending the strengths of machines and human strategists together.

Assessing the Effectiveness and ROI of AI in Decision-Making

Implementing AI for strategic decision-making offers tremendous potential, but preparing thoughtfully is critical to harnessing the full benefits while proactively managing risks. Savvy organizations take a balanced yet positive approach, thoroughly evaluating return on investment across both financial and ethical dimensions.

On the financial side, they carefully weigh hard cost reductions from improved efficiency and accuracy against the required investments. Additionally, they analyze expected revenue increases through enhanced offerings, optimized pricing and expanded addressable markets unlocked by AI. However, wise leaders complement these quantitative measures with qualitative assessments of how AI differentiates their competitive positioning and market standing. Throughout this analysis, they determine if AI systems can scale with rising data volumes over time, adapt to new applications and integrate with existing technology and processes.

Equally important, responsible adopters prioritize understanding of how AI systems arrive at outputs by emphasizing explainability, transparency, and fairness guardrails. They thoroughly assess algorithmic ethics, potential biases and adherence to regulations, recognizing that stakeholder trust is built through demonstrating these ideals in practice. Ultimately, they understand AI's value lies in augmenting human judgment, not replacing it outright.

In total, AI's real-world effectiveness for decision-making relies on comprehensive assessment of financial return thoughtfully balanced with social responsibility imperatives. This pragmatic approach allows organizations to capture AI's full advantages, while maximizing positive impacts on both business performance and the broader community. The most successful leaders therefore embrace cautious optimism on AI's potential paired with clear-eyed critical analysis to drive effective real-world implementation.

The Evolving Role of AI in Executive Decision-Making

Artificial intelligence has advanced considerably, now deeply integrated across business functions from customer interactions to forecasting and supplier logistics. This permeation enables more nuanced data analysis, providing executives comprehensive visibility into market dynamics and performance indicators that enrich strategic decisions. However, AI is best leveraged as a collaborator augmenting leaders' expertise, not replacing human judgment outright.

Thoughtful implementation first requires assessing the maturity of AI systems, particularly regarding accuracy, explainability of recommendations, and transparency of data inputs. Leading developers thoughtfully architect neural networks while engineering supplementary features that synthesize AI insights with decision-makers' experiential wisdom. This collaboration balances the weaknesses of both human and machine intelligence alone.

Yet, even the soundest AI requires validation. Organizations need talent to continually evaluate model inputs and outputs as an emerging specialty. They also must navigate evolving regulations around ethics and data privacy. More forward-looking leaders appraise AI not just for competitive returns, but also alignment with organizational values.

When strategically adopted, AI systems enable decisions substantiated by data-based pattern recognition infeasible for unaided human analysis. This new capability, unprecedented in business history, can ground growth strategies with analytical rigor across diverse market conditions. With conscientious implementation, AI promises to elevate leadership excellence via data-empowered augmentation of judgment and intuition.

While providing immense decision-making advantages, responsible AI adoption compels proactive planning around system maturity, collaboration with human experts, model oversight, ethical alignment and regulatory compliance. Executives who embrace this integrative, values-based approach are best positioned to capitalize on AI's analytical potential.

Preparing for the Future of AI-Powered Strategic Planning

Implementing artificial intelligence in a way that maximizes its strategic impact requires forethought and planning by business leaders today. Executives that are able to skillfully incorporate AI across their organizations and operations will be able to propel their companies forward and achieve new innovations and heights of success.

The first step in this process involves directly connecting AI investments and implementations to clear, predefined business goals and use cases. This alignment ensures that AI deployments provide accuracy and tangible returns back to the organization by their impact on priority growth areas.

Additionally, building internal AI talent and establishing external partnerships are both critical for responsible AI development, implementation, and ongoing optimization. The right expertise includes both technological capabilities as well as ethical orientation about AI's societal impacts. Providing training programs that teach practical AI skills while also promoting accountability allows organizations to cultivate an empowered workforce that can elevate data-informed decision-making.

Simultaneously, leadership has an opportunity to catalyze cultural change by conveying the immense possibilities of AI while also emphasizing transparent protocols around its development and use. Employees that are receptive to augmenting their intuition and judgments with AI's data-based insights are better positioned to incorporate those benefits, enhancing both personal and enterprise-wide performance. However, leaders must reinforce that AI is designed to enlighten rather than replace existing human strengths on which businesses still fundamentally rely.

By taking stock of current organizational needs and mapping future AI ambitions accordingly, dedicating appropriate resources toward ethical and responsible AI adoption, and staying grounded in human-centered design, executives can drive an era of amplified creativity, productivity, and sustainable competitive differentiation powered by AI. The future transformative potential of AI is here for leaders that proactively grasp it. Enterprises that prepare their work forces and align their cultures to embrace this new analytics-enabled environment will realize immense advantages as AI becomes further entrenched across nearly all industries. A prudent yet optimistic approach toward this transformation is key.

Chapter Eight

Case Studies—AI Transformations in Real-World Enterprises

Artificial intelligence is transforming businesses across industries and geographies. As companies increasingly adopt AI capabilities into their enterprise architectures, useful lessons can be learned from their implementation strategies and outcomes.

Industry-Wide AI Transformation Examples

AI and automation are fundamentally changing the way businesses operate across every industry. Rather than viewing these technologies as threats that will replace jobs, the key is finding ways for humans and machines to work together collaboratively. There are opportunities to leverage AI to augment human skills and capabilities.

For example, in healthcare AI is being used to analyze medical images to assist doctors in making faster, more accurate diagnoses. It can process vast amounts of patient data to help predict the onset of certain conditions, allowing for earlier intervention. However, AI cannot completely replace human expertise, emotional intelligence, and the doctor-patient relationship. An ideal scenario is combining a doctor's medical knowledge with the data processing and analysis abilities of AI—together they can achieve better patient outcomes.

Similarly in legal fields, AI can help lawyers quickly analyze large sets of legal documents and case files to identify useful evidence and connections between cases. This allows lawyers to focus their skills and time on higher value tasks like legal strategy, writing briefs, and arguing cases in court. AI makes lawyers more efficient and productive, but does not replace them entirely or remove the human touch needed when working with clients.

The key is finding this symbiotic relationship between humans and AI across sectors. If implemented thoughtfully, AI can take over repetitive and data-heavy tasks, allowing humans to dedicate their specialized skills towards the creative, strategic, emotional, and human-centered aspects of their jobs. Adopting AI is not about replacing jobs but augmenting human talent. With the right approach focused on collaboration rather than competition with AI, we can build a stronger future workplace.

Below are several illustrative case studies of how AI is transforming different sectors.

Healthcare

AI is transforming healthcare in profound ways. Machine learning algorithms can now interpret medical scans with remarkable precision, identifying diseases like cancer sooner than clinicians could detect on their own. This early diagnosis facilitates faster treatment and improved outcomes. Beyond diagnosis, AI systems help doctors predict the best treatments for patients based on their unique health profiles and medical histories. This personalized approach replaces the one-size-fits-all method of the past.

AI also assists in managing hospital logistics, allowing healthcare systems to deliver better care more efficiently through optimized scheduling, staff coordination, and resource allocation. Patients benefit from these enhancements with shorter wait times, more attention from doctors, and reduced chances of medical errors. Additionally, the emergence of AI-powered chatbots and virtual assistants has made accessing healthcare easier for patients. They can receive preliminary assessments anytime and get advice on whether their symptoms necessitate an in-person appointment, allowing them to make more informed decisions about their health.

With capabilities spanning diagnosis, treatment personalization, hospital operations, and patient engagement, AI is driving a revolution in healthcare centered on predictive, preventative, and participatory medicine. These technologies aim to anticipate medical needs, stop diseases before they progress, and empower patients to take charge of their well-being. Though still early in the transformation, AI has demonstrated immense potential to improve patient outcomes and experiences.

Finance

The finance industry has wholeheartedly adopted artificial intelligence to enhance multiple aspects of their business operations. From optimizing asset and investment management to detecting fraud to providing top-notch customer service, AI has become an invaluable tool.

Sophisticated high-frequency trading algorithms can analyze astonishingly massive datasets and make split-second decisions on trades that generate substantial returns. The speed and computational power of these AI systems allows financial firms to capitalize on even the smallest market anomalies and inefficiencies. Furthermore, AI now plays a crucial role in monitoring every client transaction and activity to immediately flag any deviations from normal patterns that may indicate fraud. By continuously updating fraud detection protocols and uncovering previously unnotice-able signs of illegal behavior, AI algorithms minimize financial risk.

Banks have also implemented intelligent chatbots and virtual assistants to transform the customer experience. Now when clients have inquiries about their accounts, need transaction assistance, or simply have a question, friendly and helpful AI agents are available 24/7 through phone, app, or website. By providing prompt, accurate, and consistent responses, the AI customer service solution delivers immense value.

The capabilities of artificial intelligence have become indispensable assets now driving improved outcomes, efficiency, and competitiveness for the financial industry. AI empowers this sector to leverage data, complex analysis, and customer interactions in new ways that were unimaginable just a short time ago. The integration of this groundbreaking technology will only accelerate in the years to come.

Manufacturing

AI is transforming manufacturing in profound ways. Rather than isolated machines on a factory floor, we now see intelligent, interconnected systems that are self-optimizing in real-time. This model of the "smart factory" leverages artificial intelligence across every component and process. Production lines feature networks of sensors feeding data to AI algorithms that perpetually fine-tune outputs for maximum quality, efficiency and sustainability.

Machines enhanced by AI no longer wait for failures and reactive repairs. Predictive maintenance algorithms instead analyze sensor data to model likely failure timeframes for each mechanical component. This enables remarkably prescient planning around service needs. Unexpected downtime is minimized, as is associated financial loss. Technicians can optimize schedules and spare part inventories, confident that requirements have been scrupulously forecasted.

Robots with AI capacities move fluidly between production line stations, adapting their programming to suit varied tasks. Unlike rigid mechanical arms requiring extensive reconfiguration to switch roles, these adaptive robots collaborate smoothly with human coworkers in shared spaces. They operate with increased speed and precision compared to manually operated equipment, while eliminating risks associated with fatigue, distraction or injury. The safety and output velocity of the entire workforce is elevated.

The net result of infusing artificial intelligence through the manufacturing environment is a self-orchestrating ecosystem that was unfathomable just years ago. Rather than reactive responses to events, processes perpetually optimize themselves through AI and machine learning. Factories require less direct control and minimize uncertainties. The sophistication and reliability of production flourishes across metrics. Essentially, artificial intelligence is enabling manufacturing processes that are self-driven, predictive and adaptable to an unprecedented degree.

Retail

Retailers are increasingly adopting artificial intelligence to enhance customer experiences and streamline operations. Rather than taking a one-size-fits-all approach, AI allows retailers to provide tailored recommendations that are more likely to result in satisfied customers and increased sales.

For example, by gathering and analyzing data on an individual customer's purchase history and browsing behavior both online and in physical stores, AI systems can determine their preferences and predict what products they are most likely to be interested in. This allows retailers to showcase personalized product recommendations specifically catered to each customer. Providing recommendations for products that the customer really wants results in a more positive shopping experience and builds loyalty.

Additionally, AI is helping retailers optimize their inventory management. By using predictive analytics and demand forecasting, AI systems can estimate future inventory needs more accurately. This means retailers can dynamically adapt stock levels across their stores and supply chains to avoid overstocking items that won't sell, while also preventing stock outs of popular products. This reduces waste and improves service levels. Automatically and intelligently calibrating inventory volumes allows retailers to meet customer demand in a more cost-effective manner.

In essence, AI is transforming traditional retail operations to be more customer-centered. Hyper-personalization of product recommendations and inventory optimization via predictive analytics are leveraging AI to enhance customer experiences. This provides retailers with competitive advantages through improved customer satisfaction, increased sales, and more streamlined supply chain execution. AI allows retailers to progress beyond a one-size-fits-all approach to truly tailor experiences to each individual customer at scale.

Transportation

The integration of artificial intelligence into the transportation sector has unlocked immense potential for optimization, safety enhancements, and improved user experiences. Rather than relying solely on human decision making, autonomous vehicles such as passenger cars, commercial trucks, and drones now utilize sophisticated AI systems to actively navigate environments and make split-second determinations. By offloading much of the operation to machine learning algorithms and predictive analytics, these vehicles can react faster and with greater precision than fallible human operators, significantly reducing the risks associated with manual control and human error.

Beyond autonomous operation, AI is revolutionizing maintenance and logistical processes within the transportation industry. Infrastructure like roads, bridges, railways, and vehicles themselves are outfitted with a vast array of sensors providing real-time diagnostics data. Machine learning models can then analyze these massive streams of information to accurately forecast maintenance needs, prevent sudden mechanical issues or decay, and greatly minimize downtime through predictive analytics. For logistics companies, AI empowers intricate route planning and cargo loading optimization according to traffic patterns, fuel usage, and hundreds of other variables—far surpassing the efficiency of traditional human dispatchers.

As these examples highlight, the unique capabilities unlocked by artificial intelligence are rapidly elevating the transportation sector in almost every respect—safety, sustainability, reliability, and customer experiences. While still an emerging technology, the machine learning models, predictive systems, and decision algorithms at work have demonstrated immense potential value. Adoption continues to accelerate year over year, and it is clear that AI will soon become an integral driver behind the operation of vehicles across land, air, and sea. The future of transportation guided by artificial intelligence is already here and fast unfolding.

Agriculture

AI is transforming modern agriculture in profound ways. Advanced AI technologies are providing farmers with invaluable insights and guidance to enhance crop yields, detect disease, and engage in precision agriculture practices. Rather than relying on instinct, past experiences, and manual monitoring alone, agricultural drones now traverse fields while capturing highly detailed aerial imagery and sensor data tracking key crop, soil, and climate metrics. The drones and accompanying AI software can analyze plant coloration, leaf coverage, soil pH levels, temperature variances, moisture content and dozens of other data points in order to generate sophisticated crop health indices and predictive analytics models.

These AI-powered insights allow farmers to identify ideal planting and harvest windows customized to their unique geographies and crops. The data enables early disease and pest detection as well, allowing for preventative action before infestations escalate. Throughout the growing season, AI helps guide irrigation schedules, fertilizer applications, and other interventions to optimize growth conditions as the AI continues to learn crop-specific needs based on the collected data over time. When harvest approaches, AI informs fruit picking or crop collection at the peak of ripeness. This precision agriculture approach powered by AI leads to higher crop quality and yield rates compared to traditional visual assessments and scheduled farming activity timelines alone.

With the wealth of crop, soil and climate intelligence gathered by the AI systems, farmers can now make every decision from seed planting to harvest backed by data-driven, actionable recommendations that reduce costs, waste, and environmental impacts while increasing productivity and profitability through greater efficiency. The AI technologies continue to quickly advance with increasing sophistication, allowing farmers large and small to leverage these tools to better understand and serve the needs of every plot of land under their stewardship. The future of agriculture enabled by AI promises more resilient, sustainable and bountiful harvests to better feed the world.

These case studies represent a mere fraction of the transformative potential of AI across different sectors. With the continuous advancement of AI techniques and algorithms, the scope and depth of AI's impact are set to expand even further, reshaping enterprises and industries in ways yet to be fully envisioned.

Lessons Learned and Best Practices

The integration of artificial intelligence capabilities is becoming increasingly crucial for enterprises across all industries to remain competitive in a rapidly digitizing business landscape. However, undergoing sweeping AI transformations requires meticulous planning and execution across all facets of an enterprise's technology architecture and business operations. There are valuable lessons to be learned from companies that have successfully implemented enterprise-wide AI—as well as cautionary tales of struggling transformations.

By studying other enterprise use cases, one can piece together an effective playbook of best practices when architecting an AI transition strategy, governing new data/development pipelines, re-skilling work forces, and managing change adoption across the organization. It quickly becomes evident that while AI drives immense opportunity, realizing its full potential necessitates a careful, phased rollout that is tailored to the specific growth priorities, talent strengths, and risk parameters of the business.

The most successful AI transformations balance ambition with pragmatic flexibility. For instance, it's better to deeply integrate AI into a few critical processes rather than hastily automate every function. And it's wise to train current employees on AI literacy before large-scale hiring. Architecting an optimal system requires assessing the readiness of datasets, back end infrastructure, cybersecurity protocols etc. as well. With a methodical, patient approach—while maintaining focus on end goals—enterprises can transform barriers into springboards for leveraging AI's full capability and value.

The arena of enterprise AI indeed presents challenges but even greater rewards. By studying patterns of positive change management and best practices around technology architectures, operational integrity, and human capital development in AI—while allowing customization for their specific business needs—enterprises can pave an accelerated path to becoming intelligently transformed organizations positioned for long-term success.

After analyzing tens of case studies we have created a comprehensive list to help you understand some of the lessons and best practices from these. While not every case study can help benefit your organization you can still use some of these points to trigger your creative potential as an enterprise architect.

Lessons Learned

Let us first take a look at some of the lessons learned from our analysis of different case studies:

Strategic Alignment

Implementing artificial intelligence capabilities should not be done in isolation—rather, it requires carefully considering how AI aligns with and supports the overarching business strategy and objectives. The most successful companies ensure that their AI projects are interwoven into critical activities, processes and systems in a cohesive manner.

Rather than viewing AI as an add-on technology, leading organizations think holistically about how AI can achieve targeted business outcomes like improved customer satisfaction, increased production efficiency, higher quality products and services, expanded market reach, and more agile operations. They assess their broader operational landscape end-to-end to determine the best areas and use cases where injecting predictive insights from AI could drive tangible improvements that ladder up to competitive advantages.

These organizations also take the necessary steps upfront to foster alignment across departments by promoting collaboration during the AI model development process. Bringing together leadership and subject matter experts from business units, IT, customer service, production, marketing and other domains ensures a common understanding of how applying AI can create value. It also leads to providing the AI teams with high quality, representative data sets to train solutions on real world scenarios faced throughout the organizational ecosystem.

By following this integrated approach to identifying and executing on AI opportunities, companies position themselves to seamlessly embed intelligence in processes and systems that are critical to delivering exceptional customer and stakeholder experiences. Rather than operating in a vacuum, their AI solutions are purpose-built to enhance decision making, optimize activities, and exceed expectations in harmonious ways that allow humans and machines to complement each other's strengths. The result is not just isolated AI wins but holistic operational excellence powered by AI's predictive capabilities.

Data Readiness

Ensuring high-quality and well-governed data is the foundation for successfully leveraging AI technology to drive business value. Many companies underestimate the investments required in proper data management when embarking on AI initiatives. They quickly learn that AI algorithms and models are only as good as the data that feeds them.

Rather than viewing data as a secondary priority, organizations should recognize that data is the lifeblood that fuels AI. Just as the human body cannot function without quality blood flow, AI systems cannot function effectively without access to quality data. This means that data must be prioritized and treated as a first-class citizen within the business.

What constitutes quality data in an AI context goes beyond what many companies are used to providing. Data needs to be clean, avoiding issues like inaccuracies, incomplete information, duplication errors, and inconsistencies across data sets. Ensuring clean data requires methodical data hygiene practices be in place.

But clean data is only the starting point. Data also needs to be relevant, meaning it must connect clearly to desired AI outcomes and provide useful signals correlating with what algorithms are trying to predict or optimize. Just amassing large volumes of data for the sake of scale will not translate to better AI performance. The data needs contextual relevance.

Making data both robust and relevant requires organizations to view data through the lens of usage requirements for AI rather than treating it as a byproduct of other systems. This means being intentional in understanding what questions the business aims to answer with AI and what data best connects to those questions.

On top of this, data needs to be made readily available and accessible to the teams and systems that interact with the AI. Data silos that hamper usage should be avoided. This makes data governance a crucial capability—assigning clear data ownership, rules, processes, and access mechanisms across the organization.

When data is clean, relevant, governed, and accessible, only then can AI technologies and techniques be effectively built on top of the data foundation to drive business value. The lesson learned by many organizations midway through their AI journeys is that data must become a first-class priority long before AI systems are put into production. Data is the lifeblood of AI success.

Talent Acquisition and Development

Managing artificial intelligence projects requires a unique combination of skills that may not currently exist within an organization. Rather than viewing this skills gap as solely a human resources challenge, leaders should see it as an opportunity to build cross-functional teams that blend complementary strengths.

The pragmatic approach is to focus first on re-skilling existing employees where possible. Assess current staff capabilities across IT, analytics, business operations, and other domains. Identify overlap with the technical aptitudes needed for AI model development, data engineering, and solution deployment. Workers with adjacent skill sets may be strong candidates for re-skilling through hands-on project participation, formal training, mentoring, and stretch assignments. Equipping internal staff for AI success stories can positively influence organizational culture while controlling external recruitment costs.

Inevitably, re-skilling alone will not address all AI talent demands. External recruiting should target both early-career professionals with emerging skill sets as well as industry veterans who offer hard-won experience implementing AI amid real-world complexity. Blending seasoned experts with enthusiastic beginners promotes knowledge sharing via peer mentoring and collaboration. Include recruiting metrics beyond academic pedigrees to reduce insider-outsider perception barriers.

AI leaders must also avoid siloed thinking by building cross-functional teams with diversity of thought and expertise. Data scientists bring analytical rigor while subject matter experts lend nuanced understanding of business operations. Software engineers enable creation of well-architected solutions. Creative thinkers spark innovation and human-centered design. Other profiles contribute strengths in user research, change management and technical writing. AI projects with multi-dimensional team composition benefit greatly from informed debate, constructive challenge and shared accountability.

The combined approach of re-skilling, recruiting, and team formation sets the stage for AI excellence by aligning complementary strengths. It enables both near-term project success and longer-term scalability across the organization. With the right talent resources, AI's potential for value creation is unlimited.

Ethics and Responsibility

Ensuring artificial intelligence operates ethically is becoming recognized as a critical priority for companies looking to implement AI, rather than an afterthought. There is growing awareness that AI systems carry risks like perpetuating harmful biases and compromising consumer data privacy. To proactively address ethical AI practices, more and more firms are building comprehensive ethical frameworks into their AI development from the initial design stages.

Rather than treating ethics as an add-on compliance item, leading organizations understand that accounting for complex areas like bias and privacy requires focusing on them throughout the AI lifecycle. For example, mitigating bias risks involves careful evaluation of not just the AI models themselves, but also the data selection, preparation, and labeling practices that feed those models. Doing so can help prevent marginalized groups from being negatively impacted by model outputs. Maintaining rigorous data privacy protections and protocols is another major consideration, including internal access policies, encryption, consumer notice and consent mechanisms, and stringent cybersecurity standards.

By establishing cross-functional ethical AI guidelines, firms can ingrain values like accountability, transparency, fairness, and explainability into their AI systems from the inside out. Some best practices include conducting AI impact assessments before deployment and creating external review boards to oversee model risk management protocols. Other components involve implementing tools to audit for bias, building AI ethics training into employee learning programs, and publishing ethical AI reports to transparently communicate with stakeholders. Prioritizing ethical AI is not only about managing legal and reputational risks but also about establishing consumer and public trust which underpins the entire AI field.

Technology Infrastructure

When implementing artificial intelligence capabilities, organizations must carefully consider their overall technological architecture and infrastructure. Rather than simply jumping into AI with an ad-hoc approach, companies need to ensure their systems provide a flexible foundation that will facilitate long-term scalability and interoperability of AI across the enterprise.

The optimal architecture might be an on-premises model, full cloud-based implementation, or a hybrid approach combining internal systems with public cloud platforms. There is no universal "best" model—the right infrastructure depends on the specific business requirements, internal resources, data governance needs, and existing technology landscape of an organization. However, regardless of the deployment approach, the underlying systems environment must address key priorities to support adaptable and extensible AI implementations now and into the future.

First, the infrastructure needs to provide adequate scalability to handle increasing data volumes, expanding AI use cases and functionality over time, and any unpredictable spikes in processing requirements. Whether leveraging internal servers or the dynamic scale of cloud platforms, architectural design must account for flexible compute, storage and bandwidth capacity that can cost-effectively scale up or down on-demand. Planning for scale provides a cushion for the rapid pace of change in AI development.

Equally important is enabling seamless interoperability between AI solutions and existing core systems, both on-premises and in the cloud. This requires using open APIs, standard interfaces, loose coupling of systems, and creating reusable libraries of functions and machine learning models rather than hard-coded "black box" implementations. Prioritizing smooth interoperability allows organizations to efficiently leverage AI alongside legacy systems, incorporate AI into new solutions, and adapt to continually evolving technologies.

By proactively building a robust, flexible technology architecture to underpin AI initiatives, companies can accelerate innovation today while laying the groundwork to rapidly adopt new AI capabilities as they emerge—gaining a sustainable competitive advantage. The right foundation enables organizations to fluidly scale AI implementations and seamlessly interoperate with both existing and future systems.

Change Management

AI adoption is transforming organizations in profound ways. Rather than viewing artificial intelligence as just another technology implementation, business leaders need to recognize that infusing AI into operations and decision-making often requires rethinking entire workflows, processes and job roles across the company. When such a deep transformation occurs, it inevitably creates unease, skepticism, fear, and even resistance among some employees.

However, with a thoughtful approach to change management, organizations can mitigate these negative reactions and smooth the transition for its workforce. The key is setting clear direction from leadership with transparent communication about why AI is being adopted, how it will impact the business, and defining any changes to individual jobs and tasks. For example, some roles may need to shift focus from repetitive tasks now automated by AI to higher-value analysis and oversight activities. Other jobs may work alongside AI co-pilots that enhance human capabilities.

Regardless of the specific AI applications, the goals and benefits need to be stated openly by leadership and discussed through multiple forums to foster employee understanding. Additionally, the organization needs to provide proper education and training to employees on working with AI systems and leveraging the technology to elevate their roles. Equipping staff with knowledge and skills for the AI-powered workplace eases uncertainty.

Finally, communication during AI adoption cannot be one-way. Business leaders must actively listen and respond to employee concerns, questions and feedback through surveys, meetings, and other channels. Making staff feel heard goes a long way toward greater engagement and willingness to embrace changes brought by AI.

Measure ROI

When organizations implement artificial intelligence projects, clearly defining metrics to track return on investment from the outset is crucial. Without this upfront strategic planning, companies risk not being able to accurately quantify the value delivered from AI implementations and struggle to justify the potentially substantial investments to key stakeholders across the business.

Rather than making vague promises of increased efficiency or ambiguous improvements from adopting AI, savvy organizations take the time to delineate precise key performance indicators that will be monitored over time. Common financial metrics include calculating specific cost savings in areas like reduced headcount or improvements in operational expenditures, tracking revenue increases that can be attributed to AI-enhanced offerings, and determining the start-up and ongoing costs associated with AI systems.

Wise organizations also look beyond purely financial returns to craft metrics that measure AI success in terms of customer and employee satisfaction, competitive advantages gained in the marketplace, improvements in product quality or service delivery, and more. Developing 360-degree metrics across multiple dimensions, including both quantitative and qualitative measures, produces a much more informative picture of the total value being driven by artificial intelligence.

Establishing this strategic practice of designing comprehensive AI success metrics upfront rather than waiting until after implementation has occurred allows organizations to set clear ROI expectations about what reasonable outcomes look like. The metrics provide accountability and give project leaders evidence to show stakeholders when milestones are reached. Defining metrics early also simplifies the assessment process to see if expected returns failed to materialize or if some unintended benefits emerged that weren't originally considered. Tracking metrics continually lets teams course correct if necessary and optimize AI performance.

With the substantial investments required for artificial intelligence today, organizations that do the groundwork to develop clear ROI metrics position their AI initiatives for the highest chance of success. They can demonstrate value and justify the costs in business terms that resonate across the leadership team and all stakeholders, setting projects up to deliver transformative capabilities that give the organization a competitive edge for the long haul.

Best Practices

Now let us take a look at some of the best practices that we have observed while analyzing these case studies. As said before, remember that not every practice will suit your organization.

Integrate Incrementally

Implementing artificial intelligence capabilities across an entire organization all at once carries substantial risk and uncertainty. However, organizations can integrate AI in a more controlled, incremental fashion by phasing AI components into existing workflows one step at a time. This gradual integration approach provides several advantages.

First, it is easier to manage potential risks upfront rather than dealing with larger unforeseen issues later on. As AI is initially implemented in limited scopes, organizations can assess performance, identify problems early, and make necessary adjustments before proceeding to the next phase. Any mistakes or failures remain relatively small and contained. Organizations can take the time to ensure AI models are properly optimized and employees are ready for the technology shift, enabling a smoother long-term transition.

Additionally, a phased approach allows for more flexibility to modify roll-out plans based on real-world testing. As AI is integrated into singular processes, organizations observe functionality firsthand, determine where enhancements need to be made, and tweak later integration plans accordingly. They can determine where AI adoption is working seamlessly and where human oversight is still required before systems are connected more broadly. This empowers managers to customize AI implementation in alignment with actual organizational needs.

Finally, a gradual integration strategy helps employees across the organization adjust to working alongside AI over time. Changing processes all at once can overwhelm employees and potentially spur resistance or anxiety. But when changes are made slowly in stages, staff have more opportunity to become acclimated with AI through hands-on experience. They gain comfort with the technology at their own pace with less disruption.

The bottom line is that implementing AI judiciously step-by-step mitigates growing pains and allows the organization to maximize value. It may take longer for AI to permeate the entire company, but the long-term benefits of managing risk, retaining flexibility, and easing employee transitions ultimately outweigh any delays.

Focus on User Adoption

Ensuring user-friendly artificial intelligence solutions that employees actually adopt and leverage is critical for any successful AI implementation within an organization. Rather than taking a technology-first approach and then forcing employees to use new AI tools, the solutions should be designed intentionally around the people who will be utilizing them day to day.

The ideal process is to first clearly understand critical pain points in current workflows, challenges employees face in their specific roles, and opportunities to automate repetitive tasks. With clear insights around user needs and use cases, AI solutions can then be customized to directly resolve existing issues while requiring minimal changes to how employees currently work. The solutions should integrate seamlessly into normal workflows rather than demanding employees learn and navigate entirely new systems.

Intuitive user interfaces, clear explanations of recommendations and insights provided by AI algorithms, and transparent processes around data being utilized can promote adoption by building trust and confidence in the technology. Users need to feel empowered by AI supporting them rather than threatened by it replacing them. Things like natural language processing and conversational interfaces help minimize the learning curve associated with adopting AI tools.

Ongoing employee engagement, communication, and training resources are also essential to drive understanding and excitement around the implementation. Training programs can not only educate on system functionality but also highlight the individual and organizational benefits different groups stand to gain. Celebrating early wins and providing forums for employee feedback foster further engagement.

By focusing first on people rather than technology, and emphasizing continuous improvement of solutions based directly on user needs, organizations can deliver AI tools that employees readily embrace rather than resist. This promotes rapid adoption and maximum utilization of AI investments.

Maintain Transparency

Implementing artificial intelligence technology can bring tremendous efficiency gains and competitive advantages to organizations across nearly every industry. However, the success of any AI initiative hinges on effective change management across the entire workforce. Rather than simply dictating a new AI-driven approach from the top-down, company leadership should focus significant effort on collaborating with employees at all levels to ensure they understand and buy into the purpose and vision behind AI adoption.

The best practice is to begin communicating early and often about why the organization is pursuing AI capability, how it stands to benefit the company and employees alike, and specifics on how each role will potentially be impacted. It is critical that people do not feel surprise or shock at a big AI announcement without context, but rather have had an ongoing transparent dialogue where their voices, concerns and ideas have been continually heard. This establishes a foundation of trust and shared vision moving forward.

For example, the executive team might schedule an all-hands meeting to announce the AI strategy and implementation roadmap. But well in advance of that, managers should have conversations within their teams to field initial reactions and questions in a more intimate setting. Peers should discuss among themselves what they are excited and apprehensive about. No question or perspective should be dismissed.

This ongoing open and collaborative communication ensures that every employee understands exactly why AI technology is being adopted, how it stands to make their individual jobs easier while accomplishing organization-wide goals, and how their roles may evolve along the way. This unified understanding and buy-in at all levels translates directly into smoother adoption, better utilization of the AI capabilities, and ultimately a higher return on the AI investment itself. The people are what make AI implementation successful, so they must be brought along every step of that journey through patient, compassionate communication.

Establish Data Governance

Establishing robust data governance is an essential building block when implementing artificial intelligence and realizing its full potential while avoiding pitfalls. Rather than simply jumping into AI with an ad hoc approach, organizations would benefit greatly from stepping back and laying the proper data foundation first.

This begins by assembling a strong data governance team encompassing leadership roles across IT, analytics, business operations, and compliance. With representation across these key areas, the team can then define comprehensive policies, procedures, and standards that place data quality and integrity as a top priority while adhering to regulatory mandates around usage and ethics.

With the right governance structure in place, the organization can institute methodical processes that collect, organize, and analyze its data assets in a manner that supports reliability and bias-free algorithmic modeling. This involves careful vetting and documentation of data sources, cross-referencing inputs, and scrutiny of analytics outputs. It also requires monitoring data practices in coordination with HR to uphold ethical standards and provide transparency around how employee and customer information feeds into AI systems.

Data governance lays a principled foundation upon which AI can then deliver robust and equitable business insights that the organization can confidently leverage for enhanced decision-making. It establishes guardrails to oversee the ethical application of predictive analytics and machine learning over the long-term and across all impacted areas of the business. When supported by a mature governance program, AI has the potential to drive dramatic operational optimization without adverse impacts.

To successfully implement AI in enterprise settings, it is a confluence of technology, people, and processes orchestrated harmoniously to actualize the potential of AI while mitigating the associated risks. Continuing to employ these lessons learned and best practices will determine the long-term success of AI in enterprise architectures.

Categorization of Case Studies by Industry

Enterprise architecture practitioners regularly develop industry-focused case studies to provide targeted insights into the challenges and opportunities within specific sectors. By organizing case studies based on industries like healthcare, finance, manufacturing, technology, and government, they can showcase how architectural frameworks, strategies, and practices address the unique aspects of each domain.

For example, in healthcare, case studies would reflect the stringent regulatory compliance requirements like HIPAA that necessitate an emphasis on security and privacy in the enterprise architecture. Patient health data requires strict confidentiality and integrity controls that span policies, processes, people, and technology. Case studies would demonstrate healthcare enterprise architectures that facilitate access controls, identity management, audit logging, and disaster recovery to mitigate risks related to sensitive personal information.

In contrast, the financial sector prioritizes different attributes within their enterprise architectures like high reliability and transactional integrity for banking and trading systems. Case studies would detail how financial institutions design resilient IT infrastructure, real-time data synchronization, redundancy, and fail over capabilities to maximize system availability and prevent loss or inaccuracy of critical financial transactions and records.

The manufacturing industry has markedly different architectural priorities centered around supply chain integration and Internet of Things technologies for production equipment and inventory management. Case studies would show innovative architectures that connect disparate manufacturing systems into a unified data environment to gain operational visibility, automate processes, and optimize manufacturing operations.

By comparing case studies across sectors, enterprise architects can discern common patterns in governance, data, application, and technology architectures while also recognizing where industry-specific customization occurs. This comparative analysis also reveals architectural best practices that succeed in one industry and hold potential for adaptation in others. Categorizing case studies by sector allows for benchmarking performance, illuminating improvement opportunities, inspiring innovation, and ultimately providing impactful illustrations of how enterprise architecture principles manifest within targeted industries.

Global Diversity in Case Studies

Artificial intelligence is rapidly transforming organizations across the globe. However, the adoption and impact of AI technologies manifests differently across regions and cultures. As companies worldwide implement AI to evolve their enterprises, distinct use cases and best practices have emerged that reflect the diverse priorities and values of local contexts.

In Asia, for example, manufacturers have pioneered 'intelligent industry' initiatives integrating AI across inventory, supply chain, quality control, and robotic automation. The priority is leveraging AI's predictive capabilities to maximize output, efficiency, and reliability. However, ethical considerations regarding data transparency, surveillance, and job automation also shape the development of Asian AI applications.

European AI development emphasizes privacy protection and human oversight reflecting public skepticism and strict regulatory controls like GDPR. Industries apply AI for enhanced decision support rather than autonomous systems. For instance, financial institutions implement AI to provide personalized portfolio recommendations and risk analysis rather than fully automated trading. Focus remains on augmenting human intellect rather than replacing the human workforce.

The open markets and abundant venture capital funding of North America, especially in technology hubs like Silicon Valley and Toronto, support widespread AI innovation. The region sets global trends in areas like conversational interfaces, computer vision, predictive analytics, and self-driving vehicles. However, barriers around data silos, talent shortages, bias mitigation, and establishing trust in AI solutions persist, requiring ongoing research.

Ultimately enterprises worldwide recognize AI's immense transformative potential, but thoughtfully integrate AI capabilities in line with local cultures, regulations, and customs. The diversity of global AI adoption yields best practices for stakeholders across geographies to emulate and adapt based on their unique priorities and constraints. Though AI is a global phenomenon, its manifestation retains local optimization.

Assessing Sustainability and Ongoing Impact of AI Implementations

Evaluating the true long-term value of AI systems requires going beyond the initial performance metrics and cost-benefit analysis. To determine sustainability, organizations need to take a more holistic view across factors related to maintainability, environmental friendliness, ethics, future trajectory and more.

From a technology perspective, it's important to analyze the robustness of the underlying AI algorithms and models. As new data flows in continuously, monitoring for degraded performance, unfair bias or skewed recommendations provides insight into when re-training or enhancement is necessary. If the models can autonomously self-assess and adapt to dynamic operating conditions, it speaks to the self-sufficiency and reliability of the solution.

In addition, examining characteristics like computational efficiency and cloud utilization helps quantify the environmental footprint of running production-grade AI. Optimizing these factors where possible ensures organizations can reap benefits responsibly while minimizing unintended negative external impact.

Furthermore, enabling transparency, auditability and explainability in AI system outputs builds trust amongst users and stakeholders. Integrating checks that trace AI reasoning, risk and compliance procedures that assure adherence and feedback loops that allow intervention in edge cases are all constructive practices. Fostering understanding engenders faith in the technology for the long haul.

And importantly, exploring what future developments are on the horizon to improve, scale or enhance the system keeps implementers ahead of the curve. Tracking the evolution of the technology itself and forecasting necessary tweaks in governance, policies and best practices ensures sustained integration.

Evaluating AI solutions along these lines of maintainability, environmental friendliness, ethical transparency and future trajectory allows organizations to better comprehend the lasting productive influence of AI. It facilitates more informed decisions around responsible scaling and continual improvement of AI capabilities.

Chapter Nine

Ethical AI—Balancing Innovation With Responsibility

E nsuring ethical and responsible deployment of artificial intelligence is crucial as companies increasingly integrate AI into business-critical systems and decision-making processes. While innovation in AI presents exciting opportunities, we must thoughtfully examine potential pitfalls and biases that can unintentionally emerge within AI algorithms and data.

From an ethical perspective, AI systems should be closely monitored to safeguard against unfair biases or harmful impacts. Biases buried within historical datasets or even in the minds of AI developers can propagate discrimination through systems built on such data. For example, resume screening algorithms have exhibited gender bias by preferentially recommending men. Facial analysis algorithms also demonstrated racial and gender bias in their accuracy levels when analyzing images of people.

To uphold ethical standards, companies should continuously audit AI systems, measure outcomes, and assess results for signs of prejudicial treatment or recommendations. Teams of ethical AI experts, sociologists, developers and business leaders should collaborate closely in this examination. Many firms also convene AI ethics boards to oversee policies. Additionally, representing diverse viewpoints in the development process can further help spot potential issues.

If systems demonstrate problematic biases, prompt mitigation should occur through data analysis, algorithm refinement and introduction of bias disincentives directly into the AI. However, this must be carefully balanced to maintain model accuracy. Fostering an ethical AI culture focused on continuous learning and improvement is critical rather than just penalizing issues as they arise.

Architecturally, AI interfaces and data flows should be engineered to easily flag biases and enable rapid response. The humans-in-command approach ensures nuanced oversight into AI decision processes versus blind automation. Explainable and transparent AI also supports better accountability if challenges emerge.

With conscientious forethought and monitoring, companies can champion AI innovation responsibly. The conversation around ethical AI must be ongoing as new frontier technologies like generative AI emerge. Maintaining public trust and mitigating harm remains imperative.

This chapter discusses further on this topic in detail so that enterprise architects can understand the importance of ethics in a ground breaking technology like AI.

Ethical Considerations in AI Implementation

Implementing artificial intelligence systems in a thoughtful, ethical way should be a priority for any organization. There are many complex issues to consider that span the entire lifecycle of an AI system, from initial planning stages to real-world deployment and operation. Enterprise architects have an opportunity to embed ethical considerations into the AI development process right from the start.

Rather than treating ethics as an afterthought, organizations would do well to take a holistic and proactive approach. During the conception phase of a new AI project, gathering diverse perspectives across teams can surface potential blind spots early on. Brainstorming sessions focused on ethical risks could cover issues like data bias, unfair outcomes, unintended consequences, and transparency concerns. Establishing clear governance policies and an ethics review board offers ongoing guidance as initiatives advance from design into testing and rollout.

There are also technical elements to weave in like developing algorithms that can explain their automated decisions to humans in a meaningful way. The algorithms themselves should be frequently audited for fairness and tested for harmful scenarios. Automated decisions with significant impacts on people's lives may require human-in-the-loop oversight before being enacted.

Enterprise architecture provides a structural foundation to make considerations like these actionable through all stages of AI adoption. With sound EA governance and planning, cross-functional teams can collaborate to create an ethical framework tailored to the organization and its AI objectives. The framework can then be integrated with concrete measures for monitoring, reporting, and refining systems over time. A thoughtful approach takes dedication, but pays dividends in public trust and responsible innovation.

Privacy and Data Protection

Ensuring individual privacy protection must be a core foundation when designing enterprise artificial intelligence systems. The architecture choices made have profound impacts on personal rights which leaders must consider with great responsibility. Any usage and handling of user data—especially sensitive personal information—carries tremendous ethical weight in our modern digital landscape.

Therefore, system designers need to embed robust privacy protection mechanisms directly within the AI's underlying data infrastructure. The specific software handling and protocols for accessing, transmitting, analyzing, and storing sensitive user data require multilayered security safeguards to prevent abuse or unintended leaks. Strict access controls and comprehensive encryption technologies provide a starting point.

Additionally, cross-departmental coordination is imperative to institute company-wide governance of data practices that comply both with legislation and social contracts of trust. In regions like Europe, regulations such as the General Data Protection Regulation, (GDPR), legally mandate user consent, data anonymization, and restricted processing—requiring a dedicated compliance strategy. But even without a regulatory mandate, proactively optimizing to minimize unnecessary collection/usage of personal information protects individual dignity.

A core technique that can be effective is carefully aggregating and anonymizing raw data sets before they are exposed to AI systems for general-purpose analytics and machine learning. This masking decouples personal identities from the facts during processing, helping preserve privacy boundaries. Overall, there are many technical and policy-based measures that, if woven together, can uphold essential personal liberties while still allowing AI advancements. But it requires conscientious design choices guided by ethical priorities—not just maximizing convenience and efficiency. The architects driving this balance hold tremendous responsibility.

Fairness and Bias

One of the most critical challenges when developing and deploying AI systems in business settings is the potential for inherent biases that can inadvertently be baked into the AI algorithms. These biases can stem from a variety of sources. During the data collection process, the datasets being used to train AI models may suffer from skews and lack representation across different demographic groups. Additionally, the programmers and developers building the models may unintentionally make prejudiced assumptions in the development and model building phase that disadvantages certain groups. And in some cases, there is the risk of reinforcing societal biases and discrimination patterns that already exist.

The implications of these biases in AI systems, even if small in nature, can be hugely consequential for customers, clients, and even employees that interact with an AI application in their daily lives. As more and more decisions, from risk assessments to financial lending, to hiring practices, become automated using AI, we must safeguard that these systems perform their functions in ethical, equitable, and fair ways.

Within a strong enterprise architecture framework, one of the most important requirements is to establish rigorous testing and validation mechanisms that can detect biases and prevent unfair outcomes. Data scientists need to analyze training data and algorithms before deployment to identify possible skew and discrimination. Teams also need to perform extensive audits through test cases to determine if certain groups are being inadvertently disadvantaged due to model limitations. And they need to put in place a process of continuous monitoring of the AI application even post-deployment to enable tuning of the models in an ethical way if biases emerge.

Constructing robust AI governance policies within the enterprise architecture stack is key to ensuring AI acts as an objective, helpful assistant in business processes rather than inadvertently causing harm. This allows companies to harness the tremendous advantages of AI while also upholding their commitments to equality and diversity. The right frameworks put in place can make this possible by design.

Transparency and Explainability

As AI continues to expand into critical domains like healthcare, finance, education, and more, there is a growing need to ensure these intelligent systems can be understood and held accountable. Though AI promises improved speed, accuracy, and efficiency over human decision-making in many cases, if stakeholders cannot comprehend the factors and logic leading to key AI-generated decisions and recommendations, responsible adoption becomes difficult.

Promoting transparency in AI system architecture enables developers, business leaders, regulators, and other relevant stakeholders to "look under the hood" to some degree and grasp why and how an AI application arrives at certain outputs or conclusions. This is particularly crucial in high-stakes sectors within medicine, law, transportation, and beyond where AI-assisted determinations and insights literally impact human lives, liberties, and well-being.

Architecting AI systems in a way that tracks and allows inspection of variables weighted, the methodologies applied, the data sources leveraged, the accuracy levels achieved, and more can help verify and validate the overall trustworthiness of the technology. It also allows those managing and monitoring these systems to identify potential gaps or weaknesses leading to unintended biases so they can be addressed responsively.

Prioritizing explainable and transparent AI architecture compels creators to build systems with inspection capabilities in mind from the start, facilitating better auditing and accountability. And it enables the humans reliant upon AI to partner these tools with an appropriate degree of caution and vigilance rather than simply accepting machine intelligence outputs blindly. The integration of emerging techniques like LIME and SHAP that produce explanations around AI decision processes shows promise on this front as well. Though full transparency may not be possible for some cutting-edge and complex AI, moving markedly in this direction serves both ethical and practical imperatives for the responsible development of artificial intelligence.

Accountability

The adoption of artificial intelligence to enhance automated decision-making brings with it a responsibility to ensure proper accountability and transparency. As enterprise architects design the integration of AI, they must establish clear lines of ownership—determining who within the organization will ultimately be held responsible when the AI system delivers sub-optimal, incorrect, or prejudicial outcomes that negatively impact customers or partners.

While the AI system is making the decisions, there should be internal visibility into the core logic, data, and reasoning fueling those decisions. To enable that visibility, governance procedures need to be put in place around regularly auditing the AI models themselves and analyzing the outcomes they produce to catch errors and prevent unfair bias. Any issues discovered can then feed back into improvement efforts so the models can be refined over time.

Equally important is enabling mechanisms for human judgment and oversight to operate in parallel with the automated AI systems. Even as AI delivers faster and more efficient decision-making, enterprise architects need to ensure there are integrated controls and procedures that give appointed reviewers the power to challenge or override AI decisions when warranted. There should also be accessible channels for those customers or partners negatively impacted by an AI decision to voice their concerns and appeal those decisions.

Embedding ongoing model accountability along with human oversight empowers enterprises to harness the advantages of AI while still maintaining responsibility over monitoring and correcting unintended consequences. This helps sustain trust and transparency both within the organization and when interfacing with the public. The end result is not just more accurate AI but also ethical integration that contemplates the shared accountability between automation and human reviewers.

Security

Ensuring the security of artificial intelligence systems is an extremely important consideration for any organization implementing AI to assist with decision-making. There is rightfully increased concern regarding potential vulnerabilities that could expose an AI system to malicious attacks, hacking, manipulation or other compromise that leads to misuse. If decisions powered by AI have the ability to significantly impact a business, its customers, or other stakeholders, the stakes become even higher for protecting against cyber threats.

Rather than simply bolting on security measures as an afterthought, organizations would be wise to take a proactive, conscientious approach to AI security from the initial design stages through ongoing maintenance. The AI system architecture should have robust cybersecurity protections woven throughout, not added as a superficial layer near the end. Security experts must carefully assess any potential weak points across hardware, software, data inputs and outputs that could allow unauthorized access or manipulation if left undetected. But assessments should not be limited to just one review. As technology evolves at a rapid pace, conducting thorough, regular security assessments enables uncovering new vulnerabilities that may emerge requiring additional safeguards to address.

Updating protocols through patches, upgrades and other system enhancements is also critical for closing security gaps and keeping protection measures current. Relying on outdated versions of operating systems, unencrypted data flows or perimeter defenses that cyber criminals have learned to breach is a recipe for compromise. Proactively monitoring technology and cyber threat landscapes to identify newly uncovered vulnerabilities allows the AI governance team to promptly install necessary upgrades and mitigate risks. For AI systems interfacing business-critical operations or sensitive user data, having these rigorous and adaptive security practices in place greatly reduces the likelihood of attacks leading to compromise or misuse that severely damages the organization and its customers' trust.

Adopting this security-focused mindset that anticipates threats and consistently enhances protections—rather than just reacting once attacked—is fundamental to developing resilient and trustworthy AI systems that support high-stakes processes.

Socio-Technical Considerations

Implementing artificial intelligence technology has consequences that reach far beyond coding algorithms or integrating software. We must thoughtfully assess and plan for the disruptive social impacts that AI will inevitably cause. Though AI promises advancements in areas like efficiency and personalization, as architects of these enterprise systems we bear a responsibility to minimize unintended harm.

Rather than taking a narrow view that focuses solely on technical capabilities, we need to adopt a broad, multidisciplinary approach to implementation. Ethicists can help assess fairness and reduce bias in these systems that make impactful decisions on human lives. Sociologists offer valuable insights into cultural norms, individual behaviors, and organizational dynamics that could be altered, for better or worse, by AI. Other stakeholders, from community advocates to policy makers, should have a seat at the design table.

Will jobs be lost to automation? How will norms around privacy change in an AI-enabled world of surveillance and predictive profiling? What happens when AI escapes carefully constrained systems and behaves in unexpected ways? These questions must be asked, debated thoughtfully, and addressed responsibly through governance, ethics training, and careful monitoring.

Implementation is not just a technical challenge: It is a deeply human one. AI will influence how we view the world and how we view one another. We cannot afford to implement ideas blindly. We have to implement them conscientiously, with our shared humanity in mind, in order to guide these transformative technologies toward justice, empowerment, and the betterment of all. The path forward requires open eyes, open minds, and open hearts.

Final Thoughts

When companies and organizations seek to adopt artificial intelligence, they are dealing with immensely powerful technologies that can broadly impact society. Therefore, the development and implementation of AI should not be treated lightly or as solely an exercise in technological innovation. There must be an ongoing commitment to responsibly shape how these technologies are integrated across the enterprise architecture.

This commitment stems from a values-based orientation that considers more than just compliance with applicable regulations, which only establishes minimum standards. And it goes beyond risk mitigation for the business itself, which still centers the institution rather than people. True ethical AI incorporates considerations around aligning with moral viewpoints and frameworks that uplift societal well-being.

Part of this is assessing both the intended goals and potential unintended consequences of AI systems from multiple stakeholder perspectives. Representatives from various groups—customers, employees, shareholders, community members, industry experts, and more—should be continually engaged for input. This diverse insight assists organizations in upholding ideals around fairness, accountability, transparency, and more in their AI tools.

This also involves establishing oversight around auditing AI for metrics beyond just system accuracy or performance benchmarks. Understanding metrics related to equitable access, user autonomy, and effects on people who may be vulnerable or marginalized is equally vital. And formal review processes are necessary to evaluate models before and after deployment in real use cases.

Ultimately, the path forward requires institutionalizing ethical considerations so they are woven directly into the enterprise architecture that guides AI implementation. This goes beyond performative actions that merely signal virtues without work to embed them. Only through an authentic commitment to responsible AI development can both societal and business value truly align.

Balancing Innovation With Ethical Responsibility

When incorporating new technologies into enterprise architectures, it is crucial we advance responsibly and align progress with organizational values. As architects, our role demands balancing cutting-edge innovation that drives growth with ethical constraints that uphold social duty.

Before deployment, we must proactively assess innovative projects, considering potential consequences, to address ethical concerns preemptively rather than reactively. One best practice is conducting impact studies to identify effects on relevant stakeholders—not just business units but also legal, customers and more. Engaging diverse voices illuminates alternate perspectives, allowing more holistic evaluation.

Embedding ethics directly into new architecture designs is also key. Shaping technical foundations and workflows to enable transparency, accountability and compliance upfront minimizes need for later rework. We must focus on building capabilities not just for monitoring regulations but also identifying emerging risks proactively.

Governance frameworks present another opportunity to institute formal ethical oversight. By creating specialized committees with risk and ethics mandates, we enable expert advisory channels for our teams. Standardizing review procedures for new technical architectures promotes consistency in sustainable, community-conscious innovation.

Of course, we operate in tension between advancing technologies rapidly and pausing for due diligence. But well-designed mechanisms help streamline diligence without severely hampering inventiveness. And culture growth is equally vital—embedding ethical mindfulness within teams through training, transparency, and leading by example.

With conscientious governance, a rich ethics-focused dialogue and a pervasive impulse towards responsibility permeating teams, we can harness technology's immense potential for good while avoiding detrimental societal impacts. Our architecture decisions resound across communities—so we must ensure they reflect wisdom and care.

Let's analyze some case studies that showcase responsible innovation.

Case Study 1: AI in Healthcare

A healthcare organization recently implemented an artificial intelligence system to assist doctors with diagnosing diseases. Recognizing the sensitivity of this technology and its impact on patients' well-being, great care was taken from the onset to ensure an ethical approach.

The development team made ethical considerations a priority throughout the design process. One key measure was ensuring the AI was trained on diverse and comprehensive datasets, seeking to eliminate biases that could negatively impact certain demographics. The team understood that if the foundational data used to train the AI was incomplete or skewed, the system's recommendations could overlook entire segments of the patient population. By sourcing training data that captured a wide spectrum of health backgrounds, histories, and demographics, they aimed to shape an AI that could serve all patients with equal precision.

Additionally, the organization mandated rigorous multi-phase testing of the AI before deployment. They created testing environments that simulated real-world diagnostic scenarios and had medical professionals analyze the system's disease assessments. Doctors reviewed hundreds of the AI's diagnostic outcomes for accuracy while also evaluating if any recommendations exhibited prejudices or disproportionately negative impacts. This comprehensive testing enabled fine-tuning of the technology to align with ethical medical standards.

By keeping the pillars of diversity and medical oversight at the forefront of development, the healthcare organization designed the diagnostic AI as not just a cutting-edge system but also one that patients and doctors alike can trust. The project stands out as an exemplar for embedding ethical responsibility into AI systems destined to impact human well-being. Through conscientious efforts, they created technology for improving lives—guided by the moral principle of doing no harm.

Case Study 2: Financial Services and Data Encryption

Protecting client data is an ethical imperative in the financial industry. Understanding this duty, one forward-thinking financial services firm recently updated its technology systems to better safeguard sensitive user information. The company integrated a state-of-the-art encryption solution directly into its client-facing application to enable strengthened data privacy across all internal and external touch points.

Encryption works by using complex mathematical algorithms to scramble information so that it becomes indecipherable to unauthorized parties. By building this natively into their software, the financial services provider enabled end-to-end safeguarding of client data in transit and storage. From the moment customers input any sensitive data, it is fully secured and remains that way throughout its journey across company systems. This top-grade encryption solution exceeds industry standards for data protection.

The firm made this innovative move because they recognized both the risk of failing to properly secure personal financial information as well as their ethical responsibility to prioritize user privacy. Especially in today's data-driven world, clients rightfully expect their chosen financial partners to be good stewards of any shared information. By fully encrypting data entries directly in the client portal, this forward-looking company has demonstrated their commitment to that fiduciary duty. The encryption not only prevents leaks but also reassures customers that their privacy comes first.

This end-to-end encrypted system now provides the company's clients with best-in-class protection of their sensitive information and financial transactions. It was a prudent innovation investment that pays dividends through enhanced trust and peace of mind. The company sees this as both a moral imperative and a competitive differentiator. Other firms would do well to follow their example.

Global Perspectives on AI Ethics

When examining artificial intelligence governance and ethics across different nations and cultures, it becomes evident that there is significant diversity in perspectives, priorities, and regulatory approaches. These variances are underpinned by the distinct cultural norms, legal traditions, and political dynamics within each country and region.

For instance, in the Western liberal democracies of the European Union, there is a strong emphasis on personal rights and privacy. This manifests in stringent regulations like the General Data Protection Regulation which mandates that AI systems enable user control over private data while also incorporating privacy and ethics by design. However, in authoritarian countries like China, state interests and social control supersede individual privacy. Consequently, Chinese AI deployments enable broader surveillance capabilities by the government coupled with less protections over how personal data is utilized.

The United States harbors a more decentralized outlook, with an emphasis on innovation and market-centered solutions over direct regulation. However, in light of rising concerns around algorithmic biases and data abuse, regulatory oversight of the AI industry is increasingly being recognized as necessary. Beyond these dominant spheres, countries like India are fostering vivid discussions around balancing AI's economic upsides with its potential downsides. India's proposed national AI strategy stresses the importance of ethics for sustaining public trust while supporting AI adoption across industrial and social settings.

In Japan, human-centrality is the focus of its Society 5.0 program, which aspires to seamlessly integrate AI and data-driven technologies across every segment of society and industry. The objectives are oriented towards augmenting societal values and welfare to tackle demographic challenges. Supranational bodies like the United Nations and OECD have also introduced ethical guidelines and best practices for cultivating responsible AI development across borders.

In totality, this comparative analysis reveals a multiplicity of ethical paradigms based on unique cultural and political ecosystems. These differences hold key implications for international cooperation within the AI space, possibly requiring shared universal principles that respect sovereign perspectives while also furthering commitment to ensuring socially beneficial and ethically aligned AI systems.

Panel Discussions on AI Ethics

When designing and deploying AI systems, transparency of the algorithms powering them has become a pivotal concern. While public disclosure of every intricate detail may not be feasible or advisable, there is consensus that these AI systems should have enough transparency to ensure trust and accountability. Architects and developers need to facilitate observableness into how these algorithms make decisions, learn from data, and adapt over time. Opaque "black box" systems can hide biases and other issues. Thoughtful transparency allows for fairness and non-discrimination.

This connects directly to the urgent need to address potential biases encoded within AI algorithms and data. Left unmanaged, biases can manifest in many forms during modeling, training data collection, and real-time decision-making. Expert panels emphasize that proactively identifying, understanding, quantifying, and mitigating biases through testing and governance is a cornerstone of ethical AI architecture. Doing so facilitates more fair, explainable, and equitable systems. The field is rapidly evolving best practices around bias detection and fairness quantification.

Intertwined with transparency and bias mitigation is the obligation to ensure responsible data privacy and governance practices. AI subsists on data, needing vast volumes of quality, labeled training data. This data is often personal and sensitive. Architecting compliant data management protocols and access controls aligned to regulations and ethical expectations is non-negotiable, according to experts. Failing to do so erodes public trust and poses legal risks.

Furthermore, unambiguous accountability is required in ethical AI design according to thought leaders. Complex socio-technical systems can diffuse responsibility across stakeholders. So governance models that clearly delineate obligations among developers, users, and the systems themselves are needed. This includes recourse mechanisms and monitoring for responsible development and deployment.

Looking beyond algorithms and data, some discussions highlight that AI interaction paradigms with humans themselves require ethical forethought. Enterprise architecture should discourage over reliance on AI, safeguard user autonomy and oversight, and nurture constructive augmentation. Manipulation and coercion should be avoided.

Zooming out, responsible AI architecture must analyze and address potential undesirable impacts on society—displacement of human roles, manipulation at scale through media, exacerbation of inequities, and other externalities. Internal governance alone is insufficient; Holistic analysis of environmental and community impact is prudent.

Finally, most experts concur that the fast pace of AI advancement demands adaptive policy and legal apparatus. Regulation lags innovation, so reactive governance is needed to incentivize ethical research while supporting rapid progress. Policy and legal guardrails should catalyze accountability without excessive impedance.

Chapter Ten

Predictive Analytics in Enterprise Planning

P redictive analytics is an emerging capability that is fundamentally transforming how leading organizations leverage data to optimize operations and strategy. By employing advanced statistical and machine learning algorithms, predictive models can forecast events, reveal systemic efficiencies, and re-imagine decision frameworks based on probabilistic modeling of potential futures. This is providing tangible preparedness and performance advantages to those integrating these capabilities compared to peers anchored in reactive paradigms.

Let me walk through a practical example: A global retailer is combining large historical datasets from across its operations including supply chain, inventory, sales, marketing and macro-economic shifts, with prescriptive scoping techniques to power its predictive models. These models uncover complex, multivariate correlations between inputs like supply chain strains, regional rainfall, promotions, and key outputs like demand forecasts, inventory needs, and customer churn risks, store-by-store. Powerful machine learning correlations surface insights that would have been impossible to manually piece together. Statistical methods then quantify the likelihood and range of outcomes—encapsulating uncertainty versus simply identifying possibilities.

Equipped with these predictive insights, the retailer preemptively adapts business plans across the enterprise based on probability. For example, supply chain orders are adjusted months in advance to prevent stock outs. Customer retention marketing campaigns are targeted based on high churn risk scores before attrition occurs. Store labor schedules optimize based on demand forecasts. They describe feeling empowered by the persistent visibility into previously otherwise opaque systemic forces.

As more data pours in, the accuracy of algorithms continues to compound over time. Predictive analytics integrates with existing reporting and planning processes, cementing confidence in executing decisions today despite inevitability of change. With expertise leveraging predictive insights, leaders optimize strategy amid a sea of uncertainty by seeing futures unfold months before they emerge. What was once reactive is now proactive. What was once based on gut feel is now data-driven. This readiness advantage will only widen over time as predictive capabilities continue maturing across operations.

This chapter focuses mainly on explaining how enterprise architectures can utilize predictive analytics by combining it with the wonders of AI to get better results for their organization.

Defining Predictive Analytics and Its Significance in Enterprise Planning

Predictive analytics empower companies to navigate uncertain futures wisely. By studying historical patterns in data, statistical models unveil key performance drivers, from sales to customer loyalty. Sophisticated machine learning techniques quantify connections between leading indicators and results. This visibility into likely scenarios and probabilities grants foresight beyond the immediate horizon, spanning months or years.

The first step entails identifying priority business outcomes for predictive focus. Reliable forecasting requires substantial structured data capturing relevant domains over time. Data mining tools extract insights from operational records and external data sources per the predictive goal. Specialized algorithms efficiently process immense datasets too large and complex for human examination.

With quality data secured, analysts construct frameworks encoding hypotheses about indicators and dynamics. Statistical approaches like regressions can quantify precise numerical relationships and variability. Machine learning classification uncovers subtle predictive factors difficult for unaided human detection. Together mathematical precision and computational power reveal hidden causal mechanisms.

Leaders, thus, obtain data-grounded event probabilities, from regional demand changes to new entrants. This foresight allows preemptive strategy adjustments and informed risk assessments instead of reactive guessing. With predictive foundations in place, organizations can execute multi-year plans with greater clarity on potential impacts versus alternatives.

The future inevitably holds uncertainty. However predictive analytics expand the horizon of visibility. Probabilistic exposures to market forces and systemic connections elevate conversations. Rather than await disruption, organizations can proactively shape destinies through data-driven investments and innovations. Predictive analytics promise greater control where once dwelled only mystery.

We will discuss in detail how predictive analytics can impact enterprise architecture.

1. Forecast Demand

Accurately predicting customer demand has always been tricky. Companies need to stock enough products to avoid losing sales if something is out of stock. But storing extra inventory strains budgets and resources. There's a difficult balance between meeting availability expectations and controlling costs. Even slight forecast inaccuracies mean spoilage, back orders, and margin hits over time.

So what causes these demand forecasting headaches? Customer preferences naturally fluctuate, sometimes rapidly. No company can perfectly predict next month's hot item or anticipated volume. Suppliers also struggle with reliable delivery schedules, further obscuring upcoming needs. Yet, shoppers want what they want, when they want it—no excuses. This leaves leaders struggling to see into the future using imperfect data.

Fortunately, predictive analytics leverages probability models to estimate purchase rates ahead of time. By blending historical sales patterns with leading indicators around competitor promotions, search trends, weather forecasts, local events and broader economic undercurrents, algorithms can quantify likely demand scenarios weeks or months in advance. Mathematical techniques also calculate confidence levels expressing the reliability of each product's forecast.

Armed with these data-driven projections, companies can tailor supply chain and marketing tactics to likely extremes. Manufacturing adjustments prevent imminent inventory shortages, preserving continuity during expected demand spikes. Informed reorder points eliminate overstock situations. Personalized promotions even retain highest-risk customers. In total, predictive analytics deliver the crucial visibility needed to optimize budgeting, storage, and operations based on calculated guesses of the future.

But even the best predictive models rely on input data integrity and awareness of inherent limitations. Businesses must continually verify assumed relationships between demand drivers and actual purchase behaviors across customer segments. Periodic model refreshing also adapts to evolving preferences over time. Still, anchored in rich datasets and governance, predictive demand analytics promise profound inventory efficiency, cost control and customer satisfaction advantages. The future remains unpredictable, but mathematical scrutiny applied prudently elicits likelihoods upon which organizations can confidently prepare.

1. Improve Marketing Effectiveness

For decades, unlocking what motivates customers and compels purchase behaviors has been the holy grail pursuit of marketing organizations the world over. Advancements in data volumes and processing technologies have steadily shed increasing light on the psychological drivers and triggers that determine market engagement. Today, analytics techniques enable unprecedented visibility into why, when and how customers respond to specific promotional elements and campaigns.

Of particular benefit is the rapid maturation of predictive modeling capabilities that marketing leaders now wield to run simulated promotions and campaigns months before public launch. The journey begins by compiling extensive historical datasets that capture past campaign performance across customer segments and channels. Leveraging these rich archives, statistical learning algorithms can discern intricate relationships between variables like creative messaging attributes, promotion types, target customer psycho-infographics and resulting engagement or conversion metrics.

From there, response curve analysis reveals nonlinear interplays and thresholds between creative variants and audience variables that surface highly nuanced optimization pathways hidden from conventional marketing wisdom. Meanwhile, multivariate testing frameworks quantify complex interaction effects between promotional variables that uni-variate perspectives essentially mask.

Concurrently, machine learning classifies individual customers based on predicted behaviors to discern addressable demand from marketing noise. Propensity models highlight certain target profile characteristics that offer an optimized balance between conversion volume and response likelihood.

And algorithms readily re-segment target populations upon the launch of new products based on updated predictors of interest and engagement.

Together these analytical assets afford marketing leaders unprecedented granular visibility into the very promotional levers that can be actively adjusted towards revenue goals. Scenario analysis weighs the financial impacts of various campaign designs and budgets to inform strategic planning. The outputs promise profoundly elevated marketing efficiency and effectiveness through bespoke messaging grounded in mathematical rigor.

1. Enhance Customer Experience

Today's customers have high expectations when it comes to engaging with brands. They demand experiences that are tailored specifically to their individual preferences and needs instead of broad one-size-fits-all interactions. Meeting these heightening expectations relies profoundly on organizations leveraging advanced analytics. By statistically analyzing diverse sources of behavioral data and customer feedback, companies can uncover nuances within large consumer populations that allow for deeper personalization.

The analytics process typically begins by consolidating cross-channel customer activity into unified profiles that incorporate information on attributes like purchases, browsing history, service contacts, and survey responses. Skilled analysts filter these rich datasets into groups of customers that share common behavioral traits and intentions. Statistical modeling reveals subtle distinctions between micro-segments that typical grouping paradigms fail to capture.

Machine learning further enables personalization by analyzing complementary indicators pulled from search keywords, payment patterns, mobile app usage and more to identify prospective customer needs. These insights empower recommendation algorithms to tailor product suggestions, messaging timing and channel optimization strategies to each individual. This level of understanding makes customers feel valued rather than bracketed by broad generalizations.

Business leadership gains invaluable visibility into rapidly evolving interests across finely graded sub-populations through these advanced analytics. They can continuously re-calibrate targeted offers that align with the latest trends and project long-term value across rising customer cohorts and declining bases. Ultimately, the level of personalized engagement cultivated through predictive insights promises improved customer experiences, sustainable revenue growth and priority status for the brand. In time, data and analytics may even come to know consumers better than they know themselves.

Discussing the Evolution and Current State of Predictive Analytics in Business

Predictive analytics has established foundations in statistical and probability theories developed over past centuries. However, only in recent years have technologies matured sufficiently to enable the full-scale commercial application of these predictive techniques across enterprises. This progression from pure theory to transformative business strategy has been facilitated by several pivotal technological advancements over the last decade.

The proliferation of "big data" now provides the essential raw materials for analysis. As organizations have digitized an expanding proportion of operations and customer interactions spanning supply chains, production systems and marketing channels, they now capture granular digital traces of activities at massive scale. Billions of temporal transactions and external data points paint intricate pictures filled with insights invisible to limited human examination alone. This presents fertile ground for predictive algorithms.

Equally important, machine learning techniques, especially complex deep neural networks, now offer exponentially expanded modeling capabilities compared to classical regression approaches alone. These flexible non-linear methods automatically extract signals from noisy data that stymie traditional techniques. They also continually learn from latest outcomes to recursively refine their algorithms, evolving their predictive acumen over time through hands-off automation.

Underpinning these expansions, the exponential growth in raw computing power now allows organizations to apply these sophisticated approaches at full scale for the first time. Cloud data storage and flexible processing facilitate timely analysis of immense datasets to enable real-time responsiveness. Leaders can rapidly retrain predictive models as new inputs expand scope.

Together these technology inflections have unlocked a new era for predictive prowess, elevating organizations from reactive tracking to proactive steering. Leaders gain accurate visibility into second-order effects and probabilistic futures that promise optimal positioning amid industry transformations. The maturity arc continues ascending even now as pioneering implementations reveal new data frontiers and analytic innovations ready for adoption.

Enhancing Predictive Analytics With AI

Artificial intelligence and machine learning techniques are poised to fundamentally transform predictive analytics capabilities for businesses. By utilizing advanced neural networks that can detect intricate nonlinear relationships in massive, fast-growing datasets, AI-driven analytics solutions can uncover valuable insights that traditional statistical approaches may miss. The scale of this data processing expands exponentially when combined with cloud-based computing frameworks. Whereas legacy analytics applications were limited to surface-level correlations, multi-layer neural networks have the ability to discern complex chains of higher-order causation that drive enhanced forecasting.

These AI systems have feedback loops that allow the models to continuously learn and improve their accuracy over time. The networks learn to adapt to new behaviors and scenarios automatically. In effect, the AI transforms rigid analytical rules into flexible and "intelligent" learning systems. This means predictions and insights generated by the systems grow more precise with use. Processing advances enable the analysis of billions of records, recognizing subtle patterns even in unstructured text-based data sources.

The AI analytics tools also feature intuitive and transparent interfaces. Leaders without specialized data science expertise can interactively probe the data through visualizations to understand the key drivers and uncertainties behind strategic forecasts. Offering accessibility and transparency, these systems democratize analytics across organizations. This both spurs creativity in applying predictive insights and also streamlines the integration of data-based probability models into day-to-day decision flows and business intelligence tools used company-wide.

In total, the scalability, adaptability, precision and intuitive nature of modern AI-powered predictive analytics promises to revolutionize the capacity of organizations to reliably peer around corners. By revealing insights from immense datasets in understandable ways, AI gives leaders at all levels the profound ability to look ahead with confidence and act decisively amidst uncertainty. Savvy organizations will harness these capabilities to own their competitive futures, armed with science-backed foresight exceeding the limits of human data processing.

Exploring How AI Technologies Enhance the Capabilities of Predictive Analytics

Predictive analytics refers to the use of statistical modeling and data mining techniques to make predictions about future outcomes and trends. It has become an essential practice across industries, enabling organizations to forecast key metrics more accurately. However, traditional predictive analytics methods do have some limitations in scale and complexity. This is where artificial intelligence closes significant gaps and takes predictive powers to new levels.

At its core, AI amplifies predictive capability through its two fundamental traits—the ability to process astronomical data volumes that no human team possibly could, identifying patterns that would have otherwise remained hidden; and the capability to continually learn from the copious data it analyzes, refining its logic, spotting new correlations, and providing recommendations. By combining these strengths with the established statistical and mathematical processes in predictive analytics, AI facilitates extremely high-dimensional modeling far beyond what traditional computation can handle.

For instance, deep learning algorithms, a subset of AI, can churn through endless streams of big data on multiple parameters and detect obscure interactive effects between variables that even the savviest analysts may not have considered. It removes blind spots. Additionally, as the AI ingests more data, its self-learning mechanisms constantly update to uncover new predictive insights without any explicit additional programming. It removes the limitations of human bandwidth.

Furthermore, AI adds new forms of data to the predictive mix—images, video, speech, and text data can now all be incorporated into forecasting models, an enhancement unattainable via conventional predictive analytics. This applies predictive intelligence to a wider, more contextual set of problems.

In summary, AI leverages its innate data processing superiority and perpetual self-learning capability to significantly boost the speed, complexity, accuracy, and scope of predictive analytics. It drives predictive modeling to new frontiers as a smarter, indefatigable companion to traditional statistical methods—one that keeps learning, keeps improving, and keeps predicting.

Examples of AI-Driven Predictive Models in Action

A global shipping company integrated a machine learning algorithm into its logistics planning operations. By analyzing tens of thousands of data points around weather patterns, fuel costs, warehouse availability, and customer delivery locations, the AI model can forecast shipping times, routes, and resource allocation needs for thousands of packages each day. This allows the shipping company to optimize delivery plans to reduce fuel expenses, speed up shipping, avoid warehouses at capacity, and provide customers with reliable estimated delivery windows.

A major retailer developed a deep learning neural network to predict customer purchase behavior. By ingesting data on past spending habits, browsing history, purchase frequency, and product preferences, their predictive model can forecast each customer's likelihood of purchasing certain items or product categories in a given time frame. These AI-generated purchase predictions allow the retailer to tailor promotions, advertisements, and recommendations for thousands of customers individually across channels to drive higher conversion rates.

A global bank built a machine learning model to analyze market volatility and political event data to predict foreign currency exchange rate fluctuations. By determining the probability of exchange rates moving outside expected bands, the bank can minimize transaction risks in foreign trades and settlements. This allowed them to avoid major losses and ensure liquidity by leveraging the AI's forecasts before rates become affected by emerging financial or political situations in specific countries.

These use cases demonstrate applied AI predictive models handling massive datasets to forecast outcomes for complex real-world situations. Whether optimizing logistics, targeting marketing, or mitigating financial risk, the pattern recognition and predictive capabilities of these AI systems deliver tangible benefits by allowing organizations to plan more effectively for the future.

Comparing the Effectiveness and Efficiency of AI-Driven and Traditional Methods

When it comes to leveraging data to forecast future outcomes and trends, organizations have typically relied upon traditional statistical modeling techniques. However, with modern advances in artificial intelligence, there are now AI-powered predictive analytics capabilities that can automate and enhance the prediction process remarkably. Evaluating the pros and cons of each method is imperative for organizations exploring which approach to adopt.

On the whole, AI-driven predictive analytics solutions allow businesses to process vastly larger volumes of structured and unstructured data than traditional techniques. The self-learning algorithms used can continually fine-tune predictive models and uncover previously unseen correlations and patterns buried deep in complex datasets. This leads to greater overall accuracy and reliability of predictions compared to traditional regression analysis or time series forecasting. The automated machine learning also reduces the need for intensive human preprocessing and analysis of data prior to modeling.

Additionally, AI empowers organizations to achieve much faster model development cycles, iterating to improve predictions in near real-time rather than waiting days or weeks. It also enables more adaptability to changing market conditions. As new data emerges, AI algorithms can retrain predictive models seamlessly. This combination of improved prediction accuracy, speed, and adaptability serves to enhance operational efficiency and informed decision making significantly compared to status quo statistical methods.

However, AI is not a magic wand. It still requires careful curation of quality, trustworthy data inputs by internal experts to ensure "garbage in, garbage out" does not occur. Interpreting AI predictions also necessitates human judgment and oversight to put insights into proper business context for impactful decision making. Additionally, traditional techniques remain simpler for less complex prediction needs, while AI excels at multifaceted forecasting.

For the majority of predictive analytics needs in today's data-rich business landscape, AI-powered solutions drive considerably greater effectiveness and efficiency gains—both directly through enhanced automated modeling and indirectly via the compounding benefits of more accurate, timely, and frequently updated forecasts. But prudent evaluation of each organization's resources, data infrastructure, and use case complexity is still warranted when determining if AI adoption is justified.

Introducing Interactive Models and Simulations for a Hands-On Understanding

Enterprise architects are responsible for translating business needs into technical capabilities by designing and governing the structural blueprint of organizations. With data and analytics becoming integral to strategic decisions, there is a growing need for enterprise architects to develop practical knowledge of higher analytical methodology like predictive modeling. Mastering predictive analytics allows architects to incorporate data-driven insights into their architectural designs.

However, gaining hands-on experience with predictive modeling can be challenging for busy enterprise architects. Attending lectures or reading theoretical concepts rarely provides sufficient understanding. A more impactful approach is to offer interactive demonstrations that allow enterprise architects to learn-by-doing.

Interactive simulations and models provide realistic, customized environments where architects can actively experiment with predictive analytics concepts using artificial intelligence capabilities. For example, an interactive simulation can present a digital prototype of an enterprise system. Architects can modify inputs and system parameters, execute predictive models on the simulated data, and immediately visualize outputs and analytical trends. This closed-loop, cause-effect experience brings theoretical concepts to life through practical application.

Unlike passive learning, simulations empower architects to gain first-hand experience of how introducing AI-enabled predictive analytics into enterprise architectures can optimize systems, inform business strategies and transformations, improve resource allocation, and meet other desired objectives. The hands-on process helps architects comprehend the tangible value propositions at a deeper, more intuitive level.

Providing a risk-free virtual space fuels creativity, exploration, and builds confidence with new techniques. Architects can tweak scenarios and re-run simulations endlessly until they are adept at leveraging predictive intelligence to enhance architectural outcomes. Guided support during these engagements ensures architects develop capabilities that readily transfer to real-initiatives. The engaging learning process equips architects to become proactive advocates of embedding predictive analytics into enterprise designs.

Predictive Analytics Success Stories With AI

When examining how organizations have successfully leveraged artificial intelligence in predictive analytics, there are a few compelling success stories worth highlighting that demonstrate tangible impacts across various industries. By evaluating the precise results of these AI implementations, we can better understand the tangible value derived as well as some of the broader implications.

One example is how shipping giant Maersk partnered with IBM to employ AI-powered predictive models to optimize ocean cargo routes and volumes. By leveraging massive datasets and machine learning algorithms, the models provided granular forecasts on expected delays for tens of thousands of container shipments each day. This enabled Maersk to boost cargo delivery performance, avoid costly delays, and reduce excess fuel consumption by 6–8% annually after deployment. The environmental impact was also substantial with annual CO_2 emissions decreased by over 40,000 tons.

In the automotive sector, BMW was able to double its production capacity for quality assurance without adding new staff by instituting an AI visual inspection system in its manufacturing facilities. The machine vision system was trained on BMW's stringent quality standards for components and can automatically detect production defects with higher accuracy levels than human inspectors. This implementation enabled accelerated defect detection in real-time, allowing issues to be corrected faster. It also provided valuable manufacturing analytics to inform better design decisions and prevent future defects.

Retailers like Starbucks and Dominos Pizza have also employed AI-enabled predictive ordering systems to anticipate customer demand at local stores based on historical data patterns. By automatically placing food and beverage orders tailored to expected sales volume for each location daily, this technology allows the companies to minimize waste, maintain optimal inventory levels, and boost sales. Starbucks reported over $100 million in cost savings from reduced waste in the first year using this AI technology in its US stores.

These examples exhibit the widespread capabilities of AI in predictive systems to automate complex forecasting and optimize everything from supply chain logistics to manufacturing operations to inventory management. Tracking both the quantitative performance gains as well as qualitative benefits across areas like sustainability, product quality, and customization reveals the full business value being unlocked, leading to higher adoption in more industries. This allows us to better grasp the tangible impacts possible as AI continues permeating critical organizational analytics and decisions.

Chapter Eleven

Rise of the AI Architects— Evolving Roles in Tech Teams

The role of enterprise architects is evolving in this era of artificial intelligence integration across organizations. Architects can no longer simply design technological systems, but must now also understand how to effectively incorporate AI into those systems in a way that brings the most business value. This requires not only technical skills, but also a deeper comprehension of the business goals, processes, and data flows underlying enterprise operations.

Some of the key skills becoming essential for architects in the AI era include data modeling, statistical analysis, machine learning operations, AI ethics, and conversational interfaces. Architects must expand their data modeling expertise to categorize information in ways usable for machine learning. Statistical capabilities help architects assess limitations of AI systems and better communicate development needs with data scientists. Machine learning operations skills allow streamlining of model development, monitoring, and maintenance. Knowledge of AI ethics assists architects in avoiding biases and ensuring transparency in AI systems. Finally, conversational interface design allows human-AI interaction for business processes.

AI can accelerate the work of enterprise architects through automated data consolidation, code generation for prototyping, and testing scenario simulations. It essentially serves as a collaborative "rubber duck" to bounce ideas off throughout the design process. Architects can iterate system designs more quickly with these AI capabilities. However, integrating AI does create challenges in up-skilling existing talent. Organizations may need to provide extensive training programs on machine learning techniques, data science tools, model interpretability methods, and AI governance best practices to allow architects to leverage these technologies effectively.

The infusion of AI also influences collaboration dynamics within technology teams and across the enterprise. AI systems require extensive coordination between architects, data analysts, subject matter experts, and business leaders to deploy solutions tailored to organizational needs. Cross-functional project charters, committees, and working groups help guide AI strategy and ensure business objectives are met. Ultimately, AI is compelling architects and technologists to engage more actively across the enterprise in shaping how these technologies transform operations, decision-making and competitiveness.

This chapter fundamentally focuses on helping you have a much clearer vision about the duties of an enterprise architecture during this AI era.

Tracing How the Role of Enterprise Architects Is Evolving With the Advent of AI

Enterprise architecture is an integral function within modern organizations, focused on aligning technology solutions and IT infrastructure with overall business goals and strategies. The role of enterprise architects is becoming even more vital with the rapid acceleration of artificial intelligence capabilities transforming industries and redefining competitive landscapes. Rather than simply recommending technologies, enterprise architects must serve as strategic advisors guiding executive leadership on AI adoption to drive innovation while managing inherent risks.

In the past, enterprise architects may have focused more narrowly on technology integration for current IT systems and infrastructure. However, the proliferation of AI is forcing enterprise architects to expand their purview. They must now track emerging technologies and evaluate how various AI tools like machine learning, natural language processing, robotics, computer vision, and more, can be woven into business processes to enable enhanced data analysis, insights, automation and decision-making.

This requires enterprise architects to partner closely with lines of business to identify pain points ripe for AI solutions. Rather than just technical experts on systems, they must lead multi-functional teams to envision how AI can refine everything from customer engagement to supply chain to product personalization and beyond. The essential skill-set is morphing from tactician to strategist—assessing AI's potential applications and implications across the entire organization.

In addition to opportunity identification, enterprise architects have a growing responsibility to develop guardrails and governance to ensure AI is implemented ethically and safely. As AI informs increasingly impactful decisions, architects must institute appropriate controls for data transparency, algorithmic bias checks, and outcome explanations while still promoting innovation. Moreover, they play a pivotal role in change management as AI disrupts workflows, job functions and even business models. Helping transition staff and leadership into new augmented roles is now part of the enterprise architect's duty.

The transformational nature of AI means enterprise architects must be flexible, creative, and responsive to keep pace with technology shifts.

Rather than execute static plans, they are now continuous orchestrators—scanning the landscape for emerging capabilities, assessing organizational readiness for AI, aligning business objectives with AI tools, and enabling responsible experimentation. As AI grows more prevalent, enterprise architects will continue seeing their sphere of impact expand.

Examining New Responsibilities and Skill Sets Required in the AI Era

Examining the evolving role of enterprise architects is crucial as organizations continue adopting artificial intelligence and other advanced technologies. In the AI era, the responsibilities and skill-sets required for enterprise architects fundamentally shifted to enable AI integration, govern data, and bridge technical and business objectives.

Rather than purely focusing on current IT infrastructure and application needs, enterprise architects must expand oversight into data architecture, AI model development, and cross-functional impacts of algorithms on processes, users, and the broader business. Architects must master technical AI concepts to evaluate different machine learning approaches, understand inherent biases and ethical risks, and guide models toward priorities like accuracy, auditability, and transparency.

Furthermore, as vast data becomes AI's most vital asset, architects are increasingly responsible for enforcing data protection, mining meaningful insights, and ensuring quality data flows securely between systems. This requires excelling at data modeling, analytics, governance procedures, and communicating insights to stakeholders. Architects must also anticipate data dependencies for AI applications and infrastructure needs for future model integration.

Beyond technical adeptness, enterprise architects are relied upon to interpret AI capabilities for senior leaders, align AI projects with strategic roadmaps, and spearhead critical governance frameworks as AI infiltrates decision making. This demands sharp business acumen, communication skills, and ethics training to account for AI risks amid pressing business objectives. Architects must future-proof roles and processes vulnerable to automation while coordinating AI talent development.

Integrating AI redefines the enterprise architect as part technologist, part data scientist, part consultant, and part change agent. Mastering this balance of technical depth, business leadership, governance, and future vision is key for organizations to transition smoothly into an AI-powered paradigm. The architects who lead this shift proactively will be tomorrow's strategic advisors powering responsible innovation.

Identifying Key Skills and Competencies Needed for Future Architects

Architects play a critical role in shaping the built environment around us. However, the advent of artificial intelligence and related technologies is rapidly changing the future landscape of the architecture profession. Architects who hope to thrive in the years ahead should focus on developing key human-centered skills and competencies that will complement AI's data-driven capabilities rather than compete against them.

Creativity, for example, will only become more vital—envisioning innovative designs, building forms and urban plans that uplift and inspire. While AI can generate countless options, architects must leverage intuition and imagination to determine which ideas hold the greatest potential. Architects adept at the creative process will bring immense value by pioneering visionary concepts that embrace both aesthetic beauty as well as qualities like sustainability, accessibility, resilience, and more in the built spaces they conceive.

Likewise, communication abilities around illustrating these forward-thinking visions will be pivotal to rally diverse teams, clients and communities to bring them to fruition. Architects must compel others through compelling storytelling, interpretive models, and even experiential simulations that make innovations tangible. They will need to listen deeply to user needs and collaborate across broad stakeholder ecosystems that today's complex building projects require.

Furthermore, as architects increasingly integrate smart systems and new materials into designs, understanding user-centered design principles will be paramount rather than just engineering specifications alone. Buildings must thoughtfully enhance comfort, convenience and health/well-being based on how diverse people actually inhabit and experience spaces. Guiding technology to best serve human needs rather than detract from them will separate progressive architects from those falling behind the curve.

Ultimately, embracing AI as a collaborative partner that complements inherent human strengths in imagination, empathy and intuition—rather than trying to compete with it—will position architects to continually expand the art of what is possible in built spaces that fulfill the needs of people today and tomorrow. The profession will no doubt be transformed, but architects committed to leveraging both cutting-edge technology as well as timeless human values will surely thrive in the process.

Strategies and Resources for Skill Development in AI and Enterprise Architecture

Mastering artificial intelligence requires architects to adopt a learner's mindset. While foundational technical skills are important, such as proficiency in Python and machine learning frameworks like TensorFlow, architects should focus more on cultivating soft skills that enable an AI-powered enterprise. For instance, sharpening analytical abilities to identify high-value AI application areas or honing communication skills to obtain executive buy-in and collaborate cross-functionally.

In terms of resources, architects have an abundance of options. Enrolling in online courses and certifications offered by providers like Udacity, Coursera, and edX allows architects to learn at their own pace. These develop well-rounded AI skills spanning computer vision, natural language processing and predictive analytics. Architects can also join industry communities like AI Network to share best practices or participate in hack-a-thons to gain hands-on experimentation. Conferences like AI World provide exposure to real-world AI use cases while podcasts like AI Today offer bite-sized learning.

Regarding enterprise architecture, the paradigm is shifting from traditional static models to more adaptive approaches. Architects now need the ability to design flexible and intelligent architectures. This requires grasping concepts like event-driven architecture, micro-services and smart automation. Impactful resources include Gartner's research notes, the MIT Center for Information Systems Research, and the Enterprise Architecture Center of Excellence. By studying leading organizations, architects gain insights into cutting-edge EA practices.

Two overarching skills underpin both AI and modern enterprise architecture—creative problem-solving and change management. Architects must apply creative thinking to uncover innovative ways of delivering business value. Simultaneously, change management abilities are crucial for driving organizational alignment and adoption. Resources like Harvard Business Review's blog provide tactics on blending these skills to shepherd enterprise-wide transformation.

By continually exploring these kinds of multidimensional skills and resources, architects can stay at the forefront of both AI and EA to drive maximum technology-powered business impact.

Featuring Insights and Experiences From Architects Who Specialize in AI

Architecting artificial intelligence systems requires expertise spanning technology, business strategy, and design thinking. Leading AI architects provide invaluable perspectives from the front lines of innovative implementations across various industries. Their real-world experiences highlight best practices and lessons learned for transforming organizations through applied AI.

Seasoned veterans emphasize starting with the business problem rather than the data or technology itself. The architects endorse collaborating closely with business leaders and domain experts first to deeply understand needs, challenges, and desired outcomes. This domain-first approach based on a strategic business mindset allows them to then explore questions around what types of patterns could emerge from relevant data and how AI techniques can drive toward solutions.

These AI trailblazers stress the importance of curating, cleaning, and labeling training data sets with precision and care. They have learned the hard way that bias and error propagation can stem from faulty data practices. Methodical governance and continuous monitoring processes are mandatory. Architecting flexibility into the system for easy retraining purposes is also critical, as new data becomes available over time.

On the software engineering side, modular design and development techniques allow the architects to incorporate AI components efficiently into tech stacks. They create robust pipelines and workflows to streamline moving models from research into production, reliably and safely. Governance around model risk management and model ops helps contain technical debt.

Above all, these experienced AI innovators emphasize that success requires a healthy dose of experimentation and learning mindsets. They approach architecting AI solutions as a continuous journey to incrementally capture value, measure impact, and adapt based on data and user feedback. A strong vision coupled with pragmatism to adjust along the way is key to transforming organizations with artificial intelligence.

Discussing the Challenges and Rewards of Working in AI-Driven Environments

Working as an architect in an AI-driven environment certainly poses unique challenges, but it also presents exciting rewards for those willing to push the boundaries of design innovation. Rather than simply integrating AI into existing methodologies, the most visionary architects have an opportunity to completely transform architectural practice through a synergy of human creativity and machine intelligence.

Of course, adapting existing skills to unfamiliar AI-based workflows can prove difficult initially. Architects pride themselves on hard-won design talents—an intuitive sense of space, light, and form—developed over years of training and practice. Delegating creative control to opaque algorithms can feel uncomfortable, even threatening. However, the key is viewing AI as a collaborative partner, not an adversary. The most successful architects approach AI with open curiosity, asking how emerging technologies can augment versus replace human strengths.

By outsourcing tedious, routine tasks to AI assistants, architects gain freedom to focus uniquely on human skills: strategic thinking, imagination, aesthetic sensibility. AI handles data-heavy technical requirements, rapidly iterating through design permutations to meet specifications like sustainability, accessibility, client needs, and budget. Freed from grunt work, architects can concentrate on the visionary conceptual work that first stirred their passion for the field. Both architect and machine do what they do best.

This human-AI collaboration also enables previously unimaginable creative possibilities. With AI able to instantaneously analyze and visualize thousands of options based on an architect's initial design impulse, there is no limit to the organic, nonlinear, even *avant garde* forms such partnerships can generate. Architects may glimpse design principles and otherworldly solutions in machine-learning feedback that expand their own visual vocabularies. The built environment of the future will combine the best of human creativity, ethics and empathy with the scale, efficiency, and precision of artificial intelligence.

For those architects willing to risk uncertainty in adoption of unfamiliar tools, AI promises to resolve the mundane constraints that have always hindered realization of creative ambitions. More than assistants, AI design partners promise to enhance what is uniquely human about the art, engineering and social responsibility of architecture, liberating the brightest design visionaries of the 21st century and beyond. The rewards for those brave enough to work in AI-driven design environments are nothing short of the revelation of creative potential beyond imagination.

Projecting Future Trends in Skills and Knowledge for Enterprise Architects

Enterprise architecture is a complex and evolving field that requires architects to have a diverse set of competencies. As technology and business landscapes shift rapidly, enterprise architects must continuously evaluate the latest developments in infrastructure, software, automation, organizational dynamics, and more in order to provide effective guidance and leadership.

To accurately forecast the skills and knowledge that will be most relevant for enterprise architects in the coming years, both quantitative and qualitative methods are required. On the quantitative side, studying industry research on technology adoption trends provides insight into shifts that will tangibly impact enterprises. For example, as artificial intelligence and cloud computing become mainstream in business operations, architects will need stronger capabilities around integrating and optimizing these emerging tools. Likewise, cybersecurity is projected to be a major focus area in the face of increasing threats, indicating architects will require advanced understanding of systems safeguarding.

Qualitative approaches are also imperative to identify intangible but critical capabilities. Connecting directly with IT leaders, enterprise architects, and C-suite executives can offer rich perspectives. Through networking, interviews and analyzing prior architectural approaches that succeeded or failed, key themes around important mindsets, communication styles, analytical thinking and leadership qualities can emerge that influence job requirements. For instance, findings may show that architects who take bold and creative approaches reflect the agile, growth-oriented way senior management intends to steer the enterprise going forward.

By blending quantitative intelligence around rapidly advancing technology with qualitative insights on strategic direction and soft skills from leadership, enterprise architects can map detailed projections of the most beneficial knowledge, skills, and abilities to acquire in order to provide maximum value as their role evolves. The specific technical and interpersonal competencies that underpin an enterprise architect's success are destined to transition over time, making continual assessment vital to staying relevant. Anticipating these shifts rather than reacting to them ensures architects can proactively realign their capabilities.

A Day in the Life of an AI Architect

The day starts early for John, an enterprise architect who specializes in artificial intelligence solutions. After waking up at 6 AM, he heads into the home office to catch up on the latest AI news, research papers, and breakthroughs in the industry. Staying on the cutting edge is crucial in his role. He spends an hour reading briefings and articles to understand the state of play in areas like machine learning, neural networks, natural language processing, robotics, and more.

At 7:30 AM, it's time to get ready and head out for the office. During the commute, John continues his learning, switching to podcasts and audiobooks related to AI and enterprise IT architectures. Once he arrives at the office at 9 AM, he reviews objectives for current projects he is working on and plans out deliverables he needs to complete. As an AI enterprise architect, his job focuses on developing technical plans and blueprints to integrate AI capabilities across the business, whether for enhanced analytics, automated workflows and processes, or even internal virtual assistants.

Mid-morning is often spent in cross-functional meetings, collaborating with stakeholders in departments like operations, product development, customer service, finance, and more. He needs to deeply understand their pain points and objectives in order to design customer-focused AI solutions. In the afternoon, John switches gears to analysis and design work. This involves researching AI vendor offerings, mapping out integration needs for data and analytics platforms, determining compute and storage requirements, and diagramming conceptual architectures.

Later in the day it is focused on documentation, report writing, and presentations to different audiences like executives and technical teams. Clear, simple communication is imperative as the bridge between business needs and technical implementation. After wrapping up loose ends for the day around 6 PM, John takes some time on his commute home to continue strategizing innovative ideas for AI adoption to push his architectures to the next level for the organization. AI moves fast, so there is no shortage of new capabilities to evaluate and integrate.

Highlighting the Challenges, Decision-Making Processes, and Satisfaction of the Role

Serving as an enterprise architect is a complex job with immense responsibilities across an organization. When artificial intelligence capabilities are introduced to enhance data-driven decisions, the role becomes even more multifaceted and strategic in nature. Enterprise architects serve as the bridge between technological innovation and practical business implementation.

One of the main challenges enterprise architects face is identifying where and how AI can drive the most impactful business outcomes without disrupting critical systems and operations. The decision-making process requires carefully evaluating each existing process, data source, and infrastructure component to determine where AI analytics and automation could boost performance and efficiency. This is a delicate balancing act of business needs versus technological capabilities. Architects must also keep in mind ease of integration when assessing where to pilot test AI applications before considering company-wide implementations.

Another critical part of the decision process is managing expectations across C-suite leaders and line of business heads eager to rapidly scale AI for competitive advantage. Setting realistic timelines for AI implementation and conveying transparent limitations of emerging AI technologies is imperative. This helps enterprise architects maintain trust and credibility as key technological advisors guiding strategic AI adoption.

Finally, job satisfaction for enterprise architects depends heavily on organizational AI governance. Defining policies for data management, system oversight, and ethical AI standards helps contain shadow IT sprawl. Having cross-functional governance committees provides forums to discuss AI priorities, funding allocation, and measure impact. This enables architects to focus on maximizing business value delivery through AI rather than getting mired in regulatory policy issues.

With proactive planning, enterprise architects can thrive as AI adoption grows. But it requires upfront analysis of decision flows, stakeholder alignment, and governance guardrails to ensure smooth integration of AI capabilities over time across the enterprise. The role stands to gain immense influence and satisfaction guiding productive AI implementations.

Chapter Twelve

AI and the Cloud—A Symbiotic Relationship

C loud computing and artificial intelligence have developed an increasingly interdependent relationship, with each field benefiting greatly from advances in the other. By leveraging the vast on-demand computing resources, scalability and flexibility of the cloud, companies have been able to rapidly accelerate the development and deployment of innovative AI applications. At the same time, AI is enabling cloud platforms to become smarter, more adaptive and greatly enhanced in their capabilities.

Several case studies clearly demonstrate the power of this AI-cloud synergy. For example, healthcare providers are leveraging machine learning services on the cloud to detect cancerous tumors, predict patient outcomes, and customize treatment plans. The massive parallel processing capacity of cloud data centers allows them to train complex neural network models on vast medical datasets. The cloud also enables easy scaling of model training, as more patient data becomes available.

E-commerce leaders like Amazon and eBay are leveraging automated AI assistants on the cloud to provide personalized recommendations, predictive user searches and real-time customer support at a global scale. The dynamic provisioning and high availability of cloud resources allows them to offer reliable, low-latency AI services that keep improving through continuous learning.

As more and more devices and appliances get connected to the internet, AI applications on the cloud can collect and analyze their data to uncover usage patterns, predict failures, optimize performance, and customize experiences based on behavioral insights. The cloud's almost unlimited storage capacity makes this possible.

Emerging edge computing architectures are bringing cloud capabilities closer to the data source by having localized mini data centers. This allows time-sensitive AI processing to happen at the edge, while leveraging the cloud's superior computing power for offline model building and training. For example, autonomous vehicles can benefit from real-time collision detection running locally on edge nodes, while updated driving policies get periodically refreshed from the cloud mothership.

As cloud-AI adoption grows across industries, enterprises are rethinking their application design, data management and processing architectures to best harness the power of this symbiosis. Key focus areas include building AI-ready data lakes on the cloud, crafting hybrid on-premise and cloud workflows, and embracing cloud-native development strategies. With the meteoric pace of innovation in this sphere, organizations that can strategically leverage cloud-enabled AI will have a substantial competitive edge.

This chapter focuses on providing information about the interdependence of AI and cloud for an enterprise architect and provides tips to improve your knowledge on the subject to make you work for your organization's prospects.

The Interdependence of Cloud Computing and AI

Cloud computing and artificial intelligence have developed an increasingly interdependent relationship that allows both fields to evolve in impactful ways. At the most basic level, cloud computing offers the foundational infrastructure of storage capacity, fast processing speeds, and networked access that enables artificial intelligence systems to operate effectively. The demanding computer processing and high data storage needs of artificial intelligence applications, especially machine learning algorithms which require immense amounts of data for model training, are fulfilled by the flexible and scalable resource capacity of cloud-based services.

Without the instantly provisioned computing power and scalability that cloud platforms provide, most organizations would lack the IT infrastructure to support extensive artificial intelligence initiatives. The cloud allows AI innovation to thrive. At the same time, artificial intelligence adds higher levels of intelligent optimization to cloud computing environments. The capabilities of AI algorithms help cloud services become smarter, more efficient, and more effective at serving organizational needs. For example, AI can allocate cloud resources more strategically based on real-time operational data, ensure robust data security, provide proactive monitoring and maintenance of cloud performance, and automate responses to system outages or overloads. These and many other enhancements powered by artificial intelligence translate to better overall cloud solutions.

Essentially, cloud computing offers an essential foundation that artificial intelligence innovation is built upon, while artificial intelligence conversely elevates cloud platforms to be more adaptive and responsive. The interplay creates a cycle where cloud-based infrastructure gives rise to progress in AI, and AI returns the favor by infusing cloud services with smarter functionalities. This symbiotic relationship is a key driver propelling both cloud computing and artificial intelligence to play bigger roles in streamlining and enhancing organizational processes across industries. Their interconnected growth trajectories present exciting possibilities for the future as researchers and technologists find new ways to leverage their complementary strengths.

How Cloud Platforms Enable AI

Cloud computing has opened up exciting new possibilities for organizations leveraging artificial intelligence. By providing vast amounts of computational power and storage on demand, cloud platforms enable companies to pursue AI capabilities that previously may have been cost prohibitive or technically challenging to implement.

Rather than needing to invest in and maintain an extensive IT infrastructure internally, the scalability of cloud resources allows organizations to ramp up processing capacity almost instantly as their AI needs grow. This scalability is crucial for powering the data and computation-intensive work that goes into developing and training intelligent algorithms. Companies can significantly cut expenses by leveraging the cloud's near-limitless scale while only paying for the specific resources used.

The cloud also provides storage capacities necessary for amassing and accessing the huge datasets that feed modern AI systems. Whether for image recognition systems, natural language applications, predictive analytics, or other uses, machine learning is fueled by data. Cloud platforms enable this data to be stored in a centralized location where it can be readily accessed to train AI models as new algorithms are developed. And again, companies avoid capital outlays by leveraging the cloud's storage on an as-needed basis.

By handling the heavy lifting of processing power and data capacity in a highly scalable environment, cloud computing removes infrastructure barriers to AI adoption. Companies can focus resources on developing intelligent models and applying them to business opportunities rather than managing on-premises hardware demands. The cloud's versatility, accessibility, and pay-as-you-go economics are helping to accelerate AI innovations across industries.

Cloud platforms address this by offering services such as mentioned below.

Infrastructure as a Service (IaaS)

Infrastructure as a Service, commonly referred to as IaaS, has become an invaluable resource for artificial intelligence practitioners looking to develop and deploy AI systems without incurring major upfront costs. With IaaS offerings, AI developers can effectively rent access to a highly scalable range of virtualized computing infrastructure resources via public cloud providers rather than purchasing and maintaining physical servers outright.

This on-demand provisioning of virtualized infrastructure—including servers, networking, storage, and more—allows AI teams to spin up and spin down compute capacity with tremendous agility. Teams no longer have to predict resource needs upfront and make large initial capital investments in data center equipment. Instead, they can start small and scale up seamlessly as project demands grow simply by paying for more cloud-hosted infrastructure resources only when they need them.

This pay-as-you-go pricing model not only helps AI teams avoid over-provisioning but also contains ongoing operating costs by removing the need to hire dedicated personnel to manage physical hardware on-premises. With cloud providers handling the hosting, maintenance and updates of virtual infrastructure, in-house staff are freed up to focus their efforts on innovation rather than IT administration.

In essence, Infrastructure as a Service offerings provide AI developers ready access to an elastic pool of infrastructure capacity for training models, running inferencing, and more without upfront capex investments. This allows for greater experimentation early on and cost-efficient scaling to support production workloads down the road—a pivotal enabler fueling rapid AI adoption.

Platform as a Service (PaaS)

Developing and deploying artificial intelligence capabilities can be complex, requiring specialized skills and infrastructure. Platform-as-a-Service, (PaaS), solutions aim to simplify the process by abstracting away many of the complicated back end details, allowing organizations to focus more on using AI to solve business problems.

In essence, PaaS offerings provide pre-configured frameworks designed specifically for building, training, and deploying intelligent algorithms at scale. This empowers teams to get applications up and running faster, without getting bogged down in the intricacies of hardware provisioning, data pipelines, model governance, and IT operations. The platforms provide robust tooling to ingest quality datasets, apply techniques like data labeling, develop models using popular algorithms, monitor for accuracy and bias issues, and promote the best performing versions into production.

These prepackaged functionalities handle many of the undifferentiated heavy lifting aspects, allowing organizations to concentrate more on the custom elements that create competitive advantage. For example, data scientists can dedicate their specialized skills solely on feature engineering, hyper-parameter tuning, and debugging model logic rather than infrastructure maintenance.

Leading PaaS solutions also automate best practices for efficiency, accuracy, and operationalization. Built-in MLOps promotes collaboration between data scientists and IT teams using DevOps-like practices for faster, more reliable updates. Automated model monitoring and benchmarking against quality thresholds simplifies governance. And robust explainability features provide transparency into model behavior and recommendations to improve outcomes.

By handling the complex model building pipeline from ingest to production, PaaS solutions empower enterprises to quickly and efficiently harness the possibilities of AI. Abstracting away infrastructure complexity allows teams to focus their high-value skills on customizing, optimizing, and deploying intelligent algorithms tailored to their specific business needs. This combination of ease-of-use with cutting edge capability allows even AI novices to operationalize the technology across their organizations.

Software as a Service (SaaS)

Software as a Service, (SaaS), represents a category of cloud computing that allows end users to access software applications over the internet. Rather than having to purchase, install, and maintain software on individual devices or servers, SaaS applications are hosted in the cloud and accessed seamlessly through web browsers. This on-demand access provides immense flexibility and cost savings for organizations.

Within the evolution of SaaS offerings, certain cloud-based applications have begun utilizing artificial intelligence for enhanced features and functionality. Specifically, many SaaS platforms leverage AI capabilities in areas like advanced data analytics, predictive modeling, and business intelligence. This enables the SaaS applications to process and interpret large volumes of data, identifying actionable insights and trends. It also allows them to predict future outcomes using algorithms and machine learning.

By building in these AI functionalities natively into SaaS platforms, it brings sophisticated AI abilities to non-expert users across various business roles. For example, a sales manager accessing a SaaS customer relationship management tool can benefit from integrated AI analytics that provide detailed reports on factors that influence deals to close or fall through. Or a warehouse manager using an inventory and order management SaaS app can leverage AI-driven recommendations on optimal stock levels to maintain.

The AI capacities handle the complexity behind the scenes, while the managers simply interact with the information and insights presented to them in real time through dashboards, notifications, and predictive recommendations. This democratizes the advantages of AI for enhanced decision-making and efficiency gains among everyday organizational users. And it does so through the user-friendly SaaS interfaces they are already accustomed to, rather than separate AI tools requiring advanced expertise.

The combination of the flexibility of SaaS delivery and the intelligence of AI holds tremendous potential for organizations to elevate a wide range of business functions in a scalable way. This drives greater productivity and competitive advantage across the workforce. As more SaaS vendors continue incorporating aspects like machine learning and natural language processing into their solutions, you can expect AI adoption and impact through the cloud to keep accelerating in the coming years.

Data Management

Managing and analyzing large volumes of data is essential for developing impactful AI systems that provide actionable insights. Cloud computing offers a flexible and scalable approach to storing and processing all that data. Rather than relying on local servers with limited capacity, companies can leverage the power of cloud-based storage and computing to cost-effectively amass and harness huge datasets.

For example, vast quantities of information on customer behavior can be gathered from sources like web traffic, purchase transactions, social media, and more. All that raw data is of little use until it can be aggregated, organized, and examined for meaningful patterns. This process is known as big data analytics. Cloud services enable businesses to ingest data from many distributed sources and consolidate it into massive databases for analysis. The cloud's distributed storage systems allow limitless expansion as the data pools continue to grow over months and years.

The insightful outputs from big data analytics then allow AI algorithms to find correlations that would previously have remained hidden. By discovering new relationships and trends within expansive datasets, AI tools can uncover valuable insights that transform decision-making. A cloud-based architecture provides the connectivity, bandwidth, storage capacity, and computing power to fuel these AI applications. It's the foundation enabling advanced analytics.

For example, retailers may discern unexpected affinities among certain products by analyzing billions of purchase records with AI, then generate targeted marketing campaigns accordingly. Or healthcare systems can find new disease risk factors by combing through comprehensive medical histories from millions of patients. The cloud serves as the back end platform making such use cases possible. By unleashing big data analytics and AI algorithms on vast datasets in the cloud, businesses and organizations can uncover insights that provide strategic competitive advantages.

Scalability

Scaling AI workloads efficiently is critical for organizations implementing artificial intelligence. Traditional on-premises infrastructure often struggles to manage the ebbs and flows of AI model development and usage. Cloud platforms provide an ideal back end for AI because of their ability to elastically allocate compute, memory, storage, and other resources in real-time to meet changing demands.

For example, the training of deep learning models is an extremely computationally-intensive process that requires high-powered GPUs or TPUs. Organizations may over-provision on-premises servers just to handle occasional model training needs, leaving resources idle in between. Cloud platforms allow precise provisioning during bursts of training activity and release just as quickly. This ensures organizations pay only for resources used, optimizing costs.

On the inference side as models are deployed into production, usage can similarly fluctuate dramatically depending on factors like time of day or sudden spikes in traffic. By leveraging auto-scaling capabilities, cloud platforms can immediately spin up more AI servers to handle heavy loads and spin down seamlessly during lighter loads. This delivers consistent model performance for end users while minimizing infrastructure expenses.

In addition, as AI workloads inevitably evolve—with new models being developed and old ones retired—cloud provides the agility to resize infrastructure up or down. On-premises systems often require wholesale upgrades and replacements to rightsize, whereas cloud offers endless elasticity to match resources to current processing demands.

By dynamically scaling compute, memory, storage, and more to align with the variable resource requirements intrinsic to AI development and deployment, cloud platforms enable efficient and cost-effective execution of AI workloads over time. The cloud's inherent scalability ensures that AI models deliver maximum value by being trained quickly and led through consistent inference at the optimal infrastructure footprint.

Advancements in AI Through Cloud Technologies

The exponential growth in computational power unlocked by cloud platforms has been an immense catalyst for artificial intelligence progress. By leveraging the vast on-demand compute, storage and services of the cloud, researchers and companies have accelerated AI capabilities in areas that were previously constrained by limited access to high-performance computing resources.

One domain that exemplifies the synergistic advancement between cloud and AI is deep learning. These data-intensive algorithms for pattern recognition and predictive analytics were restricted in their potential prior to cloud services providing flexible access to GPU and TPU processing at scale. Teams can now iterate on neural network models rapidly, conducting extensive experimentation by training deep learning models across huge datasets. For example, generative adversarial networks, (GANs), that are used to produce synthetic media like images and videos have benefited tremendously from scalable cloud-based model training. The creative applications that GANs have enabled would not be feasible without the cloud's vast parallel processing capacity.

Natural language processing is another domain where cloud-powered AI has unlocked new potentials. Cloud platforms enable users to tap into advanced pre-trained NLP models like BERT and GPT-3 that can analyze text data and linguistics with far greater sophistication than previous generations. By democratizing access to these complex models via cloud APIs, organizations have integrated language translation, sentiment analysis and other capabilities into their products much more efficiently. The utility of search engines, conversational bots and other applications relying on NLP has improved markedly as a result.

Healthcare AI has also progressed meaningfully due to cloud acceleration. Cloud storage and computing has enabled more effective analysis of large volumes of medical imaging data using techniques like convolutional neural networks. These deep learning models can identify abnormalities in scans with higher accuracy and at greater scale, by leveraging the parallel processing capacity of the cloud. Cloud-based AI is also facilitating personalized medicine by allowing healthcare institutions to run genomics workloads for precision diagnosis and treatment.

The scalable on-demand access to high-performance computing that public cloud platforms provide has removed infrastructure barriers for AI innovation. As cloud service providers continue enhancing their machine learning tooling and hardware optimizations, we can expect AI advancements across industries to be propelled even further through this symbiotic relationship.

Cloud Computing Evolution With AI Advancements

Cloud computing and artificial intelligence have evolved together in recent years, with each innovation in one area enabling new capabilities in the other. Let's trace this symbiotic relationship and see how these technologies have advanced hand-in-hand.

In the early days of cloud computing, the primary focus was on providing flexible and scalable storage and computing infrastructure on demand. As cloud platforms matured, machine learning became widely used to optimize resource allocation and automate management processes. For example, AI now allows cloud providers to efficiently assign server capacity based on fluctuating usage patterns. It has also enabled self-healing capabilities where infrastructure automatically recovers from outages and failures.

On the other side of the equation, the vast computing resources available via the cloud have accelerated AI development. The massive parallel processing power of cloud data centers allows companies to train machine learning algorithms faster. Cloud storage provides the vast datasets required, while tools make it easier to prepare that data for modeling. Without the cloud infrastructure, few organizations would have the means to run the computations necessary to advance AI.

Looking ahead, we can expect AI to infiltrate even more deeply into cloud architectures. Cloud platforms may begin optimizing everything automatically—not just infrastructure allocation, but data integration, application deployment, database tuning and more. AI will help manage increasingly complex cloud environments and enable autonomous decision making.

Another trend is the emergence of AI cloud services—such as natural language processing, computer vision and predictive analytics—that can simply be called via an API. This allows companies to leverage advanced AI capabilities without needing in-house machine learning expertise. The democratization of AI through the cloud will make these technologies accessible to organizations of all sizes and across all industries.

Cloud computing has provided the foundation for recent AI breakthroughs, while AI itself has become integral to operating and optimizing cloud platforms. As these innovations continue to support each other in a virtuous cycle, they will unleash a new wave of products, services and capabilities that will shape the future of business.

Forecasts on Future Cloud-AI Synergies

Many technology leaders envisage a deeply intertwined relationship between cloud platforms and AI capabilities unfolding over the next decade. As cloud infrastructure continues to evolve, it is expected to provide an increasingly fertile foundation upon which organizations can build and scale their AI applications to drive more informed business decisions and optimize processes.

One advancement we are likely to witness is the integration of more robust data analytics and machine learning tools directly into cloud platforms. This could significantly simplify AI adoption for companies, allowing them to hit the ground running instead of configuring complex AI infrastructure from scratch. AutoML technologies may also help automatically tune and optimize AI models in the cloud for improved performance and efficiency.

Some experts predict virtually every enterprise application leveraging the cloud will eventually incorporate some layer of AI. Supply chain platforms, customer relationship management systems, business intelligence software, and beyond could all be enhanced with predictive analytics, recommendation engines, conversational interfaces, intelligent process automation, and more. This could enable organizations to extract greater value from data across domains.

Another potential milestone for cloud-AI integration is the capability to train AI models with data distributed across different cloud services and data centers. By spreading computation and model building across a mesh of cloud nodes, organizations could overcome previous barriers around data movement and privacy. This could massively scale AI training to leverage more data sources.

However, as cloud-AI capabilities become more powerful and ubiquitous, ethical considerations around potential biases and pitfalls will heighten as well. Cloud providers and organizations implementing AI will need to ensure transparency, auditability, and integrity so that automated decisions can be explained and systems are not propagating unfair biases. With responsible oversight, experts anticipate cloud-AI synergies transforming businesses and society for the better in the years to come.

Chapter Thirteen

Preparing for an AI-Enhanced TOGAF Journey

I ntegrating artificial intelligence capabilities into complex enterprise architectures requires careful planning and execution. Enterprise architects utilizing the industry-standard TOGAF framework must take a methodical approach to integrate AI in a way that aligns with overall business goals, governance structures, and system interdependencies.

The first step is assembling a cross-functional team with the appropriate skills. This includes enterprise architects fluent in TOGAF methodologies, data scientists experienced in developing and deploying AI models, software engineers to handle system integration activities, and business leaders to align priorities. Securing executive buy-in and budget is also critical upfront.

With the right team in place, architects should conduct assessments to identify integration points compatible with AI capabilities. Which business processes or decisions could be optimized using machine learning algorithms or predictive analytics? What datasets offer input signals suitable for powering AI models? The assessments should enumerate specific use cases, requirements, and success metrics to guide the integration.

When potential AI integration points have been identified, the team can begin following TOGAF guidelines to incorporate the new capabilities into logical and physical application and technology architectures. For example, AI components like data pipelines and model inference engines can be represented in architecture diagrams. Security, scalability and governance considerations should also be addressed through TOGAF work streams.

With logical architectures defined, physical integration can commence. TOGAF artifacts like interface specifications, migration plans and testing procedures will help drive successful system integration. Continuous monitoring and improvement of integrated AI components should follow based on defined metrics. Updates may require iterating through relevant TOGAF disciplines around architecture governance and change management.

Following this methodical approach combining TOGAF's proven enterprise architecture methodologies with AI-specific assessments, design considerations and integration techniques allows organizations to effectively integrate artificial intelligence, minimizing risk and alignment issues. Reaching out to external consultants or partners with experience in AI-TOGAF integrations can also supplement internal capabilities.

This chapter focuses on providing information about this journey in detail for an enterprise architect.

Steps for Integrating AI Into TOGAF

Integrating artificial intelligence capabilities into enterprise architectures guided by The Open Group Architecture Framework offers intriguing potential to amplify the value of architectural efforts. However, thoughtfully mapping the introduction of AI across TOGAF's four architecture domains—business, data, application, and technology—is essential for smoothly embedding intelligent automation in a way that aligns to overarching business goals and target operating models.

When initially envisioning an infusion of AI, architecture teams would be wise to thoroughly understand the problem spaces and user needs within the organization where intelligent features would provide the most lift. This allows for segmentation of opportunities where applying AI-powered pattern recognition, predictive insights, recommendation engines, or autonomous workflows would drive disproportionate benefits. These use cases then become architectural guardrails for constructing AI technical solutions purpose-built for enhancing specific business capabilities.

The capabilities and associated data inputs required for training and continually optimizing AI to meet performance benchmarks should be clearly mapped out next. Assembling quality datasets for model development while properly governing access, lineage, and provenance of data elements are important foundations within the architecture process at this juncture.

Finally, the components and services enabling the AI capabilities can be framed within TOGAF's application and technology layers, aligning integrations, infrastructure, and performance attributes to intended functionality. Architecting with re-usability, scalability, explainability, and trustworthiness as guiding principles can produce more adaptable solutions.

Done correctly, embedding AI within TOGAF-based enterprise architectures can accelerate realizing strategic goals and target operating models. Maintaining human oversight and understanding of AI system behaviors will remain instrumental in managing risks and ensuring business priorities are fulfilled by the promising but often complex combination of TOGAF ecosystem architectures and artificial intelligence.

Here is a step-by-step approach, along with practical guidelines, for successfully blending AI into the TOGAF methodologies:

Step 1: Establish an AI Strategy Aligned With Business Goals

Integrating artificial intelligence into an organization's operations and strategy requires careful planning and consideration even before implementation begins. Rather than jumping into AI adoption, leadership teams would be prudent to take a methodical approach that first involves deeply analyzing their business to determine where and how AI could drive substantive impact and value.

The foundational steps would be to elucidate what the core objectives are that the company aims to achieve through the use of AI technology. These objectives should tie directly back to the overarching corporate vision and priorities that have been defined regarding where the organization sees itself in the coming years. This enables executives to figure out where AI aligns and can move the needle most meaningfully.

With these AI objectives clarified, the next move is assessing potential use cases across the enterprise evaluating where introducing AI-based solutions could significantly enhance performance, efficiency, decision automation, competitiveness or other critical aspects in relation to the business objectives. The goal is to home in on the highest value application areas—whether operations, customer engagement, market positioning or others.

By taking this strategic approach, organizations can determine where integrating AI will provide substantial upside and positive outcomes before making any system investments. They can target AI integration in a precise manner to maximize business impact. And they can establish measurable markers of success upfront based on the clarified objectives. This allows leadership to track progress and returns in a transparent way. Following these steps thoughtfully at the outset helps ensure that AI adoption efforts achieve what the business needs rather than functioning as shiny new tools that fail to add real material value. It also enables the enterprise to fluidly evolve its strategy as technology capabilities scale further.

Step 2: Update the Enterprise Architecture Vision

The Architecture Vision is a key phase in TOGAF for defining the overall shape and priorities for an organization's initiatives. Typically this vision centers around business goals like improving customer satisfaction or increasing operational efficiency. When an organization is embarking on major AI transformations, the Architecture Vision would need to expand to make AI a central priority.

Rather than treating AI implementation as an isolated IT project, it should be woven throughout the vision as integral to achieving the organization's most vital strategic goals. The objectives within the Architecture Vision should explicitly detail how leveraging AI technologies will help automate processes, generate insights from data, and enhance decision-making across departments. Setting these objectives for AI will steer the initiatives to follow in order to transform essential functions through intelligent automation and analytics.

Additionally, the stakeholders communication plan used for sharing the Architecture Vision should appropriately address the AI component. This communication is critical for securing buy-in and support across impacted business units, partners, customers and more. The plan should include content specifically tailored to explain the capabilities of AI, highlight use cases relevant to the audience, and convey how AI will take the organization to the next level competitively.

Gaining stakeholder awareness and backing is imperative for the changes entailed with embedding AI into operations, workflows, and systems. By dedicating focus on AI directly within a revised Architecture Vision, the rationale and promise behind upcoming AI transformations becomes clearer. Stakeholders will ideally become advocates for the pursuit of AI

and the long-term benefits it can offer if properly integrated organization-
ally through a well-constructed architecture roadmap.

Step 3: Perform a Business Architecture Assessment With AI in Focus

When incorporating artificial intelligence into business architecture, it's
imperative to thoroughly evaluate potential impacts on existing processes,
roles, and capabilities. Rather than bolting on AI technologies to legacy
ways of operating, organizations have an opportunity to re-imagine how
work gets done after carefully analyzing the transformations AI may catalyze.

For example, routine tasks like validating invoices, authorizing transactions, and drafting reports can be redesigned around automated systems powered by machine learning algorithms. As these AI components
handle mundane responsibilities with higher quality and throughput, the
human roles responsible for supervision and exceptions management of
these processes may be refocused on more strategic, creative interventions.
Finance managers previously bogged down with manual approvals may
have capacity to provide more value-added analysis to executive leadership.

These types of process augmentations warrant drafting new operating
models, workflows, and maps that clearly delineate between automated
versus human-driven tasks. Organizations should avoid viewing this as a
one-for-one replacement of people for technology; thoughtfully balancing
the two is key. Cross-functional teams with insights into the nuances of
existing processes must work in tandem with AI experts that understand
inherent technical constraints. Together, they can co-create and simulate
enhanced processes that play to the strengths of both people and AI systems, realizing synergies neither could achieve independently.

The outputs of these collaborative sessions should produce new process
architectures—the models, maps, and documentation of how work gets

executed within the business. These artifacts establish clarity for how responsibilities will shift across roles when the reinvented processes are launched. They also serve as critical guides for change management initiatives that proactively up-skill and re-skill the workforce for operating in concert with AI. Adopting this future-state orientation toward process and role redefinition unlocks immense potential. Rather than simply enhancing what exists today, re-imagining work streams through the lens of AI integration lays the foundations for the next chapter of efficient, innovative operations.

Step 4: Incorporate AI Into Information Systems Architectures

As organizations adopt artificial intelligence technologies, a critical yet often overlooked aspect is integrating AI capabilities within existing information systems architectures. Rather than bolting on AI tools without proper planning, companies should conduct in-depth assessments of their data, application, and overall digital infrastructures to support robust and sustainable AI implementations.

This process would fall under common information systems architecture planning methodologies, but with an AI-focused lens. Activities would likely involve enterprise architects, data engineers, application owners, and AI specialists working collaboratively. A logical first step entails cataloging, mapping, and evaluating current data structures and models across business units to determine suitability for powering AI algorithms. Assessments will reveal availability, quality, and accessibility of data sources that machine learning models can leverage for optimal training and performance. Architects can then pinpoint and prioritize any data infrastructure upgrades, consolidation initiatives, or new data pipelines that must precede AI integration.

In tandem, application architectures require similar audits based on AI needs. Teams should survey which applications and software systems will directly interact with AI technologies versus those that will remain unchanged. This mapping exercise also uncovers applications that may require modifications, upgrades, or replacements to enable the ingestion and processing of predictions, insights, and other outputs from AI systems. Activities could range from relatively simple tweaks to user interfaces all the way to significant reengineering efforts for handling AI functionalities within legacy systems.

With thorough evaluations of existing data and applications, information systems architects can develop integrated roadmaps that align AI solutions with the necessary data, application, and infrastructure foundations for sustainable success. Rather than one-off AI experiments, companies can take an architectural approach that embeds AI capabilities holistically across systems, enabling greater value and competitive differentiation over the long-term.

Step 5: Adjust the Technology Architecture for AI

When integrating artificial intelligence capabilities into an organization's technology environment, it is important to thoroughly examine the existing architecture first to assess and determine what adjustments may be necessary to support and accommodate AI computing needs. Rather than simply bolting on AI components, a thoughtful analysis of current infrastructure along with an understanding of AI processing requirements can inform strategic upgrades that will optimize for AI while keeping the entire ecosystem aligned.

At a basic level, legacy hardware that may be outdated will likely need to be replaced with modern high-powered graphical and tensor processing units designed specifically to handle the intense mathematical computations that AI and deep learning algorithms necessitate. Servers with increased capacity for storage, memory and processing ability will tangibly improve AI system performance. Beyond servers, evaluating edge devices and endpoints to support localized AI applications can provide more organization-wide infusion of intelligence.

Another area requiring scrutiny is network capacity and information pipelines since AI systems are extremely data hungry. AI not only analyzes real-time data but also learns from historical data. This makes a high-bandwidth, low latency network imperative for connecting disparate data sources via reliable information flows. Upgrading network connectivity across the enterprise data infrastructure ensures AI algorithms can efficiently access the immense data volumes required for accuracy.

Finally, existing cybersecurity tools and policies need to be assessed considering AI brings with it unique vulnerabilities that can be exploited if not properly protected. Governance models accounting for factors like data privacy, system transparency, AI ethics and safety will help minimize organizational risk. Embedding cybersecurity earlier rather than later in the design process through measures like multi-layered defense and continuous monitoring helps secure AI integrity over the long term.

This examination and strategic upgrade of technology architecture to natively support evolving AI capabilities avoids inefficient one-off changes down the road. It also prevents performance bottlenecks that adversely impact AI reliability for decision making. Establishing an agile, resilient and secure technology foundation ultimately provides scalability for expanding organizational adoption of artificial intelligence now and in the future.

Step 6: Address Opportunities and Solutions With AI in Focus

When integrating artificial intelligence solutions into an organization's enterprise architecture, it is strategic to carefully evaluate and identify the projects that will derive the most business value from AI implementation. Rather than taking a scattershot approach, companies should thoughtfully prioritize and sequence the incorporation of AI into initiatives and processes that are both high-impact for achieving organizational goals and also highly feasible from a technological and resource perspective.

As an overarching best practice, developing a comprehensive yet flexible roadmap for rolling out AI aligns to the Architecture Development Method cycle within TOGAF. This allows for effectively planning the adoption timeline, mapping AI integration points to the key phases from preliminary vision through migration planning, allocating budgetary and talent resources, and plotting how both new AI capabilities and legacy systems will intersect. Having a phased roadmap also enables adjusting on the fly as market conditions and internal needs take shape.

For example, an e-commerce company may rank personalizing customer recommendations and predictive inventory management as top-tier AI opportunities that can elevate competitiveness, revenue growth, and operational excellence. After confirming technical requirements, data inputs, and availability of data science skills, these one or two high-potential AI use cases can become the focus of a 12–18 month execution roadmap. This roadmap would detail activities from conceptual architecture through implementation roll-out and measurement. Concurrently, other secondary AI opportunities can be nurtured for future roadmap inclusion while maintaining focus and resources on quick wins with broad organizational impact.

Step 7: Adapt the Migration Planning to Include AI

Integrating artificial intelligence capabilities into an organization's systems and processes often necessitates substantial modifications to existing technology infrastructure and workflows. Rather than treating AI implementation as an isolated IT project, companies should take a more holistic approach that maps out an enterprise-wide modernization journey to support ongoing innovation.

To start, IT departments may need to upgrade their data pipelines and analytics tool-sets to consolidate siloed information sources, provide data scientists with the inputs required to train machine learning algorithms, and generate detailed reports that track AI effectiveness over time. Legacy systems may not have the data storage capacity, processing bandwidth, or algorithmic functionality to power complex predictive models and optimization techniques. New cloud-based AI services often provide these features out-of-the-box but will require careful integration with on-premises databases and applications.

The procurement and deployment of AI technologies also introduces new steps into the development life cycle. IT project managers without ML expertise may struggle to evaluate vendor solutions or properly monitor prototype testing for model drift over time. They will need to oversee collaboration between engineering teams who develop algorithms and subject matter experts in the business units who define key performance indicators and guard against bias in training data. Rather than deploying static software updates, the organization must now also continually feed fresh data into ever-evolving analytical systems.

Above all, companies should avoid tech-first approaches to AI adoption or digital transformation more broadly. The most successful IT modernization strategies begin from an understanding of business goals and user needs. Technology serves as an enabler to enhance human capabilities and workflows. So AI integration should focus on augmenting individual workers with decision support tools and automating only repetitive low-value tasks. With the proper infrastructure upgrades, deployment tactics, and change management support, AI can take enterprise optimization and innovation to new heights. But integration plans must start from a human-centrist perspective first.

Step 8: Implement Governance and Manage Risks Involving AI

When integrating artificial intelligence capabilities into business operations, organizations must take a thoughtful approach to governance, risk management, and compliance. Rather than treating AI systems as autonomous entities, they should be viewed as integral components of a broader enterprise architecture. As such, existing governance frameworks, policies, and procedures should be extended to encompass AI development, deployment, and management.

Specifically, organizations can incorporate AI governance into their overall enterprise architecture governance structures. The goal should be to implement a consistent, company-wide methodology for managing AI systems just as one would manage any other enterprise capability. This starts by defining AI development life cycles that align with IT development and implementation standards. Model development, testing, production deployment, monitoring, and model refreshing should adhere to the same rigorous protocols as other enterprise software.

In addition, organizations must establish company-wide ethical guidelines for AI usage. Human review processes should be built-in to AI systems to safeguard against potentially unfair, biased and dangerous algorithmic decisions. And AI systems should be continuously monitored and audited for model drift or decay over time. Essentially, ethical AI governance means putting people at the center of technology deployment rather than simply letting algorithms and machines run free without oversight.

Additionally, organizations must understand regulatory compliance considerations around AI. As governments enact new data privacy, algorithmic accountability and AI ethics laws, companies must ensure they adapt their governance policies accordingly. This makes it essential to perform robust AI risk assessments and mitigation strategies as part of a comprehensive governance plan. Risks around data quality, model bias, platform robustness, explainability, and more, must be evaluated and managed to ensure both ethical and compliant AI systems.

The key is to stop thinking about AI as an independent, abstract capability. Rather, it must become intertwined with broader enterprise governance. By implementing AI development cycles, ethical guidelines, risk frameworks, and regulatory compliance into their existing architecture governance, organizations can more safely, responsibly and effectively leverage AI capabilities while managing risks.

Step 9: Execute the Architecture Change Management With AI Deployment in Mind

Managing organizational change brought on by artificial intelligence requires forethought and care to ensure a smooth workforce transformation. Rather than simply implementing AI systems and expecting employees to adjust, leaders should take proactive steps to equip staff across the company with the proper training, resources, and support they need to adapt to evolving roles and workflows.

By taking an empathetic approach and recognizing that AI integration will fundamentally change how many employees work, managers can mitigate issues that come with change management. For example, providing comprehensive training sessions will help staff better understand how their day-to-day responsibilities may shift alongside new AI technologies meant to enhance specific tasks and decisions. Hands-on learning experiences with the AI systems will make integration less abstract and more tangible.

Providing ongoing professional development opportunities as workflows continue to progress with AI will also be crucial to avoid skills gaps or confusion down the line. Designating expert peer mentors who can offer guidance as on-the-job questions arise will encourage regular feedback loops and bolster internal knowledge sharing. Managers should continuously assess training needs and offer new programs accordingly.

Leadership should also supply various learning resources like online courses, reference guides, and cheat sheets staff can leverage as daily reminders of the best ways to collaborate with AI. This supportive content will empower employees to support each other through the transformation journey. Facilitating internal discussion boards and community groups around the AI rollout can also help teams share best practices.

With strategic planning, resource allocation, and compassion for the very human impacts of technology change, leaders can enable employees to feel motivated and capable when adapting to new AI-driven processes. A culture focused on communication, knowledge development, and collective learning will pave the way for successful integration over time across the organization. The AI transformation will be as smooth and positive as management makes it for staff.

Step 10: Review and Update Architecture Requirements With AI Considerations

As companies increasingly adopt artificial intelligence technologies to enhance products, services, and decision-making, it becomes critical that they also implement robust architecture change management. Rather than taking a static approach, organizations need to view AI integration as an ongoing process that evolves in step with shifting business goals and emerging technological innovations.

By instituting clear governance and review cycles, companies can continually re-evaluate AI requirements against current business objectives and realign them accordingly. An initiative that showed great promise a year ago may now be less strategically relevant due to alterations in corporate strategy or competitive conditions. Architecture change management provides a structured methodology to ensure AI projects continue fueling data-driven decisions that help achieve corporate goals.

In addition to business objectives, architecture change management also allows companies to assess AI integration in light of the latest technology developments. The rapid pace of innovation in machine learning, predictive analytics, neural networks, and other AI-related fields means platforms and algorithms are constantly advancing. Through iterative evaluation, organizations can determine where enhanced or entirely new AI solutions may improve upon existing ones. They can then architect optimal integration of these AI capabilities to replace or work alongside previous implementations, allowing for improved functionality.

Fine-tuning architecture also involves ongoing performance optimization as data volumes, user loads, and algorithmic complexity scale upward. As with any enterprise-wide infrastructure, what works initially may begin showing performance lags or bottlenecks as demands increase. Proactive stress testing, capacity planning, and architecture re-configurations can help minimize disruptions. This allows companies to cost-effectively scale AI alongside business growth.

Effective architecture change management requires companies to treat AI integration as the continuously adaptive process that it is. By iteratively realigning objectives, embracing new technologies, and optimizing architecture, organizations can achieve maximum business value from AI investments over the long term. The process enables data-driven decisions to evolve in step with the company's needs.

These guidelines, when applied thoughtfully, will enable organizations to integrate AI into their TOGAF-guided Enterprise Architecture effectively, ensuring that AI capabilities are leveraged strategically to drive business value.

Necessary Resources and Skills

Integrating artificial intelligence capabilities into an organization's existing enterprise architecture requires careful planning and preparation to ensure access to the necessary resources and skills. Rather than simply listing requirements, I would like to provide some guidance by walking through this process in the context of TOGAF, the industry standard enterprise architecture framework.

First, it is important to fully understand the target state—what does the organization hope to achieve by deploying AI? The goals could include improved customer insight, increased efficiency in operations, higher product quality—any number of objectives. With the goals clarified, the next step is determining what AI tools and techniques can get you there. The power of AI comes from combining advanced algorithms with large, high quality datasets. Stocking relevant datasets and confirming data quality standards must be addressed early on.

Next is identifying resource requirements—this ranges from infrastructure like GPU computing capacity for running complex machine learning models to personnel with skills in areas like mathematics, statistics, software engineering and domain expertise related to the AI application. Many organizations discover they need to re-skill or hire for these capabilities. Developing partnerships with AI vendors and consultants can supplement internal skills. Education programs for employees focused on AI literacy and ethics also smooth adoption.

Finally, the inputs gathered—target state, technology approach, resource needs—shape the development of new enterprise architecture components like information management policies, security controls, technology standards and procurement processes that enable sharing, governance and scaling of AI solutions across the business. With the groundwork laid, integration of AI can be accelerated in a responsible way—transforming decision making, operations and products to create substantive business value.

Checklist for AI Integration in TOGAF

Integrating artificial intelligence capabilities into an organization's enterprise architecture can deliver tremendous value, but it requires careful planning and preparation. Rather than simply jumping into AI implementations, architects should take a methodical approach aligned with industry best practices for enterprise architecture, such as The Open Group Architecture Framework.

When envisioning how to seamlessly weave AI into business processes, data flows, and technology systems, architects would be wise to conduct an assessment using a comprehensive checklist that covers the essential areas to consider. This evaluation enables architects to map out an integration plan for AI that works in harmony with existing IT landscapes while meeting the current and future needs of the business.

First, the checklist should assess the readiness of the organization and its enterprise architecture. This involves examining the maturity of existing infrastructure and applications, availability and accessibility of quality data sources, cultural dynamics across leadership and employee levels, availability of internal AI skills and knowledge, and governance practices and change management processes. Understanding strengths and gaps informs the integration approach.

Another key area is conducting a detailed audit of business requirements and use cases. This means collaborating with business leaders and other stakeholders to identify and prioritize goals for applying AI. It is imperative to catalog where in processes and operations AI can add the most value, whether through automated insights, improved customer experiences, or increased efficiency. The use cases determine the AI methods and tools needed.

Equally important is performing a full evaluation of impacts and dependencies. Adding AI capabilities affects multiple components across an enterprise architecture, including processes, data stores, applications, infrastructure, and even staffing roles. Architects have to analyze the downstream effects on these areas to address integration complexities. And dependencies must be examined so AI integrations enhance rather than hinder other systems.

Adhering to a thoughtful checklist when planning for AI integration enables organizations to reap the full benefits of AI while minimizing disruption. It is an opportunity to optimize architectures for the future through a solutions-focused lens. With an enterprise architecture centered around enablement of emerging innovations like AI, substantial competitive advantages await.

Templates and Frameworks for AI Integration Planning

Integrating artificial intelligence capabilities into an organization's enterprise architecture can seem daunting without the right guidance and tools. Utilizing standardized templates and planning frameworks tailored for AI integration can help streamline this process and overcome adoption barriers companies often face.

Rather than tackling such a complex initiative in an ad hoc fashion, many leading organizations are now providing AI-focused iterations of existing enterprise architecture frameworks like TOGAF to give all stakeholders a common language and methodology. These updated frameworks offer templates, best practices, and step-by-step methodologies for each phase of planning, designing, and integrating AI across business, data, applications, and technology architecture domains.

For example, an AI-enhanced version of TOGAF would provide organizations with AI integration templates for documents such as vision statements, capability assessments, gap analyses, requirements catalogs and design principles. These templates have been pre-formatted to include important AI-specific considerations upfront, saving time and ensuring key factors are addressed from the start.

The framework would also provide dedicated guidance for architects on adapting essential TOGAF artifacts like the Architecture Development Method and Architecture Content Framework to cover common AI integration pain points across different architecture layers. This can accelerate foundational activities for organizations earlier in their AI journey.

Additionally, TOGAF-aligned AI planning frameworks cover detailed steps on evaluating, designing, prototyping and governing AI capabilities in alignment with business motivations and architectural best practices. This end-to-end guidance combined with adaptable templates gives architects an accelerated launchpad tailored to AI-driven digital transformation initiatives.

leveraging templates and prescriptive frameworks designed specifically to support integrating AI can provide organizations a structured methodology for planning, executing, and governing AI implementations holistically across people, process and technology. The increased ease of adoption also opens the door for companies struggling with ad hoc AI experimentation to scale in an architectural way.

Risk Assessment Models for Long-Term AI Strategies

When an organization is looking to incorporate AI capabilities into its long-term plans, it is crucial to thoroughly assess the potential risks that may emerge. Risk assessment models provide methodical and evidence-based approaches for identifying, evaluating, and addressing the unique risks introduced by long-span AI initiatives.

By leveraging risk modeling, organizations can quantify the probability and business impacts of various unfavorable scenarios, from mild impediments to operations to major technological failures or public backlash. Common risk factors for ambitious AI programs include data errors propagating through machine learning systems, algorithms behaving in unexpected ways over time, technical debt accumulating as systems scale, and reputational damages if AI recommendations are deemed unethical.

However, simply recognizing long-term AI risks is not sufficient. Organizations must also implement mitigation strategies and controls to properly account for these risks in planning stages, rather than reacting retroactively. Examples include improving explainability measures for AI systems, instituting stronger model governance practices, proactively auditing for biases and errors, creating contingency plans for AI failures, and fostering a risk-aware culture throughout the AI development lifecycle.

With prudent risk planning in place, organizations can then focus efforts on enabling sustainable AI integration over the long-term. This involves both technological and organizational best practices, like architecting flexible and modular AI infrastructures, maintaining strict version control as models iterate, building partnerships across functions to nurture AI literacy, and providing ongoing education for staff as AI capabilities progress.

The combination of risk modeling, mitigation strategies, and an emphasis on sustainable integration helps ensure that AI initiatives amplify business capabilities rather than introduce destabilizing factors over long time horizons. A pragmatic view of emerging risks alongside AI's opportunities allows organizations to plan ambitiously while also grounding innovations in strategic reality.

Chapter Fourteen

Future-Proofing Your Architecture—AI as a Long-Term Ally

D eveloping sustainable artificial intelligence strategies in enterprise architecture requires navigating a complex and rapidly evolving technological landscape. As enterprise architects, we must take a far-sighted yet pragmatic approach to integrating AI capabilities in a way that drives value over the long term while being flexible enough to adapt to future advancements.

Rather than pursue AI initiatives in an ad hoc manner, it is prudent to develop an overarching strategy that aligns to the overarching business strategy. This starts with identifying target use cases that address key enterprise priorities whether improved customer engagement, optimized operations or managed risk. The focus should be on rolling out AI solutions for targeted needs rather than generalized applications.

In order to future-proof these strategies, architects need to emphasize interoperability, scalability and transparency in underlying AI platforms and models. Choosing flexible, modular AI solutions over monolithic alternatives affords greater agility in upgrading, replacing or expanding capabilities. Establishing sound data management and governance practices also increases extensibility moving forward.

Additionally, maintaining technology monitoring processes and participation in expert communities enables architects to stay abreast of the latest innovations. While new does not always mean better, periodic reevaluation of existing strategies against the evolving state-of-the-art allows for keeping strategies aligned to best practices. This balanced, evidence-based approach prevents over-correction when new technologies emerge while still allowing for adoption when appropriate.

By instituting these pragmatic practices, enterprise architects can develop AI strategies that target current business priorities, optimally leverage AI capabilities over time, and adjust course appropriately when the underlying technological landscape shifts, in earnest. With the guidance of experts and continued learning systems, what can seem an overwhelming task given the dynamics of technological change, becomes within your grasp. With the right framework in place, architects can confidently navigate the complex route towards institutionalizing ethical and sustainable AI.

This chapter is designed to help you future proof your enterprise's architecture as an enterprise architect.

Developing Long-Term AI Strategies

When companies look to integrate artificial intelligence capabilities into their long-term plans, it presents both opportunities and challenges across the organization. Enterprise architects in particular have an important role to play in mapping out an AI strategy that allows for innovation but also keeps the company grounded in practical execution and measured risk-taking. Rather than pursuing AI advancements in isolation, they must be woven into the fabric of the enterprise architecture itself.

As AI strategies are formulated, maintaining balance is critical. The promise and hype surrounding AI calls for tempered enthusiasm; organizations must walk the line between being visionary and being realistic. Architects must foster experimentation and proof-of-concept testing for high-potential AI applications, but also be pragmatic when determining what solutions can work right now with existing infrastructure and data ecosystems.

The architects' role is to develop integrated roadmaps for AI that outlast ephemeral trends. That requires advising stakeholders on the responsible development of AI systems—implementing governance practices surrounding data privacy, algorithmic bias, and ethical considerations. Risk management ensures regulatory compliance, but also guards against data vulnerabilities and maintains public trust. AI is not a panacea, nor is it advisable to embed it into every process. Architects determine where it can augment human capabilities most effectively for the organization's specific needs.

With a balanced set of guiding principles rooted in pragmatism, governance and a vision for value-driven AI integration, enterprise architects can translate promising innovations into practical realities. They connect the dots between AI's emergence and its assimilation into the daily workings of the business. The end state is where the art of the possible for AI meets the reality of current-state systems and future-state potential in a long-term strategy. With architecture guiding its evolution, AI can become an integral element that drives sustainable competitive advantage.

Establishing a Foundation With Enterprise Architecture Principles

Developing long-term artificial intelligence strategies requires laying a strong foundation. Rather than jumping straight into AI initiatives, organizations should take the time upfront to ground their efforts within the context of enterprise architecture principles.

Enterprise architecture guidelines that companies have codified provide an invaluable and objective reference point for technology decision-making of all types. Some examples of common EA principles include maintaining adaptability to accommodate change, enabling scalability to support growth, and promoting alignment between technology solutions and business goals.

Using these EA principles as a North Star while formulating an AI strategy enables organizations to produce more future-proof plans. For instance, prioritizing adaptability guides technical teams to build flexibility into the AI systems they develop and purchase. This allows the AI to more gracefully handle new data sources, changes to models, and shifts in operational requirements down the road. Designing for scale from the outset lays the groundwork to efficiently expand AI usage across the enterprise as the benefits materialize. And the alignment principle ensures the objectives for AI tie directly back to overarching business priorities, targets, and needs.

Anchoring AI strategy development firmly within EA principles helps convert lofty AI ambitions into executable roadmaps. It also makes the solutions more sustainable. Applying design standards and best practices upfront increases the likelihood that AI deployments will deliver value long into the future, even as the technology and business environments inevitably evolve. Organizations that devise AI strategies rooted in their EA principles gain an advantage—they are strategically leveraging AI's capabilities today while methodically preparing for continued AI innovation tomorrow.

Conducting a Thorough Current State Assessment

When initially considering integrating artificial intelligence capabilities into an organization's technological architecture and operations, it is vitally important that leadership teams conduct a comprehensive assessment of the current state across all facets of the business. Rather than jumping straight into AI implementations, devoting the necessary time upfront to thoroughly analyze existing data, infrastructure, applications, workflows, and processes allows companies to determine current readiness levels and identify potential gaps that may need to be addressed in order to support ambitious AI innovation down the road.

I would advise constructing a cross-functional team combining business strategy leaders, technology experts, and key stakeholders from priority functional areas to carry out this architectural analysis. By collaborating together, they can map out an accurate baseline understanding of factors such as data maturity, infrastructure scalability, application interfaces and interoperability, process efficiency opportunities, regulatory requirements, and overall digital transformation readiness for machine learning and automation.

The next step would be performing an insightful gap analysis between the assessed current state and the desired or required conditions for launching enterprise-wide AI systems. This analysis should reveal crucial intelligence around data deficiencies, infrastructure limitations, application modernization needs, disconnected processes, lack of AI talent or understanding, and remaining digital transformation steps integral to optimizing results from machine learning tools over time. Identifying and agreeing on priority gaps allows organizations to then develop comprehensive roadmaps, allocate proper investments, and establish execution timelines to ready the technology stack and workplace for maximizing the promise of AI at scale.

Understanding the AI Landscape

When it comes to leveraging the power of artificial intelligence, it's essential that organizations have a detailed understanding of the innovations taking shape in the AI landscape. This empowers enterprises to strategically evolve their architectural capabilities in alignment with the latest advancements that offer transformational potential.

By continuously tracking emerging AI trends, companies can identify cutting-edge tools and techniques that can drive enhanced productivity, efficiency and decision making across critical business functions. This might encompass the emergence of revolutionary machine learning frameworks that enable predictive modeling at scale or breakthrough developments in natural language processing that vastly improve capabilities like contextual customer service.

Maintaining a pulse on these trends allows enterprises to envision where the AI field is headed and determine which capabilities show promise in generating greater value—whether it's empowering data scientists through automated machine learning, enabling knowledge discovery through AI search functions or driving optimization through self-adjusting algorithms. The enterprises who keep an eye on the horizon can readily assess where integrated AI can take their architectures in the years ahead.

In parallel, it is important for organizations to monitor best practices for effectively leveraging these innovations within large-scale environments. By understanding how leading institutions are using methodologies like human-in-the-loop oversight and AI ops to implement AI responsibly, enterprises can incorporate similar governance, monitoring and control mechanisms into their own operating models.

Taken together, comprehensive awareness of what is state-of-the-art along with real-world implementation guides and frameworks lays the foundation for enterprises to assimilate AI's rapid evolution into their architectures today and into the future. It empowers transformation that aligns with ethical imperatives while maximizing AI's potential.

Aligning AI Initiatives With Business Objectives

Developing an effective artificial intelligence strategy requires clear alignment to overarching business goals and measurable objectives. Rather than operating in a vacuum, the implementation of AI technologies should directly correlate to tangible improvements in operational and financial performance. This integrated approach enables organizations to articulate the purpose behind AI adoption in the context of business value—whether through increased revenue, greater efficiency, lower expenses, or improved customer experiences.

When building out an AI roadmap, leaders should continuously evaluate how specific use cases and proof-of-concepts in areas like machine learning or natural language processing might drive cost reduction by automating manual processes. They should examine how AI-fueled insights gleaned from data analytics could optimize supply chain management or inventory control workflows. Organizations should also explore new market opportunities made possible through AI-powered innovations in products, services, or business models.

By maintaining a tight linkage between AI technologies and business value, companies can pivot their strategy in alignment with shifting market dynamics or new opportunities on the horizon. This agility is enabled by a clear line of sight between AI investments and the specific business goals they are moving, whether today's cost-focused initiatives or tomorrow's revenue-driving capabilities. Rather than siloed projects, AI adoptions should be strategic imperatives integrated across all levels of the organization. The businesses that will lead the future are taking this integrated view today to ensure that every AI strategy directly supports overarching success.

Adopting a Modular and Agile Approach

Implementing artificial intelligence can seem daunting, but it doesn't have to be an all-or-nothing approach. The most effective strategies view AI as a flexible, adaptable toolkit that can be integrated over time to achieve business goals.

Rather than a single monolithic initiative, the ideal AI implementation roadmap comprises modular components that are thoughtfully phased in. This agile, iterative process allows pieces of the strategy to shift without undermining the overarching vision. For instance, a manufacturer may initially leverage AI for predictive maintenance of equipment, then expand capabilities to optimize supply chain logistics and production quality down the line.

The key advantage to modular integration is that it parallels how organizations naturally learn and refine complex processes. Starting with a few high-impact AI proofs of concept, early successes can demonstrate tangible value while building critical internal skills and enthusiasm for expanding. This sets the stage for methodically scaling while allowing strategy to fluidly evolve with emerging data and changes in the competitive landscape.

Approaching implementation in targeted stages also reduces disruption by giving operations and employees time to adapt to each wave of optimization. And if certain AI applications do not achieve hoped-for returns, they can be retooled or replaced without sinking the whole initiative. Above all, modular integration enables AI to permeate the organizational culture and decision-making DNA over time, becoming a driver of continuous improvement rather than just a one-off tool. The most transformative benefits happen when human and artificial intelligence seamlessly amplify each other.

Incorporating Ethical Considerations and Compliance

AI strategies should be developed carefully, keeping in mind the ethical implications of this powerful technology. As organizations determine how to best leverage AI to achieve business goals, they need to prioritize responsible and fair use.

Foremost, the collection and use of data that feeds AI systems should respect individual privacy. Policies must enable people to understand what data is being used and give meaningful consent. Furthermore, AI strategies should ensure unbiased outcomes. Teams should proactively assess and mitigate issues, like unfair bias or lack of transparency, that can arise in AI systems.

In regulated industries like finance and healthcare, strategies must align with relevant laws, regulations and industry standards from the outset. The same vigilance applies even for consumer-focused AI applications to prevent unfair or predatory practices.

Responsible AI practices also consider environmental sustainability. Things like energy efficiency, reuse of datasets, and overall model governance are important.

Crafting an ethical AI strategy protects both the business interests and public interests. It ensures AI positively impacts business results without infringing on stakeholder rights or important societal values. With conscientious planning, AI can be tremendously beneficial, and organizations have an obligation to deploy it in a way that earns public trust.

Risk Management Framework

A robust framework for managing risk is critical when deploying artificial intelligence capabilities across an organization. Rather than viewing risk management as an isolated compliance activity, organizations should embed it within AI adoption strategies to create an integrated, living program that provides ongoing vigilance.

This begins with identifying potential risks across the spectrum—not just technological, but also operational, reputational and ethical. Technological risks assessment involves an audit of the robustness, security and transparency of AI systems, ensuring accuracy and reliability as well as mitigating biases. Operational risk assessment encompasses evaluating dependencies on AI to avoid business disruption. Reputational risk management is also imperative as brand perception and customer trust could be impacted by AI systems. Finally, organizations must assess ethical risks around data usage, accessibility, transparency and accountability within AI tools.

Once risks have been identified, quantifying the likelihood and potential impact of each one is essential. This assessment informs appropriate mitigation strategies to put in place that align to risk severity and organizational priorities. This could involve setting governance policies, implementing technological controls like access management, creating redundancy in capabilities, monitoring systems, and establishing review processes for high-risk AI models.

By taking an expansive, forward-looking approach, risk management transforms from being a one-time project into an iterative capability that moves in lockstep with AI adoption. It becomes a key enabler in scaling AI confidently while upholding customer and stakeholder trust. With robust risk assessment and mitigation practices, organizations can tap into the promise of AI-driven transformation with greater confidence.

Iterative Testing and Learning

Implementing artificial intelligence capabilities within an organization should start small before being scaled up. The most effective approach is to deploy a series of proof of concepts and pilot projects that test out the feasibility of using AI for specific applications across different parts of the business. These controlled experiments expose the technology to real-world conditions on a limited basis to ascertain its viability while also allowing for adjustments and refinements as the teams learn what works well and what doesn't.

For example, AI could be piloted for a customer service chatbot on the company website or for an inventory management algorithm in a ware-house. In each case, the capabilities are restricted to very defined parameters and use cases. Performance is closely monitored to see if the AI delivers value without disrupting operations. Lessons from both successes and failures are captured to guide the evolution of the solutions.

By taking this iterative, focused approach to developing AI applications, enterprises can foster a culture of continuous improvement and innovation around their AI strategies. It allows them to build internal capabilities in the technology safely, enabling the organization to harness the full potential of AI across the architecture. And it prevents expensive, enterprise-wide implementations of AI that prove ineffective or counter-productive. Through a series of pilots, the most promising use cases rise to the surface which then warrant being scaled up.

This methodical, test-and-learn process is vital for unlocking transformative value from AI in a responsible, sustainable manner. It sets up the foundation for competitive differentiation over the long run. Rather than viewing AI as a one-time project, the organization can start embedding it into its fabric through targeted proof of concepts that eventually mature into core components of the business model.

Building AI Literacy Across the Enterprise

Developing an organizational culture that truly embraces artificial intelligence is an essential, yet often overlooked, aspect of effectively integrating AI solutions. More than just implementing AI tools, businesses need to nurture an understanding and appreciation for AI across all levels of the organization. This starts with fostering overall AI literacy through training and development initiatives aimed at creating a baseline comprehension of what AI is realistically capable of achieving versus where its limitations currently stand.

Equipping staff with this foundational knowledge helps diminish unfounded fears about AI taking away jobs which can impede adoption. Leadership should encourage ongoing transparent communication about each department's needs and challenges to identify high potential AI applications. When staff are actively included in brainstorming workshops to creatively explore how AI could augment and elevate their contributions, it drives engagement and inspiration along with a tangible understanding of AI's utilities.

Continuous learning opportunities through AI mentorship programs, new hire orientations and regular training updates can help sustain employee excitement and technological competencies. Focusing efforts on nurturing this supportive, innovative culture across the entire company is just as integral as the technology implementation itself when it comes to optimizing processes through artificial intelligence over the long-term. The businesses that will realize the full advantages of AI are those that openly embrace it holistically as a collaborative tool to enrich the human elements that have always been their core competitive advantage.

Sustainability and Evolution

When it comes to leveraging AI, organizations can't afford to become complacent or operate on autopilot after the initial implementation. The landscape of AI technological capabilities and business impacts evolves rapidly. What may have been an optimal strategic approach last year could quickly become outdated or inefficient if unexamined.

That's why preserving agility with regular check-ins is so vital. Companies should put time on the calendar—say every 12–18 months—to wholly review their current AI strategies against the present realities. New solutions and use cases are constantly emerging that could make AI applications even more intelligent and valuable to an organization if integrated. And competitive pressures or economic shifts may demand new AI-powered optimizations not previously considered.

Essentially the smartest leaders realize AI strategy transformation doesn't end at go-live. They plan to collaboratively re-explore where present innovations could drive an even stronger competitive edge or cost efficiency. And how the existing AI approach syncs with changes in corporate vision or industry disruption. Companies who continually refine and tune their AI roadmaps based on these recurring check-ins will sustain more dynamic, responsive, and ultimately fruitful AI pursuits over the long haul. They see AI oversight as an ongoing journey rather than a one-and-done project.

Staying Ahead in the Evolving AI Landscape

As AI capabilities continue to rapidly advance, it poses an exciting yet complex challenge for organizations seeking to harness these innovations. In order to fully capitalize on the promise of AI, companies must establish a strong foundation in their enterprise architecture to properly integrate these emerging technologies and methodologies. This requires enterprise architects to take a strategic and adaptable approach based on continuous learning and evolution.

Ongoing education is the fuel that powers one's ability to keep pace with AI developments. Enterprise architects should actively participate in formal coursework, workshops, and seminars focused on the latest trends, tools, and best practices in AI. Reading academic and industry research publications also provides invaluable insights into pioneering AI technologies still in development. Since AI intersects many disciplines, expanding one's knowledge into areas like data science, machine learning techniques, and ethical AI can further enrich perspective and strengthen cross-domain abilities.

Armed with cutting-edge learning, enterprise architects can then incorporate AI advancements into their organization's frameworks and processes. This may involve revising existing standards to accommodate unique aspects of AI systems and data. Pilot projects enable hands-on experimentation with AI capabilities in a controlled setting without disrupting enterprise-wide operations. These small-scale initiatives help enterprise architects understand the broader implications introducing AI may have on an organization's culture, workflows, and technologies. With AI being an emerging field, uncertainties and risks still exist. Applying robust risk management strategies allows potential disruptions to be identified and mitigation steps outlined proactively.

Given the fluid evolution occurring in the AI sphere, an agile approach to enterprise architecture design is recommended. Modular components and flexible integration mechanisms empower rapid adoption of new AI technologies without requiring extensive re-engineering efforts. Compliance with ethical AI best practices and regulations is also integral throughout the development lifecycle to instill responsible AI behaviors company-wide. Finally, forging partnerships with AI leaders, tech innovators, and industry groups provides access to leading-edge insights and tools to inform architectural enhancements.

By championing a culture of learning and adaptation, enterprise architects enable organizations to embed AI capabilities deeply within their business DNA—creating intelligent, responsive, and resilient company architectures built to thrive today and into the future. This sustained commitment to understanding and integrating advancements positions organizations at the forefront of the rapidly changing AI landscape.

Expert Predictions on Long-Term AI Trends

Artificial intelligence is expected to become deeply integrated into enterprise architectures going forward. It will serve as an integral technology for optimizing processes, enhancing decision-making, and driving innovation across organizations.

One major area experts predict AI will impact is enabling augmented analytics. With techniques like machine learning and natural language processing, AI can help prepare data, generate insights, and explain these insights to users. As enterprise architecture deals with complex systems, AI will likely become vital for unraveling these complexities and advising strategic decisions to improve efficiencies.

Additionally, experts forecast the advent of autonomous systems powered by AI in enterprise IT infrastructure and operations. These systems can self-manage, self-heal, and self-optimize without human intervention, in real-time. This marks a notable shift, as traditional monitoring and maintenance rhythms transition into more autonomous frameworks.

Governance and ethical considerations around AI are also expected to come to the forefront. As adoption accelerates, the need for transparency, fairness, and accountability will heighten. Enterprise architects will likely lead the formulation and implementation of robust governance policies and ethical AI practices.

Furthermore, AI is predicted to enhance enterprise security in a major way. With capabilities to rapidly analyze vast data and discern patterns, AI shows promise in bolstering threat detection and response capabilities. Enterprise architects will be tasked with seamlessly baking these AI-powered mechanisms into the broader security infrastructure.

Edge computing, entailing distributed data processing near the source, is another area primed for an AI boost. Architects are seen incorporating

AI algorithms at the edge to allow real-time analytics and foster innovation across the enterprise network periphery.

Finally, AI collaboration platforms are envisioned to drive organizational synergy. By providing insights and automating tasks, these platforms can monumentally improve collaboration, creativity, and productivity. Enterprise architects will play an instrumental role in integrating these systems into the organizational tapestry.

The overarching notion is that AI will catalyze foundational shifts across industries. While transforming operational constructs, it will also spawn new innovations and efficiencies. However, ethical implications must remain top-of-mind, and integration must be conducted strategically. The enterprise architect's role will morph from system planner to AI orchestrator.

Scenario Planning

Scenario planning aims to help organizations actively adapt and steer themselves through complex, uncertain environments instead of passively letting the future happen to them. This structured strategic planning technique allows companies to envision several alternate but plausible future scenarios related to artificial intelligence advances and then form flexible long-term plans to effectively prepare for multiple possibilities.

Rather than making decisions based on projections or forecasts, scenario planning encourages organizations to think more broadly about emerging AI developments and trajectory, opening their minds to divergent ways the future may unfold. Companies invent and then consider multiple scenarios that could plausibly occur including best case, worst case, and other realistic outcomes for AI. By deeply analyzing various plausible scenarios and implications, organizations become more agile and strategically equipped to handle uncertainty and sudden shifts in the AI landscape.

The multi-scenario planning process for emerging AI also drives productive discussions about monitoring key indicators in areas like government policies, social attitudes, technological innovations and adoption rates that may substantially influence the AI environment. This helps management spot early signals related to impactful AI changes and challenges as well as new opportunities. Thoughtful scenario planning around AI ultimately allows companies to uncover key vulnerabilities, future-proof strategies, and uncover hidden growth prospects that traditional predictive planning methods may overlook. This leads to more robust policies, investment decisions, and responsive business strategies that perform well even if the future AI scenario is unexpected.

The scenario planning methodology requires visionary thinking about AI's evolution. But it yields resilient strategies and policies that can bend but not break when the actual future deviates from the expected. That nimbleness to adapt to a range of potential AI outcomes makes scenario planning an extremely valuable tool for organizations operating in very fluid, rapidly advancing technology environments.

Example: Healthcare Provider Leveraging AI for Diagnosis

Artificial intelligence is believed to transform medical diagnostics over the coming decade thanks to rapid advancements in machine learning. However, healthcare organizations must thoughtfully explore how to integrate this emerging technology into their workflows and processes.

As a first step, this healthcare provider would clearly define their objectives—namely enhanced diagnostic accuracy and efficiency. Understanding the potential value AI could bring to diagnosis is essential. The provider must also begin preparing their staff, data infrastructure, and electronic systems for seamless AI integration in the future.

A critical next step involves identifying current uncertainties that may impact an AI diagnostics rollout. Will machine learning algorithms progress to reliably detect complex conditions? How will patient privacy and data security be maintained? Can AI systems interoperate with the provider's electronic health record platform? By outlining these uncertainties, the provider can envision multiple potential scenarios.

In one scenario, AI diagnostics become extremely accurate and widely adopted across healthcare. Here the provider would invest heavily in best-in-class AI and partner with tech innovators. In another, patient concerns about data misuse slow AI diagnostic adoption, pushing the provider to instead focus on data governance while judiciously applying AI. A third scenario may find AI diagnostically solid but incompatible with existing tools. The provider would then devote resources to developing compatible systems and encourage industry-wide participation.

By analyzing the implications of each scenario and formulating adaptable strategies to succeed within their constraints, this healthcare provider can strategically activate the most fitting plan when the uncertainties of the future begin to resolve. Staying alert to emerging trends in the space will signal which strategy to initiate. This proactive scenario planning approach allows the organization to access the benefits of AI diagnostics while building resilience to unpredictable changes ahead.

Risk Assessment Models for Long-Term AI Strategies

When integrating AI capabilities into business operations, organizations must thoroughly evaluate the associated risks, not just to technological performance but even more critically to overall business continuity, regulatory compliance, ethical boundaries, and social impacts. The foremost priority is safeguarding the interests of both the business and its customers in an AI-enabled landscape.

A thoughtful approach to AI risk assessment will methodically progress through several key stages. First, all pertinent risks require careful identification—spanning inherent AI risks around opaque machine learning algorithms, data privacy, algorithmic biases as well as risks related to integrating AI within existing systems and processes. Next, an analysis phase evaluates each identified risk for its probability of occurrence and potential impact, utilizing quantitative techniques like Fault Tree Analysis or qualitative approaches such as Preliminary Hazard Analysis to gauge severity. These analyzed risks then undergo evaluation and prioritization based on the risk matrix methodology that plots probability versus consequence to distinguish critical risks demanding priority mitigation.

For high-priority AI risks, developing mitigation strategies is essential—putting in place redundant systems to contain technical failures, robust data governance frameworks to prevent privacy violations and embedding AI ethics across development and usage. With risks and mitigations in place, the process still requires ongoing monitoring and reviews to account for an evolving technology landscape.

Enabling this adaptive and resilient approach requires building enterprise architecture with modularity, interoperability, and governance as central tenets while also emphasizing workforce skills development. Additional techniques like AI explainability tools, CI/CD pipelines tailored for AI, and proactive cybersecurity measures specialized for AI threats, foster resilience. Most crucially, aligning AI pursuits to business goals, continuous model training and maintaining stakeholder dialogue sustains AI's strategic value. In essence, methodical assessment and mitigation of risks combined with enterprise-wide vigilance not only minimizes pitfalls but also amplifies AI's substantial benefits.

Chapter Fifteen

AI Literacy for Leaders—Guiding the CIO and Tech Teams

B uilding artificial intelligence literacy among an organization's technology leaders is critical for driving informed adoption and effective implementation of AI capabilities. Rather than siloed expertise, Chief Information Officer, (CIOs), must spearhead an integrated understanding across their teams. This distributes knowledge and skills at all levels, creating a culture adept at deploying AI tools for maximum business impact.

The fluid nature of AI development necessitates continuous learning. Tech leaders well-versed in AI's evolution are better positioned to envision applications that transform processes and user experiences. When leadership models openness to emerging technologies, they motivate teams to actively enhance their literacy through shared learning.

Curious and informed CIOs ask forward-thinking questions around use cases and their ethical implications. They understand AI success depends on people and processes, not just machines. These leaders recognize AI's limitations along with its potential. With patient persistence and realistic expectations, they pilot AI judiciously, scaling value and insights over time.

Enterprises leading the AI revolution provide ample resources for developing talent. Sponsoring external training, conferences, and workshops allows teams to absorb the latest AI thinking. Internal mentorship, lunch-and-learn sessions, and hack-a-thons encourage curiosity and skills application. Rotational assignments distribute expertise across departments, mitigating concentrated dependencies.

With deliberate learning strategies woven into operations, CIOs transform their IT groups into adaptable, AI-ready organizations. More than acquiring cutting-edge tools, they build institutional knowledge to propel AI innovation and adoption for the long term. Their emphasis on people-focused literacy fosters a motivated culture that thinks critically about AI each step of the integration journey.

This chapter focuses on helping enterprise architects become tech leaders that their organization needs and deserves.

Building AI Literacy in Leadership

As artificial intelligence progressively makes its way into organizations across all industries, it is crucially important that technology executives build a strong understanding on both the possibilities and limitations of AI. Without proper comprehension of what today's AI technologies can and cannot achieve, technology leaders run the risk of either overestimating the current state of the art, leading to poor planning, or underestimating what is possible, opening the door to competitors racing ahead.

Gaining AI literacy gives CIOs and IT directors a grounded framework for developing digital strategies that play to the strengths of AI while recognizing its constraints. Rather than reacting to vendor hype cycles, an AI literate leadership team can set pragmatic roadmaps for piloting and adopting AI that matches organizational readiness.

Leading technology practitioners emphasize that AI literacy is not about becoming a data scientist or coder. Rather, it simply involves cultivating a strong grasp on how various common applications of AI like machine learning, natural language processing and robotic process automation can be leveraged to tackle business challenges. An AI fluent CIO knows intelligent automation holds tremendous potential but needs careful scoping and governance.

Just as importantly, embracing AI through an ethical lens enables technology heads to implement AI solutions responsibly. Monitoring factors like data bias, transparency and accountability allows executives to build trust in AI among customers and employees. Prioritizing ethics pays dividends through enhanced brand reputation.

Taking the time to nurture in-house AI expertise gives CIOs the confidence and credibility to serve as strategic advisors on AI adoption. Leading by example in developing one's personal AI IQ establishes the knowledge base to guide management conversations and decision making at the executive table. A little bit of learning goes a long way to set up IT leaders and their teams to drive AI advancement the right way.

Approaches for Enhancing AI Understanding and Competency

While improvising on AI literacy, taking a multi-pronged approach helps integrate AI understanding at different operational and strategic levels.

Structured Education Programs

Implementing artificial intelligence capabilities requires more than just the technology itself. To truly unlock the potential of AI, organizations need to foster understanding and build critical skills across all levels. Rather than treating this as an afterthought, strategic leaders would benefit from weaving training and educational programs into their AI implementation plans right from the start.

By developing customized masterclasses, workshops and collaborations tailored specifically to one's unique business needs, companies can accelerate competency development in a way that off-the-shelf programs may not offer. For example, an automotive manufacturer could partner with academic institutions to create an "AI in Engineering" curriculum for its design and production teams. An AI Lab could be embedded within headquarters where employees rotate through intensive technical cohorts focused on practical applications. Leadership can enroll in executive sessions that demystify what AI is and how it drives value while honing their ability to ask the right questions.

The scope and variety of offerings are endless, bound only by the organization's imagination. The key is crafting programs holistically designed around current skill levels and desired competencies while aligning to overarching AI strategies. This level of customization requires effort but pays dividends through a more prepared and AI-fluent workforce. With the right knowledge foundation infused across the business, employees can then actively support and enhance AI solutions rather than passively consume them. This allows companies to maximize returns on their investments both in the underlying technologies and the people who interact with them. In-house training and academic collaborations are critical tools to build this foundation for long-term advantage.

Cross-Disciplinary Learning

When it comes to embracing artificial intelligence, leaders have a responsibility that extends far beyond just adopting the latest technology. There is a critical need for managers and executives to have a deeper appreciation for the broader implications of these advanced systems if they are to be successfully integrated in a manner that provides maximum benefit for organizations and society.

Rather than remain isolated in their particular domains, leaders should be actively encouraged to engage with experts across different disciplines that touch AI. For example, having an open dialogue with data scientists would allow leaders to grasp the realities, tradeoffs and risks around aspects like model accuracy, transparency and bias. Reaching out to those specialized in cognitive psychology could provide valuable perspective on how AI systems process information and interact with human judgment differently. Discussions with ethicists could uncover potential pitfalls surrounding the morality of AI and machine learning algorithms.

The insights gleaned from exploring these diverse fields could profoundly shape the way an organization applies AI. Leaders may adopt new protocols around auditing algorithms to check for unfair bias. Policies could mandate certain levels of transparency or human oversight to ensure proper accountability. Training programs may be enhanced to prepare workers to comfortably use—and even challenge—AI where needed. Fundamentally, the organization's AI strategies would improve, with leaders benefiting from a knowledge base far more interdisciplinary in scope.

The technologies may be cutting edge, but avoiding insular thinking is key. Leaders need to recognize the core strengths of AI while balancing them with a realistic view of current limitations. Encouraging engagement with different disciplines helps provide the broad perspective required to maximize the strategic upside of AI while developing the safeguards and policies appropriate for an emerging technology that touches so many aspects of business and society.

Partnerships and Collaborations

Staying competitive in the age of artificial intelligence requires more than just implementing AI solutions. It demands that organizations proactively foster relationships with those on the cutting edge of AI innovation—the pioneers pushing the boundaries of what's possible. By collaborating with AI experts, startups, and think tanks, forward-thinking companies can ensure they have a finger on the pulse of emerging developments in AI and machine learning.

Building connections with AI thought leaders, influential researchers, and acclaimed scientists allows an organization to stay in tune with breakthroughs in neural networks, advanced prediction systems, natural language processing, and beyond. Ongoing dialogue and idea sharing with these experts ensures leaders can incorporate the latest AI capabilities into their products, services, and decisions quicker. Sponsoring or participating in technology conferences and seminars to interface with these experts expands exposure to pioneering AI use cases.

Developing relationships with AI-focused startups through partnerships, investments, and acquisitions plugs an organization directly into the energy and ingenuity of these agile innovators. Tapping into their creativity and venture capital-powered rapid experimentation in AI applications keeps established companies aware of new technologies redefining what's achievable. Ongoing collaboration allows larger organizations to deliver fresh AI solutions ahead of rivals.

Finally, partnering with AI-centered think tanks, research institutes, and innovation labs ensures companies can evaluate the latest concepts in ethical AI development, protocols for human-AI collaboration, future policy making around AI, and cutting-edge ideas still in incubation. Maintaining ties to these knowledge hubs provides invaluable context and perspective to inform an organization's AI pursuits in alignment with thought leadership steering the field.

By making AI experts, startups, and think tanks allies instead of competitors, organizations can ride the wave of progress in artificial intelligence instead of being swept away by it. Aligning with these centers of excellence secures a competitive edge.

Knowledge Sharing Platforms

Building widespread AI fluency across an organization requires moving beyond traditional top-down knowledge dissemination. While executive leaders and data scientists may possess valuable AI expertise, restricting the flow of understanding around artificial intelligence to certain levels of leadership can severely limit how broadly AI gets embedded into company culture and day-to-day operations.

Some forward-thinking companies are pioneering clever new approaches centered on cultivating shared learning around AI innovations. One method gaining traction involves fostering internal communities of practice that provide forums for peer-based AI skill-building and knowledge exchange. These communities deliberately bring together cross-functional teams ranging from front-line staff to managers to IT specialists, offering a space to participate in activities like analyzing AI case studies, discussing AI ethics considerations, and exploring practical applications of AI relevant to members' respective roles. They essentially help democratize foundational AI fluency.

Other organizations are leveraging user-friendly digital collaboration platforms with built-in AI features to encourage company-wide learning. By making instructional AI content, training modules, and digital twin models easily accessible on a common hub, employees across leadership levels can voluntarily develop AI acumen. And digital tools provide data and feedback loops on member participation, allowing companies to track AI knowledge growth across the enterprise.

The goal with both approaches is to step away from limited, top-down AI enabling, and instead tap into models centered on collective learning and dialogue. This not only accelerates AI understanding but also uncovers more diverse applications of AI innovations coming directly from operating teams rather than prescribed solely by executive mandates. The outcomes can include faster assimilation of AI technologies and more creative, role-based implementations scalable across the organization.

Resources for Enhancing AI Understanding and Competency

Gaining a working knowledge of AI is crucial these days across industries. With AI technology advancing so rapidly, we all need to keep pace! I find that staying on top of the latest developments and having meaningful exposure to real-world applications puts the concepts into perspective.

There are some great online courses available now for building baseline AI literacy. I recently came across an introduction to AI course that provides very accessible explanations of key terms and applications. Completing a course like this can give you a fundamental vocabulary and framework for thinking about AI.

Another approach that I think helps consolidate learning is to participate in workshops or seminars that showcase AI innovations in your company or industry. Seeing AI systems in action and being able to ask questions really brings the technology to life! Meetups and conferences centered around AI trends can also let you probe experts directly on the intricacies of machine learning or natural language processing.

And we can't forget about all of the expert perspectives shared online through podcast episodes, blog articles, whitepapers and more. Following some top thinkers in the AI space by subscribing to their content can expose you to the latest breakthroughs and ethical considerations in a very timely manner.

Finally, don't underestimate the value of experimenting with AI first-hand with tools meant for non-experts! Whether using pre-trained machine learning models or testing chatbot solutions, hands-on exploration lets you grasp AI functionality quickly.

Educating and Empowering Teams With AI Knowledge

A key priority for any organization adopting AI solutions should be ensuring their technical teams fully understand this emerging technology and have the skills to effectively leverage it. Rather than just throwing information at them, we need a thoughtful approach to actively empower these teams and create an innovative environment conducive to AI integration.

A good first step is to map out an AI learning roadmap aligned with the organization's broader objectives. This creates a structured pathway for team members to follow as they build their AI competencies. It allows individuals to digest complex concepts in stages, with milestones tailored to each job role. This personalization keeps people motivated and engaged, rather than overwhelmed.

Collaborative digital platforms are invaluable here too. They remove silos and enable knowledge sharing between team members at all levels. E-learning resources, discussion forums, even informal AI tutorials facilitated by colleagues—this peer-to-peer approach means learning is iterative, hands-on and collaborative. It mirrors the agile techniques we use in software development.

That hands-on ethos is so important when mastering applied technologies like AI. We can complement online learning by running in-person workshops where teams tackle real-world problems with AI. Internal experts could facilitate, or we can bring in external specialists to advise. This experiential approach allows members to witness the tangible impact AI can have. It motivates them to continuously expand their skills.

Finally, nothing beats learning through doing. By encouraging cross-functional project teams to incorporate AI components into their work, we fast-track up-skilling. Team members experience first-hand how AI can enhance process automation and innovation. It stimulates creative thinking, as people feel empowered to experiment with new technologies.

Creating a Culture of Continuous Learning and AI Readiness

Incorporating artificial intelligence literacy as a fundamental corporate value reflects an organization's commitment to continuous learning and development. Leaders should set the tone by actively engaging in AI education themselves, modeling an attitude of openness and curiosity. By establishing internal AI competency centers—essentially hubs of expertise that can provide guidance on best practices—companies can enable employees to easily access knowledge resources and obtain clarity on AI-related queries.

Furthermore, implementing systems that formally recognize and reward achievements in advancing AI skills fosters an environment where employees are motivated to push the boundaries of their aptitude. Growth opportunities, certification badges, and awards for milestones demonstrate that professional progress is both valued and supported. Most importantly, organizations need to promote a culture that tolerates failure as a natural part of innovation.

Experimentation with emerging technologies stimulates vital learning—from both successes and mistakes. Employees should feel empowered to test thoughtful risks with AI tools without fear of repercussions. For human-AI collaboration to truly thrive, the human element must have space to harness their creative potential through a flexible framework marked by psychological safety. By taking these comprehensive steps, companies can cultivate team-wide AI fluency that becomes a differentiating organizational advantage. With continuous education balanced by practical application, they will gain the insight and confidence to navigate both existing and unforeseen AI-driven shifts in the market landscape.

Workshops and Training Modules for AI Literacy

When looking to develop workshops and training modules to improve understanding and effective utilization of artificial intelligence across an organization, it is critical to recognize the foundational importance these educational tools play in cultivating comprehensive AI literacy amongst all personnel. Thoughtful design and strategic implementation of such AI literacy programs serves as a necessary starting point to equip employees with the knowledge base required to appropriately leverage AI technology within their respective professional capacities.

In conceptualizing robust and multidimensional AI literacy curricula, one must consider a diverse array of topics spanning theoretical foundations, practical applications, and critical thinking skills development. Training modules should offer dynamic, tailored content that speaks to varying mastery levels, ensuring accessibility and progressive learning for all attendees regardless of previous subject familiarity. An effective program might explore fundamental AI concepts like machine learning, natural language processing, and neural networks to establish baseline understanding. Hands-on skill-building workshops could then provide direct experience applying AI tools already integrated across the company's operations. Training should also cultivate analytical aptitudes and ethical discernment, guiding participants through case study examinations, risk/benefit analyses, and assessments of how emergent AI could impact regulation, labor economies, and society overall. Discussing both existing and prospective applications would empower personnel to anticipate and adapt to AI's rapidly advancing capabilities and integration.

By blending exposure to core ideas, technical proficiency, critical awareness and future-focused insight within iterative AI literacy workshops, companies can empower employees to safely, responsibly and optimally leverage AI technology to drive innovation and growth across the organization. The knowledge cultivated in these sessions serves as a vital foundation for AI adoption and strategy within the enterprise.

Real-World Example

The marketing leadership team at the retail company decided to pilot an AI-powered customer segmentation and targeting tool to see if it could provide novel insights compared to their traditional data analytics methods. Recognizing both the promise and concerns this emerging technology presented, the Chief Marketing Officer, (CMO), helped frame the implementation as an experiment that could reveal supplemental intelligence to empower her team, not replace them.

She encouraged her marketing analysts and campaign strategists to thoroughly examine the customer and prospect profiles the AI tool produced, looking for unexpected trends or commonalities among groups that could inform smarter messaging. By positioning the AI as an exploratory instrument for uncovering fresh knowledge, the CMO fostered genuine excitement and buy-in across her teams instead of apprehension.

Throughout the examination of AI-generated segments, the CMO counseled her teams to maintain a balanced perspective. While urging them to have openness to new discoveries from the machine learning application, she also reminded analysts to verify insights with sound statistical testing before acting. This guidance enabled marketing employees to gain confidence in progressively applying AI-based insights while still upholding responsibility for final decisions rather than blindly following its predictions.

The CMO's supportive and participating leadership style cultivated enthusiasm to expand AI usage while preventing over-trust in its outputs. Her governance and involvement throughout the rollout instilled comfort with responsibly leveraging AI to enhance data-based understanding of customer motivations and behaviors within strategic campaign development. This manifested in improved segmentation quality, higher campaign performance, and growing adoption of AI tools across the marketing organization.

Chapter Sixteen

The AI Toolkit—Essential Technologies and Skills

E nterprise architects play a critical role in guiding organizations to effectively leverage artificial intelligence technologies to achieve business goals. As AI continues its relentless integration into operations, products, and services, the architect perspective remains vital to align AI implementations to overarching infrastructure, development, data, and functionality strategies.

Rather than take a reactive stance, architects must proactively assess, evaluate, and integrate a robust set of core AI technologies to future-proof and optimize organizational success. Architects should maintain competence in machine learning, natural language processing, computer vision, speech recognition, and conversational AI to understand capabilities, use cases, and implementation methods. Fluency in Python, TensorFlow, automation, and data engineering empowers architects to directly apply AI technologies versus solely theoretical knowledge.

Emerging technologies like generative AI prompt architects to continually expand skills as well. Evaluating ethical risks, implementing responsible AI practices, and directing complex AI projects further establish architects as invaluable leaders in AI adoption. With technological disruption accelerating, architects must embrace AI's transformational potential, guiding decisions through a balanced lens of pragmatism and creativity.

The architect's perspective remains unrivaled in realizing AI's full value. Maintaining technological competence, evaluating leading-edge and emerging capabilities, and aligning implementations to overarching infrastructure and data strategies allows architects to help shape an organization's AI future amidst relentless change. With AI permeating business functions, architect readiness safeguards optimized, ethical, and sustainable AI adoption.

This chapter introduces to enterprise architects about some of the next generation technologies that can help you operate your organization effectively.

Must-Have AI Technologies for Architects

Artificial intelligence has become deeply integrated into the technology infrastructure of many organizations. Rather than just hype, AI has proven itself to be a cornerstone capability for enhancing overall enterprise architecture—the blueprint for complex modern IT environments. Practical applications of AI are driving very real improvements in system efficiency, automation of repetitive tasks, and data-driven decision support.

Behind the scenes, AI technologies like machine learning, natural language processing, and robotics process automation are being embedded into both customer-facing applications and back-end business operations. And AI adoption continues to accelerate rapidly. Organizations are applying AI to guide everything from predictive inventory planning, to dynamic pricing models, to customized marketing campaigns, to self-running network security.

And AI's benefits compound quickly, allowing people to focus their talents on more impactful work. Repetitive manual processes that once bogged down human workers are now automated. Massive amounts of data that was previously hard to analyze is now used to spot trends and make recommendations. AI has become the connective tissue that weaves through and enhances all aspects of enterprise technology environments.

Rather than replacing humans, AI actually empowers organizations to re-focus their human talent on creative, strategic tasks only people can handle. This realignment and partnership between AI and humans underpins modern, innovative enterprise architectures built for speed and agility. In today's hyper-competitive economy, having enterprise architecture accelerated by artificial intelligence has become an indispensable advantage. Those applying AI's full potential are outpacing rivals, achieving cost and time savings, making better decisions, and delivering superior customer experiences.

Here are several AI technologies and their respective use cases in the context of enterprise architecture.

Machine Learning (ML)

Machine learning represents an exciting branch of artificial intelligence that is driving significant value and transformational change across industries. At its core, machine learning refers to the ability of computer systems to learn patterns from data and improve their performance over time, without the need for explicit additional programming.

One of the most common applications of machine learning is in predictive analytics. Here, machine learning algorithms are leveraged to analyze current and historical data to detect patterns and relationships. These models are then utilized to forecast future trends and scenarios that are likely to materialize. The insights gained from predictive analytics empower companies across sectors to make more intelligent and informed strategic decisions. Everything from anticipating future sales trends, to projecting machine down times, to modeling customer churn can be enabled through predictive machine learning capabilities.

Another high-impact application of machine learning is anomaly detection. This refers to identifying abnormalities or outliers in data that deviate from historically observed patterns. By analyzing data such as network traffic, financial transactions, health records, etc., machine learning algorithms can swiftly detect anomalies and elevated risk factors. This can allow organizations to respond to issues like fraud, network intrusions, mechanical failures and medical concerns before they escalate into larger problems. The ability to separate background noise from truly anomalous events that warrant intervention is an extremely valuable application of machine learning technology for security, performance and risk management.

These are just two examples demonstrating the versatility and business value that machine learning innovation offers. Whether it be enhancing decision support, optimizing processes or identifying risks, machine learning is driving transformation across functions. As an agile subset of artificial intelligence, machine learning will continue pioneering new opportunities and applications that will define the next era of technological advancement.

Natural Language Processing

Natural language processing is focused on enabling computers to work with and make sense of human languages. Rather than relying on more rigid coding languages and commands, NLP applies algorithms and machine learning to large volumes of natural language data to perform tasks like translation, sentiment analysis, and speech recognition.

One of the most common applications is creating chatbots that can handle customer service inquiries. By programming these bots to understand common customer questions and complaints, they can provide the initial layer of response. This allows the chatbots to resolve many routine issues, freeing up human customer service agents to focus on addressing more complex and high-priority cases. Over time, as the chatbots collect more conversational data, they become even more adept at independently handling everyday customer interactions.

Another valuable use case for NLP is enhancing enterprise search capabilities. Traditional keyword matching in enterprise data and content management systems often yields frustrating, irrelevant results. By integrating NLP, these systems can go beyond matching keywords to understand the contextual meaning and intent behind queries and content. This allows them to provide employees with search results that are significantly more intuitive, accurate, and tailored to the specifics of their information needs. As a result, employees can find relevant content and answers in a fraction of the time, supporting increased workplace productivity.

The previous two examples demonstrate the diverse value NLP can provide. Whether it's interpreting complex analytical questions to extract key insights from data or helping standardize and structure documents by extracting key fields, NLP opens up many possibilities. And with continual advances in machine learning and the availability of conversational data, the capabilities of NLP will only grow over time.

Neural Networks

Artificial neural networks are an area of artificial intelligence that has seen rapid advancements in recent years. These computing systems are inspired by, but simplify, the network of real biological neurons and synapses that make up animal brains. At their core, they are formed from a large set of interconnected elements, called artificial neurons, that receive inputs, process them, and output a result.

One of the most promising application areas taking advantage of these neural networks is pattern recognition capabilities that rival even human abilities. For example, advanced image and speech recognition neural networks can analyze visual or auditory data, identify patterns imperceptible to humans, and determine the contents with high accuracy. These intelligent recognition capabilities have opened up neural networks to several impactful use cases.

For image recognition specifically, neural networks can enable biometric security measures to control access to facilities, devices, or systems by identifying authorized individuals through scans of attributes like fingerprints or facial features. They also empower self-driving vehicles to interpret visual data to safely navigate roads. In terms of speech recognition, virtual assistants like Alexa, Siri, and Google Assistant rely on neural networks to understand spoken commands and respond conversationally.

Neural networks are also proving adept at predictive analytics applications, such as anticipating equipment failures through predictive maintenance. By continuously monitoring data from sensors on industrial equipment in real-time, even slight performance deviations or subtle early warning signs of issues can be detected. The neural network models then forecast deteriorating conditions so proactive repairs can be made, minimizing downtime. This application area is estimated to create billions in cost savings across manufacturing, oil and gas, aerospace, utilities and transportation sectors.

As computing capabilities continue to expand, the possibilities for innovating with artificial neural networks will only increase across even more impactful and transformative use cases. Their advanced pattern recognition abilities, fueled by ongoing learning, make them a versatile technology for the future.

Robotic Process Automation

Automating repetitive tasks is crucial for companies to operate more efficiently and remain competitive in the modern business landscape. Robotic process automation provides a powerful solution that allows employees to configure software robots to automate well-defined workflows. By mimicking user actions, these bots can interpret data from existing IT systems, trigger responses, communicate across digital systems, and carry out a wide range of repetitive tasks without human intervention.

RPA bots shine when applied to high volume, repetitive processes such as data entry, invoice processing, and document management. By coding the software bots to handle these mundane tasks, companies can reduce operational costs and manual errors while allowing human employees to focus their time on more impactful work. Bots can be configured to log into applications, enter data, trigger confirmations and notifications, all based on predefined rules and actions. Multiplying the efficiency of a single worker.

Beyond repetitive workflow automation, RPA offers applications in IT operations functions like network monitoring, patch management, and infrastructure optimization. By leveraging bots to track performance metrics 24/7 and flag any anomalies or issues requiring human analysis, IT teams can focus on more strategic initiatives while maintaining seamless network operations. Bots can also handle the rollout of software updates across servers and end user devices saving IT teams countless hours typically spent on these mundane but necessary tasks.

With the transformative efficiency gains offered by RPA, it is no wonder businesses are eager to automate more processes with intelligent software bots. When thoughtfully implemented, RPA enables companies to reduce costs, improve compliance, and empower human employees to focus on delivering value by handing off repetitive tasks to robotic assistants. This symbiotic partnership between human and machine is key to unlocking productivity gains across an organization.

Expert Systems

An expert system is a form of artificial intelligence software that uses a knowledge base of human expertise to provide advice or recommendations. The goal is to mimic the judgment and analytical skills of a human expert to help solve complex problems.

Unlike traditional computer programs that rely on conventional procedural code, expert systems are rule-based—they apply a series of "if X, then Y" rules to a fact base to reason through solutions. This structure allows them to act as advisors, prompting users through a series of questions about an issue just as a human expert would.

Expert systems are most commonly put to use in roles that require specialized domain knowledge and analytical ability to navigate nuanced issues. For example, an expert system may be used in a corporate setting to assist high-level decision-making processes, applying rules, and logic to evaluate strategic alternatives just as an industry veteran might. The system allows organizations to leverage the judgment of their most skilled professionals on a wider array of decisions.

Additionally, due to their analytical nature, expert systems are ideal for diagnostic purposes—think troubleshooting technical problems in machinery, complex software systems, or even unusual medical symptoms. The system takes a user through a tree of possible causes, weighing evidence just as a seasoned technician, IT support specialist or physician might. This allows expert-level diagnostics to be available more broadly.

The end result is that expert systems expand access to specialized human expertise, improving decision-making and problem-solving abilities in areas that require nuanced analytical judgment. By encoding human knowledge and reasoning into automated rule-based systems, the insights of one expert can be made widely available where they are needed most.

Skill Building for Effective AI Utilization

Building the right skills across teams is essential for organizations looking to effectively adopt and utilize artificial intelligence capabilities. Rather than simply stating requirements in a list, it is best to have an integrated discussion focused on nurturing talent and competencies within architecture and related functions.

When identifying the core areas for skill building, it is important to recognize foundational domains like data and analytics, statistical modeling, and computer science. However, one should not overlook soft skills either. Cross-functional communication, creative thinking, and ethical reasoning enable professionals to apply technical knowledge responsibly. Leadership capabilities further empower them to drive enterprise-wide AI adoption.

There are many developmental resources and learning pathways that can equip staff with blended skill sets for AI excellence. Rotational programs offer on-the-job training by having architects work alongside data scientists on applications like predictive analytics. Partnerships with academic institutions facilitate specialized courses and certifications. Hack-a-thons and design thinking workshops promote computational thinking in internal teams. Such initiatives not only close skills gaps but also foster a culture of learning and innovation.

As organizations continue on their AI journey, they must nurture talent through a multifaceted skills strategy. With the right developmental focus, an enterprise can build high-performing teams that ethically and strategically apply the power of AI to create business value. The capabilities of technology and people grow together in today's landscape. Investing in skills is thus the fuel for realizing the transformative potential of AI across the organizational architecture.

Emerging AI Technologies and Skills to Watch

Emerging artificial intelligence technologies are transforming many industries. As a result, professionals working in enterprise architecture and related fields must update their skills. Keeping an enterprise architecture framework modern now requires paying attention to advances in artificial intelligence. It also means watching how jobs change as artificial intelligence progresses.

Specifically, enterprise architects need to track how artificial intelligence is altering technical abilities. For example, they must understand the latest artificial intelligence algorithms and how such algorithms get embedded in enterprise software applications. Additionally, enterprise architects have to grasp new concepts and components surrounding artificial intelligence systems such as neural networks and advanced data analytics. Mastering these evolving technologies enables enterprise architects to properly design and integrate artificial intelligence within business environments.

Along with technical competencies, enterprise architects must also stay informed on how artificial intelligence is affecting business capabilities. The technology promises to automate an expanding array of processes while also generating insights from ever growing volumes of data. Enterprise architects thus need skills for identifying where artificial intelligence can optimize operations, create efficiencies, drive revenue and lower costs. This understanding allows enterprise architects to pinpoint where deploying artificial intelligence can provide the most business value.

Upcoming AI Technologies

Let us take a look at some of the AI technologies that are going to disrupt the enterprise architecture and industry as whole.

Machine Learning Operations

Deploying machine learning models into production environments has often been challenging for organizations. There can be a lack of alignment between data science teams building the models and IT teams responsible for application architectures. This results in models that fail or provide no business value.

MLOps practices aim to solve these issues by streamlining the entire lifecycle of an ML model after it is developed. This starts right from capturing relevant data to monitoring the model's performance in production. Using DevOps principles tailored for machine learning, MLOps containers standardize the model packaging process so IT teams can seamlessly integrate them. Continuous integration and delivery pipelines make updating models easier. Detailed instrumentation through logging and metrics provides visibility into how new models are performing once deployed.

MLOps enables rapid and reliable evolution of AI components across the enterprise stack. Data science teams can focus purely on model development while ops engineers manage deployments. This division of responsibility along with automation establishes guardrails that make the progression from proof-of-concept to productive ML application faster. Companies can realize more value from their AI investments with lower risk. The key advantage is flexibility to experiment with new models and double down on those delivering the highest business impact. By closing the loop between developing, deploying and monitoring; MLOps unlocks innovation velocity otherwise throttled by technical debt accrued when scaling AI.

Explainable AI (XAI)

AI systems are rapidly advancing in complexity as they take on more integral business decision-making responsibilities. There is a corresponding growth in the demand within organizations to have clarity and visibility into how these AI technologies are arriving at key conclusions that drive strategic outcomes. Without reasonable transparency, lack of trust and adoption tends to occur no matter how sophisticated the AI solutions become.

An emerging field known as explainable AI, (XAI), aims to address this need. It involves developing a range of explanatory techniques that open the "black box" of complex AI. The goal is to comprehensively map out the underlying models, algorithms, and data that feed into the AI decision processes. By utilizing specific methods from XAI, organizations gain the ability to describe the reasoning and rationale behind AI decisions to human experts across managerial, technical, and operational roles.

Equipped with understandable explanations of AI outcomes, human experts can appropriately trust and oversee these technologies as collaborators in the decision process rather than unknown enigmas. Furthermore, this transfer of knowledge from AI to human also enables the opportunity to improve the AI systems themselves in an ongoing capacity. XAI delivers the translations needed for enterprises to tap into the rising sophistication of AI while still maintaining transparency required for adoption. The result is AI and human experts can complement one another in optimized decision-making.

Edge AI

The emergence of edge computing is transforming how organizations manage and leverage data. Rather than relying solely on central cloud servers, more processing and analytics is now occurring on local devices and systems positioned at the edge of networks—in close proximity to where data generation occurs. This edge-focused approach reduces dependence on cloud transmission and storage while also decreasing latency. With data able to be handled faster and more dynamically at the point of origin, there is less bottleneck around shuttling vast amounts of data to and from a central repository.

However, to truly capitalize on the possibilities enabled by edge computing, updates to network architectures, data management philosophies, and analytics strategies are required. Companies need network protocols and infrastructure that seamlessly blend edge capabilities with core cloud servers. Data management platforms have to provide consistent governance, security, and reliability across decentralized data pools residing far from traditional centralized stores. Analytics techniques must also evolve to conduct real-time decision-making and knowledge discovery within ephemeral edge environments while still maintaining integration with core data warehouses.

Edge computing has unlocked astonishing potential for responsiveness and computational power close to customers and devices. But it also necessitates a rethinking of how data architectures, movement, and processing are conducted in a hybrid edge-cloud ecosystem. Companies that can successfully navigate this shift are poised to achieve dramatic gains in speed, scale, and insight from their data assets. The strategies and solutions required to thrive in this new edge-centered paradigm continue to rapidly evolve.

Quantum Computing

Quantum computing is an emerging technology that is still in early development stages yet has the capacity to fundamentally transform current constraints around data processing power. Even the most advanced computer processors and servers today have limitations in how quickly and efficiently they can run complex algorithms and encrypt large data sets.

Quantum computing aims to shatter those limitations through quantum physics, allowing exponential increases in computation speed and power.

At the subatomic level, quantum computers leverage the unique physics of tiny particles to introduce new data processing paradigms. By developing quantum bits or "qubits," scientists can exponentially increase computational capacity and speed to analyze algorithms at unprecedented rates. When scaled within servers built specifically for quantum workloads, these new types of quantum processors could provide enterprises with abilities to run sophisticated encryption techniques, optimize machine learning applications, and derive insights from big data stores more rapidly than ever before conceived.

The implications of successfully commercializing scalable, high-performance quantum computing for the enterprise market are tremendous. Introducing radically faster encryption and algorithms has the potential to revolutionize industries from finance to healthcare. Existing computational barriers to running complex predictive models, identifying patterns within massive datasets, and securing networks could be lifted. Quantum computing remains highly experimental, but its future impact could be analogous to the mainstream adoption of cloud computing in digitally transforming business technology landscapes. Even in its earliest stages, quantum computing foreshadows innovations that enterprises must follow and be prepared to leverage as the technologies develop further. The processing potential of quantum systems could profoundly reshape enterprise IT, data analytics, business insights, and competitive dynamics across sectors when applied at commercial scale.

Emerging Trends in AI Tools

As we look towards the future, the evolution of AI tools is expected to follow certain trajectories that will further shape enterprise architecture.

Greater Cognitive Automation

AI tools are rapidly evolving to handle more complex cognitive tasks beyond basic automation. Where we once relied on AI just to streamline routine and repetitive processes, we now see AI systems demonstrating more advanced decision-making capabilities. This progression is opening up new possibilities for integrating intelligent automation into critical business areas to help strengthen strategic operations and workflows.

As AI platforms grow increasingly adept at analytical thinking, prediction, optimization, and even some degree of independent judgment, enterprise architects have an opportunity before them. By thoughtfully evaluating where emerging cognitive technologies can augment existing processes, architects can design next-generation architectures that successfully leverage AI's strengths. This allows organizations to offload select decisions to enhance overall productivity, insight, and competitive positioning without losing human oversight and accountability.

The key for architects will be promoting symbiotic collaboration between humans and machines. AI should not be treated as a wholesale replacement for human analysis. Rather, by combining AI's computational speed, scalability, and lack of bias with human strategic vision, ethics, and experience, organizations can achieve heightened performance. The future architecture must incorporate this hybrid approach into workflows, systems, and data flows to give enterprises the agility to remain responsive in fast-changing markets while making their strongest resource—people—more effective.

This calls for architectures centered on transparency and trust so that AI-human collaboration can succeed. Architects must engineer interpretability and explainability into AI systems to maintain accountability. And by establishing robust data supply chains from source to decision, architects uphold confidence in the AI and in downstream choices influenced by its outputs. With responsible and ethical integration, AI and human leaders together will transform decision-making and value creation across the enterprise.

AI-Driven Security

As cybersecurity threats continue to evolve in complexity, artificial intelligence technologies are poised to transform how enterprises approach system protection and response. Rather than reacting to threats, innovative AI algorithms promise more proactive threat intelligence gathering and real-time prevention capabilities. This represents a paradigm shift for enterprise architecture, which will see security tightly integrated into the fabric of business solutions rather than appended as an afterthought.

By continually scanning system activity and evaluating behavioral patterns, AI-powered cybersecurity tools can identify anomalies indicative of emerging attacks. This allows security teams to contain threats before they result in damage. AI can also analyze vast volumes of threat data to detect subtle signatures and warning signs of different attack types. This level of early threat detection is extremely difficult to achieve manually.

Additionally, AI has the capability to initiate automatic responses and countermeasures to neutralize threats in milliseconds. Traditional security tools rely heavily on human intervention, unable to match the processing speed and accuracy of AI systems. As attacks become more automated, the need for AI-enabled defenses continues to grow.

Enterprise architects must evolve their designs and processes to prepare for this new era of AI-driven security. This involves planning for integrated layers of AI security spanning core infrastructure, applications, APIs, cloud environments and any endpoints. Architecting security from the ground up rather than considering it as an add-on or afterthought will enable organizations to fully leverage AI's potential as a force multiplier for threat detection and response. It is an acknowledgment that in the modern threat landscape, AI is fundamental to achieving robust, reliable security posture. Enterprises who embrace this and architect accordingly will gain a distinct competitive advantage.

Federated Machine Learning

Federated machine learning is emerging as a promising approach for organizations looking to leverage AI while respecting user privacy and data sovereignty concerns. Unlike traditional machine learning, where all data is concentrated in one location for model training, federated learning allows models to learn from decentralized data that remains distributed on user devices or on various company servers. This avoids directly sharing potentially sensitive data.

Adopting this distributed approach poses architectural challenges, as enterprise systems will need to orchestrate much more complex data flows. Rather than simply centralizing data in a warehouse or lake, systems must coordinate data sharing and aggregation across a network of decentralized data sources. This requires meticulous tracking of data provenance across disparate systems and careful access control mechanisms to preserve data privacy and compliance.

The model itself must also be able to synthesize learning from data sources with varying formats, sampling frequencies, and populations. Robust data transformations and privacy-preservation techniques are necessary so that these diverse data points can be harnessed for collaborative model improvement without allowing any one party's data to be exposed or inferred.

For organizations, this means rethinking aspects of their analytics architecture to enable decentralized data sharing as well as centralized model aggregation. Federated learning at scale will rely on refined data streaming pipelines, security protocols, compartmentalization methods, and model versioning processes that were not required for conventional, centralized machine learning. Substantial coordination will be needed across IT, analytics, and business teams to get the data orchestration right.

With deliberate architecture strategies, however, organizations can overcome these hurdles to make privacy-preserving federated learning a viable paradigm. And they may reap benefits like improved model accuracy, user trust, and data security in the process. The path to adoption starts with understanding what new architectural elements are required to truly decentralize AI.

Human-AI Collaboration Frameworks

As artificial intelligence capabilities continue to advance, there is a growing need to thoughtfully integrate these technologies alongside human workers rather than view them as replacements. Seamless human-AI collaboration in the workplace will require system architectures and interface designs that specifically enable a symbiotic working relationship between people and AI agents.

Rather than siloed AI tools that operate independently, future platforms should provide integrated environments where AI handles repetitive analytical tasks while humans provide creative oversight, apply emotional intelligence, and make executive decisions. This could involve advanced visualization dashboards that allow human workers to rapidly process AI-generated data insights and override incorrect predictions. It may also include configurable settings that determine the balance of autonomous recommendations versus manual approvals at each stage of a given business process.

Interaction models will also need to seamlessly facilitate communication between front line employees, managers, and intelligent algorithms working in tandem. This could mean designing chat-based interfaces where people can pose clarifying questions to AI assistants, notify them of potential biases or errors, and provide periodic performance feedback. The system would then analyze these human inputs to continuously fine-tune its decision-making approach rather than operate as a rigid, rules-based system.

By proactively addressing factors such as intuitive controls, clear visibility into AI reasoning, and flexible integration with human insight, architects can work towards human-AI partnerships that accentuate mutual strengths. Rather than a hand off between people and machines, the workplace of the future will feature an efficient, integrated approach that combines AI productivity and human judgment.

Chapter Seventeen

Overcoming Challenges—Navigating AI Implementation Pitfalls

I ntegrating artificial intelligence capabilities into enterprise architectures can unlock tremendous value, but it does not come without its fair share of challenges. From complex data infrastructure needs to ethical AI concerns, organizations must navigate a web of potential pitfalls to ensure smooth and successful AI implementation.

At the core, AI integration challenges tend to revolve around data—its availability, quality, and governance. Many enterprises simply do not have the datasets required to train and validate AI to the level needed for reliable business applications. Additionally, real-world data tends to be messy, incomplete, and siloed across various sources. Combining and cleaning this data in compliance with regulatory policies requires heavy lifting.

The operational side also bears consideration. AI often faces skepticism from longtime employees who can be hesitant to embrace autonomous systems and new workflows. Change management is crucial, as is air-tight monitoring of AI models to ensure outputs align with business goals and values. From an architecture perspective, AI workloads necessitate dynamic allocation of compute resources to accommodate intensive training and inference demands.

The good news is that through proper strategic planning, sufficient financial commitment and buy-in across all levels of the organization, these hurdles can be overcome. Some proven recommendations that experts endorse include starting with a well-scoped pilot project, investing early in data infrastructure, and maintaining flexibility around AI vendors and tools. Building in-house AI skills via training programs also pays dividends.

Of course, each enterprise situation brings unique challenges. By maintaining an open dialogue with all stakeholders, asking the difficult questions early, and focusing AI efforts on the most impactful business use cases, organizations can drive tremendous productivity improvements, customer experience gains, and future-proof competitiveness. The journey requires work but the rewards warrant the effort.

This chapter focuses on helping you identify these challenges and know how to address them effectively.

Identifying and Addressing Common AI Challenges

Implementing artificial intelligence capabilities across an organization's operations and systems can unlock tremendous value, but it also comes with common growing pains. Rather than technical components like complex algorithms, the biggest challenges often arise in organizational alignment, data pipelines, and adoption at scale.

Without executive support and strategic clarity on how AI will deliver business impact, projects can stall at the proof of concept stage.

Cross-functional coordination across IT, analytics, business teams, and end-users is essential to ensure the AI solution solves real pain points. Achieving this collaborative structure is challenging but necessary.

Delivering quality, clean data to the AI models can also hamper progress. Data may get siloed across legacy systems or require considerable preprocessing. Investing in pipelines and governance early on can pay dividends.

Finally, the path from prototype to industrialized solution at scale requires planning for aspects like model monitoring, explanation, and transparency. Without focus here, adoption can fail. But by putting the proper operational components in place and with a commitment to developing talent and AI-ready culture, organizations can overcome the common struggles and get to production AI that realizes the hoped-for ROI.

The challenges are real but solvable. With methodical approaches grounded in cross-functional partnership, high-quality data, and focus on adoption, companies can pave the way for AI to positively augment business performance.

Strategies and Best Practices for Addressing These Challenges

Let us take a look at some of the practices that can help you address these challenges without affecting your organizations resources or revenue.

Ensuring Data Integrity

Collecting good data is essential for developing effective AI systems. Rather than just amassing large volumes of data, companies should focus on building systems that methodically gather, process, and validate information. This allows them to create high-quality datasets that truly capture the patterns and variations found in the real world.

With clean, robust data, organizations can train AI models that make reliable predictions and recommendations aligned with business goals. Useful models require inputs spanning the full spectrum of potential scenarios. For example, an AI model that assesses loan risk would need data on both individuals likely to repay loans and those likely to default. This diversity of information enables the model to learn nuanced differences between high- and low-risk cases.

Ongoing data collection and model retraining are also critical. By continuously ingesting the latest data, companies can incrementally improve model accuracy over time. This allows the AI to adapt as new products are launched, economic conditions change, or customer behaviors evolve. Periodic retraining prevents accuracy decay while capturing new trends and patterns as they emerge.

In summary, data is the lifeblood of AI. Investments should focus on building reliable data infrastructure and workflows. This provides the foundation for advanced analytics and intelligent systems that generate real business value. The companies that leverage data most effectively will gain competitive advantages as AI becomes increasingly embedded into operations and decision making.

Incremental Integration

Integrating artificial intelligence systems into complex organizational processes can seem daunting, but it does not have to be an overnight transition. There are benefits to taking a gradual, phased approach, slowly incorporating AI where it makes sense while assessing impact at each stage.

For example, many companies start by using AI to automate basic tasks in a single department or work stream. This allows them to free up their top talent to focus on more value-added activities while testing how employees respond to and interact with AI. Lessons learned during this initial implementation, such as the user experience or integration challenges, provide important insights before deploying AI on a larger scale.

Organizations might then look to scale their use of AI to multiple departments or teams. But rather than network-wide updates, they slowly roll out intelligent automation applications one team at a time. This controlled expansion enables adequate testing and troubleshooting within each group, minimizing disruption. It also allows other groups to observe early AI adopters and better prepare for their own integration in later phases.

This gradual deployment schedule, moving systematically from department to department, continues until AI is fully embedded across the organization. Moving slowly, assessing results, and making adjustments along the way provides lessons that lead to smoother long-term transitions. And by keeping legacy systems and AI running parallel for a period, risk is reduced if processes need to be reverted back.

The key is not to rush into organization-wide AI adoption all at once. Patience is required. But a plan of gradual integration focused on controlled testing at each stage can minimize disruption while enabling the benefits of AI to take hold. This disciplined approach allows the organization and its employees to adjust to AI-enhanced processes over time—setting up both technology and people for success.

Designing for Scalability

Architecting scalable AI solutions is crucial right from the initial design phases. As organizations increasingly embrace AI to elevate decision-making, enhance customer engagement, and drive efficiencies, planning for growth and change through flexible architectures enables sustaining performance gains over longer time frames.

Rather than monolithic designs, taking a modular approach allows AI components to be swapped in or out fluidly as algorithms mature or new techniques arise. Loose coupling the various analytics, predictive models, and data pipelines that comprise robust AI systems permits updating or expanding specific layers without rebuilding entire stacks.

Leveraging cloud-based services further bolsters seamless expansion, allowing storage, compute power, and network capacity to scale on-demand. As data volumes or user loads grow, the AI application can utilize more cloud resources through auto-scaling capabilities. This prevents overload issues that would otherwise require re-platforming solutions on more powerful infrastructure.

Architecting for scale also entails planning for connectivity across the broader enterprise technology environment. Using open APIs and interfacing with existing software systems allows the AI capabilities to be leveraged across business functions. This avoids siloed AI that cannot integrate with other critical organizational data sources or workflows.

The responsiveness and flexibility engendered through cloud-based modular design and enterprise integration enables the AI to expand its decision-making power across the organization. With robust scalability architectures, AI achieves greater ubiquity and a higher return on investment.

Addressing Ethics and Bias

Ensuring artificial intelligence systems are designed and deployed ethically is vital for building trust and confidence in this transformative technology. By weaving ethical thinking into the AI development process from the initial stages, organizations can proactively address potential downsides that could negatively impact people or society.

One recommendation is to start by ensuring the data used for developing and training AI models represents diverse perspectives. The models of the world that AI systems build are only as unbiased as the information they are exposed to during machine learning. Data diversity leads to more inclusive outputs. Cross-functional teams of domain experts, data scientists, and ethics advisors can collaborate closely on sourcing and preparing data to mitigate representation issues.

In addition, regular algorithmic audits during the build phase and continuous monitoring after deployment can detect unwanted bias in AI systems before it results in real-world harm. These audits analyze decision-making outputs for fairness regarding all demographic groups. Issues identified can be swiftly addressed through adjusting the algorithms, data, or other factors perpetuating unintended prejudice. Ongoing assessment for bias enables organizations to uphold rigorous AI ethics standards.

By working conscientiously at each development stage to evaluate AI systems through an ethical lens, consult experts on societal impacts, and implement bias detection checks, organizations can feel confident the AI solutions they launch are trustworthy and advance the collective good. The incentives are aligned—ethical AI builds user trust, enhances brand reputation, and unlocks more value.

By considering these common challenges and adopting the respective strategies and best practices, enterprises can enhance the success rate of AI implementation and diminish the risk of encountering systemic failures often associated with complex technological incorporation. Moreover, these approaches will assist in realizing the transformative potential of AI while maintaining adherence to ethical, legal, and practical business standards.

Expert Opinions on Overcoming AI Challenges

Overcoming challenges in AI implementation is a multidimensional effort, demanding expertise from various facets of enterprise architecture. Organizational readiness, data governance, and architecture scalability are some of the common obstacles faced by enterprises.

Here is an expert perspective on addressing these hurdles.

Organizational Readiness

When it comes to successfully implementing any major new technology, organizations can't just throw money and resources at it. They really need to evaluate and prepare their culture, processes and staff skills well in advance. This is especially important for a rapidly advancing field like AI. Companies that want to leverage its benefits should be proactive in cultivating an appetite for innovation across all levels—from leadership to line workers.

This starts with an openness to continuous learning and adapting to change, not being set in established ways. Management needs to communicate clearly how emerging capabilities like AI align with overall business strategy for competitive advantage. Equipping employees with growth mindsets and the latest technical skills empowers them to embrace new tools versus fear of things like workplace automation.

As for operational readiness, conducting honest capability assessments of current workflows, data infrastructure, and analytics is essential. Understanding limitations will better inform appropriate investment decisions and roadmaps. Adopting agile frameworks allows necessary tweaking as AI solutions and best practices evolve.

The organizations that put in the groundwork to ready both staff and systems will reap the most rewards. They are positioned to dynamically integrate AI in step with the ideal balance of people, processes and technologies.

Data Governance

When it comes to AI, people often focus on the sophistication of the technologies, the algorithms, and the capabilities being developed. However, what really feeds and empowers AI are data—and lots of it! Without access to quality datasets that are robust, well-organized and accurately labeled, even the most advanced AI cannot reach its full potential.

This is why implementing strong data governance must be a priority for any organization pursuing AI. I cannot stress enough how vital it is to have clear policies and frameworks governing your data—addressing everything from quality and integrity to documentation, compliance, ethics and security. AI will leverage whatever data it is given, for better or worse. So if you don't have control over the sources, accuracy, biases and appropriateness of that data, you are setting your AI up for failure—or even legal penalties down the road.

The good news is that by establishing and committing to sound data governance early in the process, you ensure that your AI has what it fundamentally requires to thrive: access to clean, reliable, well-understood data that meets your standards across the board. When people ask me what the foundation is for successfully leveraging AI, I always come back to the quality and governance of your data. Get that right from the start through solid data policies, and it smooths the path for advanced AI and algorithms to reach their full capability and deliver real business value while avoiding regulatory or ethical pitfalls. It's not the most exciting topic, but it underpins everything when it comes to capitalizing on AI!

Architecture Scalability

Achieving scalability in enterprise architecture is critical for organizations adopting artificial intelligence and advanced analytics. Rather than bolting on scalability as an afterthought, it must be woven into the fabric of enterprise architecture from the initial planning stages of AI projects. This architectural approach enables the flexibility necessary for the enterprise to grow in tandem with increasing data workloads and evolving business requirements fueled by AI.

Practically speaking, baking scalability into enterprise architecture requires leveraging specific technologies and design patterns. Transitioning to micro-services architecture allows applications to scale more efficiently through independent deployment of modular components. Containerization technologies better utilize underlying resources by virtualizing computer workloads. Cloud platforms provide innate scalability, allowing enterprises to scale up and down their computing power and storage needs on demand. And robust APIs enable flexible inter-communication between components and applications behind the scenes.

With the responsiveness and agility provided by these scalable architectural approaches, organizations can deploy innovative AI projects without being handcuffed by rigid legacy systems. The enterprise gains the capacity to handle exponential data growth as models iterate and usage expands. And innovations can be built rapidly atop stable, flexible foundations. With an eye towards scalability in enterprise architecture from the outset, companies position themselves to achieve the full transformational potential of AI.

Technology Integration

Integrating artificial intelligence capabilities into legacy business systems can prove challenging, but adopting a thoughtful enterprise architecture approach makes this process manageable and effective. Rather than directly plugging AI into existing ecosystems, organizations should take a step back and develop an overarching framework that evaluates how these new data-driven technologies can maximize interoperability, access valuable siloed information, and phase out antiquated solutions.

TOGAF as discussed before provides an industry-standard blueprint for architecting integrated systems. When preparing to implement AI,

TOGAF's model first compels stakeholders to comprehensively review what legacy systems currently support crucial business operations. It then stresses the importance of understanding upcoming data and processing requirements for AI tools under consideration. This upfront analysis subsequently informs a tailored integration strategy, allowing architects to design smart conduits, protocols, and APIs that allow AI and traditional systems to exchange insights.

Rather than a wholesale rip and replace approach, TOGAF emphasizes setting a transitional roadmap for scaling AI over time while still maintaining essential functionality. As an example, an initial rollout might focus on augmenting an existing CRM system with a virtual assistant chatbot. Future phases can then replace on-premise data warehouses with cloud-based lake storage better optimized for machine learning. This stepped strategy minimizes disruption while allowing the organization to incrementally benefit from AI's potential as part of a unified enterprise architecture vision.

Proactively defining these systems integration needs avoids attempting to force incompatible solutions together. Establishing an architectural blueprint for AI support promotes interoperability, easy data access, and a manageable bridge towards more intelligent operations. The TOGAF methodology keeps implementation grounded in this bigger picture perspective.

Talent Management

Building, implementing, and scaling AI comes with myriad complexities, many of which center around talent. As enterprises dive deeper into advanced analytics and machine learning, they often discover gaps in in-house skill sets needed to drive AI success. From core data science disciplines to user experience design to change management communication, organizations struggle to find professionals fluent in both AI technologies and their specific industry landscape.

Rather than viewing the shortage as an insurmountable barrier, we must approach it as an opportunity to build for the future. Where should enterprises start? By forging partnerships with academic institutions which serve as breeding grounds for emerging AI talent. Developing our own in-house training programs is equally critical, where employees with little AI exposure can level up through hands-on practice and mentoring. And as models are built and deployed, actively participating in external AI communities allows us to keep our fingers on the pulse of best practices and future trends.

With the speed at which AI continues to evolve, an under-investment in talent, and expertise is no longer an option. Though the lift is heavy initially, the long view is bright. Equipped with qualified and passionate teams, enterprises can transform obstacles into catalysts for true competitive advantage where AI ceases to intimidate, but rather becomes an engine for unlocking unprecedented efficiency, accuracy and innovation across the organization. The lift is heavy, but for those with vision, the view ahead gleams bright.

Each of these expert opinions provides a logistical and strategic approach to overcoming the main challenges of AI implementation. The overarching aim is to create a responsive, adaptive, and resilient enterprise architecture that can leverage AI technologies to their fullest potential.

Interactive Troubleshooting Guides

Well-designed troubleshooting guides can be invaluable for those working with artificial intelligence systems in enterprise settings. By empowering end users to properly identify, comprehend, and resolve common AI problems themselves, interactive guides nurture vital problem-solving and critical thinking abilities that serve them well in navigating intricate enterprise architectures.

Constructing truly effective interactive troubleshooting guides requires thoughtful structure. The guide should open by introducing the specific AI system's purpose and context within wider business operations. This framing sets the stage for users to better grasp how the AI functions within their organization's complex framework of data flows, software applications, hardware infrastructure, and human roles.

For each common issue, the guide should:

1. Define the Problem

The guide needs to start by having users describe the specific issues they are facing in detail, including the symptoms and manifestations within their enterprise systems. Providing a framework for problem definition acts as a diagnostic tool to pinpoint the exact failures or challenges that need resolution.

1. Trace the Source

Once the problem is clearly described, the guide should methodically walk users through a process of elimination using analytical questioning and logic flows to incrementally identify the root cause of the issue. Whether originating from data pipelines, algorithm limitations, infrastructure constraints, or integration with other systems—the goal is to unravel where the problem began.

1. Offer Solutions

The guide should put forward practical solutions in a staged manner, starting with the simplest and most probable fixes before escalating to more intricate troubleshooting techniques. For example, updating to the latest AI model or reviewing data inputs can be an early recommendation before conducting deeper algorithmic diagnostics and system assessments.

1. Engage With Critical Thinking

In addition to troubleshooting instructions, the guide needs to pose thoughtful questions and hypothetical scenarios that compel users to think critically about the interactions and dependencies within their AI solution stack. This reflective evaluation of why something is not working as intended is key for framing how design choices translate to real-world outcomes.

1. Evaluate and Reflect

Finally, the guide should provide mechanisms for users to share feedback on what troubleshooting recommendations were effective versus not. Collecting these insights over time and continuously updating the guide's logic flows and decision trees will be crucial for improving its future value in solving subsequent issues expediently. This cyclical process of learning will allow both the guide and users to mature in their approach to issue resolution.

An interactive guide should be complemented with diagrams, flowcharts, and decision trees to aid in the visual representation of troubleshooting pathways. Additionally, incorporating a feedback mechanism enables continuous enhancement of the guide itself, ensuring that it evolves with the technology and remains a relevant and dynamic resource for problem-solving within enterprise architectures.

Chapter Eighteen

Bridging the Human-AI Gap—Collaborative Systems

As artificial intelligence systems become more advanced and integrated into business operations, understanding how humans and AI can effectively collaborate is crucial for success. Companies need to proactively develop strategies, leadership approaches, and organizational processes focused specifically on facilitating seamless collaboration between human employees and AI technologies.

There are already powerful real-world examples that showcase the value derived from purposeful integration of human ingenuity and skill with AI efficiency and capabilities. In the healthcare field, AI tools have been developed that can analyze patient data and medical images to provide doctors enhanced diagnostic capabilities and early detection of diseases. However, the AI is designed to augment the specialized medical knowledge and experience of the physicians, not replace them. This human-AI collaboration ultimately leads to improved patient outcomes.

In the financial services sector, AI engines assist wealth managers by automatically analyzing investment opportunities and market conditions in real-time. But the AI recommendations must still be reviewed and validated by the human managers, combining the speed and accuracy of the machines with human judgment, reasoning and responsibility. When designed appropriately, with the strengths of both humans and AI systems working together, these collaborative models drive higher ROI.

To promote this type of collaboration, organizations need to foster a culture of transparency, trust and shared purpose between people and AI teams. Integrating human specialists into the AI development process, actively soliciting employee feedback about AI systems, and providing training on transparent AI design principles have proven effective for establishing shared vision. Leadership must also reinforce that AI should act as an enhancement tool for employees to help them focus their talents on higher value aspects of their roles.

As AI capabilities grow, emerging trends like collective intelligence systems that seamlessly combine both human and machine intelligence into unified models, will open up even more opportunities for impactful and mutually beneficial collaboration. Overall, organizations that intentionally develop cooperative frameworks and environments around human-AI collaboration will have substantial competitive advantage in their industries going forward.

Strategies and Best Practices for Promoting Collaboration Between Humans and AI Systems

When bringing AI into an organization, it's crucial that we don't view it as something alien or robotic that's separate from human intelligence. The most effective implementations see AI as an enhancement and extension of human capabilities. The goal is a seamless integration and a symbiotic relationship where both sides actively collaborate and augment each other's strengths.

To accomplish this, leaders should emphasize that AI is a tool for empowerment—not replacement. Make it clear that these technologies are here to elevate what humans can achieve by reducing drudgery and providing insights no individual could uncover on their own. Training programs that allow hands-on interaction can demystify these systems so people become comfortable working alongside them.

It's also important that AI have transparency built-in from the ground up when making recommendations or taking actions. Explanations of the reasoning and data behind suggestions helps create trust in the system. And allowing humans to give direct feedback makes it clear that the human is still the manager here. AI is there to surface insights humans would have likely missed otherwise—but final decisions and governance still firmly rest with people.

Lastly, collaboration requires communication and shared understanding on both sides. Providing AI access to organizational datasets, processes and subject matter experts during development gives it the context necessary to align with business goals and human knowledge. In turn, interpretative machine learning helps humans understand the patterns and relationships AI has uncovered. This cycle of communication between man and machine is what takes collaboration to the next level.

The key in all of this is striking the right balance. AI should not be either master or slave, but rather a symbiotic partner working in concert with humans. With the right integration approach that focuses on augmentation over automation, advanced intelligence can collaborate with people in ways that create better outcomes for all.

Exploring the Dynamics of Human-AI Interaction in a Business Context

Human-AI interaction in the business context refers to various ways in which people and artificial intelligence systems work together to enhance outcomes. There are three primary types—collaborative, supervised, and autonomous. In collaborative interactions, humans and AI augment each other's capabilities, almost like a partnership. An example would be AI-powered analytics tools that enable financial analysts to uncover deeper insights and make better investment decisions. In supervised interactions, humans oversee AI systems and guide their outputs, like customer service chatbots where human agents intervene when queries get too complex. Finally, autonomous interactions involve AI systems that operate independently with minimal human input after initial programming, such as automated stock trading algorithms executing pre-defined strategies.

Effective human-AI interaction offers tremendous benefits for companies across sectors. By automating repetitive and time-intensive tasks like data processing and report generation, AI systems boost business efficiency and productivity, freeing up human employees to focus on more strategic work. Furthermore, by surfacing patterns and insights from vast datasets that are impossible for humans alone to analyze, AI enhances decision-making across critical functions like new product development and marketing campaign optimization. AI also directly augments customer experiences via personalized recommendation engines and conversational chatbots that handle routine queries. More broadly, human-AI collaboration fosters innovation by helping companies re-imagine business processes and explore creative solutions.

However, human-AI interaction also poses some challenges that must be carefully managed. If the historical data used to train AI systems reflects societal biases, it can lead to discriminatory and unethical outcomes. Certain AI models also lack transparency and explainability i.e. it's unclear how they arrive at specific outputs. This becomes problematic especially for safety-critical and legally regulated use cases. The automation enabled by AI also raises concerns about job losses, requiring companies to re-skill employees to work synergistically with intelligent systems rather than be replaced by them. Finally, for seamless adoption across the organization, both employees and customers need to trust AI systems. Achieving this necessitates transparency, explainability, and responsible AI development.

From predictive analytics in marketing to fraud detection in finance and even recruitment process automation in HR, practical use cases leveraging collaborative human-AI interactions are rapidly emerging across business functions. Companies that thoughtfully implement such solutions while emphasizing augmentation over automation and prioritizing trust, transparency and ethics are poised to unlock tremendous synergies and outperform the competition. The future points decisively toward ever-closer collaboration between human and machine intelligence.

Success Stories of Human-AI Systems

Several compelling real-world examples exist demonstrating how teams comprised of humans and artificial intelligence systems working together can outperform either the technology or people alone. This collaborative approach strives to emphasize the unique strengths of both sides—leveraging human strengths in areas like strategic thinking, creativity, and nuanced judgment while utilizing the AI's advantages in computational speed, pattern recognition, and data processing.

One such example can be seen in freestyle chess competitions where centaur teams, made up of human chess players partnered with AI chess engines, consistently defeat even the most powerful solo chess AIs. By thinking through game strategies and move options critically before accessing the AI's expansive databases of opening moves and tactical calculations, the combined centaur group excels. The AI's instantaneous computations complement the human's capacity for developing innovative solutions.

A rapidly accelerating area of human-AI collaboration can be found in healthcare and medical diagnostics. AI imaging analysis tools used to identify tumors, infections, fractures and other conditions have proven increasingly accurate, especially when radiologists and other specialists provide oversight and incorporate these AI insights with their own expertise when making diagnoses. This approach can lead to earlier detection of issues, more precise conclusions and importantly, improved patient outcomes overall.

The finance world provides more examples of hybrid teams mixing human judgment and AI-enabled data processing and prediction generation. Leading investment management companies now regularly utilize sophisticated AI models to analyze market trends, detect pattern deviations, model probabilistic movements and provide trading signals. However, their human analysts make the final decisions by combining these statistical AI outputs with their own assessments of broader economic environments, geopolitical events, company leadership changes and more.

The customer service domain clearly illustrates how AI and people can handle different aspects of interaction extremely effectively. AI chatbots now frequently manage simple inquiries by providing consistent fact-based responses 24/7 while seamlessly escalating more complex and emotionally nuanced queries to human representatives. This hybrid approach delivers personalized and timely customer assistance while maximizing productivity.

When analyzing these success stories, several consistent key factors emerge:

- Clearly defined goals and focused use cases for AI integration rather than broad, scattered implementation.

- AI deployed to enhance and augment human capabilities rather than replace jobs and tasks.

- Iterative, step-by-step incorporation of AI over time using trial and error.

- AI model transparency, inspect-ability, and explainability to provide users trust and understanding.

- Workforce skills adapted alongside AI transformation through training programs.

- Careful, ethical AI design and testing to avoid biases and errors.

The examples provided underscore how with a thoughtful approach, AI and human collaborators can form remarkably productive teams across many industry verticals. However, achieving this symbiotic relationship requires upfront planning, communication and learning—people and machines can accomplish so much more together than apart.

Discussing Emerging Trends and Potential Future Developments in Human-AI Collaboration

One pivotal trend is Explainable AI pushing towards models that can clarify the reasoning behind their outputs. This transparency is vital for establishing trust in AI, allowing ethical deployment, and helping humans better understand complex problem domains. By making their inner workings more interpretable, XAI will enable wider audiences to actually utilize AI insights.

Additionally, the line between human and machine capabilities is blurring within hybrid intelligence workplaces. Rather than predefined job descriptions, tasks are structured to optimize the strengths of both humans and AI. This focuses on maximizing outcomes through flexible collaboration. Humans handle creative aspects, leadership, and social skills, while AI excels at analysis, prediction, and acting on large data.

Looking beyond data cognition, AI is also advancing into creative arenas like art, music, and content generation. The path is through cooperative creation, with humans providing overall guidelines, feedback, and curation to shape the direction. AI then assists by rapidly ideating, prototyping, and producing original complex work. This symbiosis combines human ingenuity with machine scale and speed.

An emerging conduit for human-AI collaboration is Brain-Computer Interfaces (BCIs). Though early stage, BCI research suggests potential for more direct, nuanced exchanges between minds and machines. This could significantly transform how humans collaborate with AI, perhaps even allowing AI to become an inner advisor.

Future trends point to AI evolving into more of a conversational colleague. As natural language capabilities grow, the human-AI dynamic may shift towards more fluid back-and-forth interactions. Imagine an AI teammate actively strategizing with you—warning of risks, suggesting ideas, and contributing data-backed insights to discussions.

Additionally, highly personalized and adaptive AI learning systems could emerge to revolutionize workplace training. These would optimize development to individual strengths and needs, helping humans adapt to a rapidly changing technological environment.

Advances in emotional intelligence and interpreting social cues can also enable AI to better collaborate with humans. Areas like conflict resolution, team building, and customer service could be upgraded by AI that provides real-time interpersonal insights and facilitates productive dialogues.

Overall, the path forward requires emphasizing ethics-first AI development governed by transparency, accountability and fairness guardrails. Understanding the promise and risks will be vital. While automation displaces jobs, history shows it also creates new industries. The key is developing human adaptability and reasoning to complement emerging AI capabilities through collaborative synthesis.

Predicting How These Collaborations Might Evolve and Impact Business Operations

As AI systems become more accessible and user-friendly, we can expect AI to spread across departments and functions, no longer siloed in specialized teams. This democratization of AI will promote its integration into regular business operations led by employees without specialized data science expertise. The nature of human-AI collaborations will also evolve from humans using AI tools that merely enhance specific capabilities to more proactive AI systems that function as creative partners. There will be more fluid, iterative exchanges where AI co-develops ideas and solutions in collaboration with human teams, even anticipating their needs. This will transform many traditional roles as more hybrid human-AI jobs emerge. People will increasingly manage and tune AI systems, train machine learning models, and interpret AI outputs for stakeholders across the business.

These human-AI partnerships will accelerate innovation cycles, as businesses rapidly prototype and test new ideas and concepts. They will also enable data-driven decision-making to be seamlessly embedded at all levels, with real-time analytics and AI-generated insights becoming fundamental. We will see customer experiences reach new levels of personalization as well, with AI systems predicting individual preferences and delivering tailored recommendations to each user. Even management functions will transform, with AI tools helping optimize complex areas like scheduling, performance reviews, and goal setting while identifying potential burnout. Ultimately, the most adaptable businesses that actively up-skill their people to fluidly collaborate with creative, scalable AI will gain the most significant competitive advantage.

However, ethical governance and responsible development of human-centered AI will escalate in importance. New regulatory standards will likely emerge to ensure transparency and accountability. Companies must also retain intuition and human judgment in decision-making, not solely data-driven AI outputs. Balancing innovative cultures with responsible AI integration will be essential. Those that re-imagine their operations around collaborative human-AI augmentation and partnerships will thrive in this emerging landscape.

Interactive Case Study 1

The market analyst has an upcoming client presentation that requires identifying high-potential investment opportunities in the renewable energy sector. With limited time for research, the analyst enlists the help of an advanced AI-powered market analysis tool that can process volumes of financial data, news, and social media to generate predictive models.

To initiate the collaboration, the analyst provides the AI with some initial instructions—focus specifically on solar, wind, and biofuels companies in Europe and other emerging markets. The analyst requests analysis on companies with potential for both short and long-term gains.

The AI generates an initial report, identifying and ranking potential renewable energy companies based on the parameters. It presents relevant financial data for each company with trend analysis. Additionally, it flags pertinent news reports and social media chatter related to some of the companies.

Armed with this AI-generated shortlist, the analyst starts digging deeper into the top-ranked companies himself. He conducts qualitative research by studying leadership profiles and reading the latest industry analysis reports on the renewable energy sector.

The analyst uses these additional insights to further refine the AI model, adjusting the weighting of certain factors like innovation potential and ESG ratings so that the next round of analysis accounts for them more prominently.

The output of this collaborative exercise is a nuanced presentation that combines the broad data-driven insights that the AI analysis provided along with the analyst's deeper understanding of the renewable energy landscape. This allows for pitching high-potential investment opportunities to the client in an effective manner.

Interactive Case Study 2

The lead customer support agent at the rapidly growing e-commerce company faces an influx of customer queries during the busy holiday season. The increased volume has led to longer than acceptable response times, resulting in rising customer frustration.

To address this challenge, the company has implemented a multi-tier AI chatbot system with escalating capabilities and integrated sentiment analysis. The goal is to maintain prompt query resolution while still providing the personalized service that builds brand loyalty.

The AI chatbot acts as the first line of defense by answering common questions around order status, return policies, and account details. It pulls up individual customer data to provide tailored responses. Additionally, the chatbot detects rising frustration levels or negative sentiment in user replies through ongoing sentiment analysis.

When the AI chatbot flags complex queries or high levels of customer dissatisfaction, it seamlessly escalates those conversations to human agents. This collaboration allows the chatbot to resolve the majority of inquiries through automation while enabling human agents to step in to handle delicate situations.

The lead customer support agent monitors live transcripts of escalated chats to oversee the human-AI collaboration in real-time. When taking over distressed conversations, the agent works to resolve the issue and simultaneously helps train the AI system by example. Over time, the agent compiles best practices from successful human-led resolutions for future chatbot refinement.

This collaborative process between the AI chatbot and human agents aims to achieve improved wait times, increased query resolution rates, and most importantly, to maintain personalized and empathetic service to address each customer's complex and delicate situations. Over time, the human guidance helps the AI chatbot learn how to resolve a growing range of customer needs with care and tact.

Profiles of Successful Human-AI Collaboration Teams

Integrating human intelligence and artificial intelligence can unlock tremendous value, but it requires thoughtful leadership and management. There are a growing number of teams that serve as inspirational models of how to bring together human and machine capabilities harmoniously.

One example is an insurance company that developed an AI system to analyze claims and recommend settlement amounts. They ensured that human claims adjusters remained deeply involved—leveraging their judgment, emotional intelligence, and legal knowledge while benefiting from the AI's data processing and pattern recognition capabilities. Core to the success was the adjusters' input in designing the AI system, ensuring they felt it empowered them by reducing repetitive tasks and letting them focus on complex claims. Leadership also deserves credit for the extensive training to ensure adjusters understood the AI's capabilities. The result—faster claims resolution along with increased adjuster and customer satisfaction.

However, the path to integrate AI is not always smooth. Another insurance firm struggled to achieve adoption of a similar AI claims assistant. In contrast to the first example, adjusters felt out of the loop in the tool's development. They distrusted the AI's recommendations, often overriding them without justification. Leadership was slow to respond, only later recognizing the lack of communication and change management hampering success. They eventually regained buy-in through adjuster involvement in ongoing tool enhancement and emphasizing that AI recommendations would improve with feedback.

These cases illustrate that while the technology is vital, factors like communication, stakeholder buy-in, training, and culture fundamentally shape how well human-AI collaboration works. Examining successes and failures offers insights into the best practices needed to enable both humans and AI to thrive together in a mutually reinforcing way.

Chapter Nineteen

Future Trends—AI's Evolving Role in TOGAF

T he integration of artificial intelligence capabilities within the confines of The Open Group Architecture Framework has rapidly accelerated in recent years as enterprises seek to harness the power of AI to enhance business processes, decisions, and data analytics. Current observations reveal a meshing of advanced intelligent algorithms and learning systems into existing TOGAF components to augment efficiency, insights, and automation across critical architectural layers.

Experts highlight the infusion of AI assistants and advisors into the TOGAF Architecture Development Method to provide real-time recommendations and guidelines for architects building out enterprise blueprints. As architectures shift from static to dynamic, AI appears poised to keep pace with and adapt to rapidly changing infrastructure, applications, data flows, and interconnections through continual learning cycles. We also see AI optimization techniques fine-tuning legacy architecture designs to bolster security, resiliency, and scalability.

Looking ahead, integrations between robotic process automation and TOGAF standard operating procedures and specifications seem inevitable. As enterprises become increasingly complex and distributed, AI shall likely play a central role in enabling enterprise architects to continually visualize, model, and maintain intricate, evolving business landscapes. We can also reasonably expect innovations in how AI helps enterprise architects seamlessly bridge solutions across on-premise, cloud, and edge infrastructure.

This final chapter predicts some of the future trends that may happen in the space and helps you understand where you need to improve to become a better enterprise architect.

Emerging Trends in AI and TOGAF Integration

Integrating artificial intelligence into enterprise architectures opens up exciting possibilities for organizations to become more agile, optimized, and insights-driven. When done thoughtfully, embedding intelligent systems throughout business frameworks like TOGAF can usher in a new era of responsive and adaptive models.

TOGAF provides a structured methodology for coordinating vital enterprise components—from business strategies to data assets, applications, and infrastructure. AI adds another layer of agility to this framework. As organizations map their existing assets granularly through TOGAF, they gain visibility into where injecting AI-enabled functionalities like predictive analytics and automated workflows can systematically reduce friction and unlock value.

With any architecture, governance is critical for cultivating environments ready for the AI age. Ethics, compliance, and responsible innovation management become integral to technical integration and data orchestration. With reliable guardrails in place, employees across units can confidently collaborate with AI, heightening collective intelligence. Intuitive interfaces allow staff at all levels to benefit from human-AI symbiosis.

When architectures provide easy access to real-time, data-driven insights and dynamic decision support, organizations gain responsiveness in turbulent markets. With AI embedded intelligently across critical business components, companies can sense environmental shifts, predict emerging risks, and simulate innovative strategies adeptly. Rather than a discrete technology, AI becomes the connective tissue enabling enterprise architectures to underpin sentient, thriving organizations.

The potential is exciting. But we must ensure people stay at the heart of these human-AI collaborative models to build our collective future together.

Current Trends in AI Integration Within TOGAF

We will take a look at some of the current trends that AI can revolutionize with its integration within TOGAF.

Automated Architecture Artifacts Generation

Enterprise architects spend a great deal of time on routine documentation tasks—assembling visualizations, catalogs, and matrices to convey complex technology and business landscapes. This is time that could be better spent on more strategic initiatives like creative problem-solving and cross-functional collaboration. AI has the potential to automate much of the repetitive, manual work needed to keep architectural artifacts accurate and up-to-date.

By continuously analyzing relationships across information silos in real-time, AI algorithms can automatically generate high-fidelity diagrams, taxonomies, and mappings. Given how labor-intensive and static these artifacts become when manually maintained, AI brings about a huge advantage—living references that organically adapt as company data and systems evolve.

Now, imagine those automatically generated architecture models becoming trusted advisors that provide perceptive guidance. As machine learning algorithms become attuned to the intricacies of an organization's schemas, capabilities, dependencies and more, it can reveal optimization pathways previously hidden. AI may surface integration opportunities that an enterprise architect would never uncover on their own.

Broadly speaking, AI-powered automation stands to inject new momentum into digital transformation efforts. By distilling extreme organizational complexity into authoritative interactive dashboards, stakeholder confidence is strengthened. Fundamentally, enterprise architecture gets closer to achieving its mission–conveying simplicity from chaos so that business vision can flourish.

Enhanced Decision-Making Through Predictive Analytics

Architects play a critical role in helping organizations align technology strategy with business goals. An emerging approach that supports this is integrating AI-driven predictive analytics into the Architecture Development Method defined within The Open Group Architecture Framework.

Rather than rely solely on backward-looking analysis of previous trends, the ADM provides a structured method for architects to design future-state architectures. Enhancing this with predictive analytics fueled by artificial intelligence allows assumptions and models to be stress tested against an array of possible scenarios. This foresight enables architects to anticipate shifts in demographics, technology, regulations, competition, risk profiles and more.

With these analytical insights, organizations can transition from reactive responses to proactive strategic planning. Risks can be identified earlier when mitigation is more affordable. Plans can be simulated across plausible futures to design more adaptable platforms and capabilities. By the time initiatives reach the later implementation phases of the ADM, there is greater confidence in the path ahead based on data-driven foresight into trends on the horizon.

This combination of AI and architecture development ultimately allows technology transformation to be synced more tightly to where the organization seeks to head. Rather than solutions chasing a moving target, they are equipped to shape conditions for success. With technology life cycles measured in years rather than months, the ability to calibrate strategy and adapt along the way is critical. Integrating predictive analytics into architecture efforts allows organizations to navigate uncertainty and accelerate into the future.

AI-Driven Stakeholder Engagement

AI-driven stakeholder engagement offers exciting opportunities to improve how organizations communicate complex strategies in a targeted, meaningful way. Rather than taking a one-size-fits-all approach, advanced AI tools can analyze the background, interests, and context of each stakeholder group and tailor communications accordingly.

For example, when presenting a new enterprise architecture strategy involving intricate technological integration, AI could assess that the executives in the room have no technical background. It would then dynamically generate slides and talking points using simple, non-technical analogies and focusing on the potential business value, competitive advantages, and ROI. At the same time, for the IT managers also present, AI could produce more detailed diagrams and specifications with technical language, ensuring they can validate feasibility and identify implementation requirements.

Rather than glossing over concepts not universally understood or diving too deep into the technology weeds, AI can determine the perfect level and format of information for each audience. This helps key stakeholders comprehend the essence and implications of the strategy as it pertains to them, facilitating more informed and constructive discussions. Audiences leave feeling heard and empowered to provide feedback based on a clear understanding of potential trade-offs, options, and next steps.

With AI orchestrating and personalizing all stakeholder communications, organizations can count on improved transparency, accountability, and collaboration on everything from new initiatives to crisis response. Both leaders and stakeholders feel their unique needs and perspectives are prioritized from the very start, setting the stage for meaningful dialogues where all feel empowered to productively question, challenge, and contribute. This drives better decision making while proactively mitigating risks from communication gaps or mixed messages that could delay or derail successful strategy execution.

Adaptive Architecture Governance

Adaptive architecture governance leverages artificial intelligence to enable more dynamic governance models within organizational frameworks like TOGAF. Rather than rely on static policies and procedures, AI can be integrated to provide real-time monitoring of technology environments and workloads, along with feedback loops that allow governance to adjust and adapt in an ongoing manner. This creates a governance approach that is proactive and forward-looking compared to more reactive models.

With continuous access to performance data, usage metrics, and operational insights across infrastructure, applications, data, and other technology areas, AI algorithms can analyze trends, model scenarios, and identify opportunities or potential risks. Governance policies can then be tuned automatically to align with changing business objectives, new initiatives, shifts in the competitive landscape, and other factors that necessitate an agile technology strategy.

This allows governance to move at the speed of business change rather than being bound by quarterly or annual review cycles that allow gaps to form between technology capabilities and business needs. The integration of AI in architecture governance provides the flexibility and responsiveness required in fast-paced digital environments. It enables organizations to accelerate innovation cycles while still maintaining appropriate guardrails through a governance model that monitors and adapts in real-time.

The end result is technology governance that is just as dynamic, in-sight-driven, and nimble as the modern digital capabilities it oversees. With AI, architecture governance can break free of static models to become a true enabler of transformation rather than a restrictive barrier. It provides the real-time visibility, automated intelligence, and continuous adaptation needed to balance innovation with appropriate risk management.

Architecture Repository Optimization

Architecture repositories contain valuable information that guides an organization's technology strategy and decision-making. However, as these repositories grow over many years, it can become challenging to efficiently leverage their contents. There is often a vast amount of unstructured data spanning documents, models, code, and informal tribal knowledge. Finding the right architectural assets at the right time or maintaining currency as systems change hands can prove difficult.

This is where artificial intelligence has emerging potential to transform the way companies interact with their architecture repositories. Natural language processing, a form of AI, can ingest and comprehend vast amounts of unstructured, text-based data. It can automatically tag, categorize, and cluster content based on contextual meaning. Rather than relying on rigid schemas or taxonomies, these AI techniques adapt on the fly, allowing people to query the repository using natural phrases. The system delivers remarkably relevant results regardless of how the question is phrased.

Architects spend less time struggling to locate artifacts, even obscure ones from past projects. Historical details remain crisp despite employee turnover. Management gains better visibility into existing architecture investments when evaluating new initiatives and roadmaps. Relying on the institutional knowledge within the repository via AI allows the organization to operate with clarity and confidence in technology decision-making. It ultimately enables companies to optimize the utility of their architectural assets.

The capabilities are already maturing through commercial offerings. Integrating AI into architecture repositories represents one of many promising ways organizations can increase productivity and sustain competitive advantage. The transformative business benefits have only begun to scratch the surface at this early stage of AI adoption. But for those investing in architecture-driven transformation, applying AI to better leverage repositories is a valuable efficiency to strongly consider.

Cognitive Computing for Complex Problem Solving

Solving complex business problems requires seeing things from new perspectives and identifying insights that may not be obvious at first glance. As enterprise architects, we regularly face the challenge of developing solutions to multidimensional issues that involve both technical and human components across an organization's systems and processes. When dealing with these intricate matters, it can feel like trying to assemble a puzzle without having the full picture to reference. This is where the emerging capabilities of cognitive computing enabled by artificial intelligence can guide our problem-solving approach in impactful ways.

By combining the pattern recognition and deep learning strengths of AI with human subject matter expertise, cognitive computing allows us to process and gain meaning from vast amounts of data far faster than if we relied solely on our own analytical skills. The technology's ability to quickly parse through intricacies within large bodies of information helps uncover connections and trends that we would likely miss otherwise. These insights shed new light on the problem's parameters and uncover avenues we should explore that our customary methods may never have revealed.

Having this more holistic view of all the variables at play allows us to then be more strategic in assessing the interdependencies and relationships between each element within complex situations. We can piece together the fragmented components in ways where the solutions' frameworks were previously obscured. This ultimately leads us to smarter, more informed decisions backed by both data-driven AI insights on emerging patterns as well as our own seasoned judgment. By leveraging the strengths of advanced cognitive computing along with our specialized knowledge, we can collaboratively tackle multifaceted problems and achieve better outcomes. With AI as an advisor, we have a robust problem-solving partner to get a comprehensive view of the most confounding issues organizations face and chart an optimal path forward.

Shaping the Future of Enterprise Architecture

Enterprise architecture is undergoing an exciting transformation as artificial intelligence becomes more deeply integrated into frameworks and governance models. Rather than following prescriptive, rigid methodologies, architects are now able to take a more agile, insightful approach that evolves with changing business conditions.

For example, AI tools can analyze real-time data patterns and feedback loops to detect shifts in priorities or market dynamics much quicker. This allows organizations to accelerate strategic decision-making and respond rapidly to new opportunities or threats. Architects have a continual pulse on emerging needs.

Additionally, predictive analytics and AI planning assists architects with higher-quality foresight into future needs and scenarios long before they unfold. By processing volumes of data from across the enterprise, guidance around infrastructure requirements, process changes, and technology investments becomes more data-driven versus speculative. Resources can be aligned intelligently to initiatives that will deliver the most business value.

AI capabilities also introduce more maturity into architecture governance. Manual governance processes often lag in providing quality guidance. Intelligent frameworks powered by continuous learning can assess new initiatives and designs for better alignment to policies and technical standards. This real-time governance enables organizations to scale rapidly while minimizing disruption.

Overall, integrating AI is empowering architects to keep pace with the complexity of modern IT landscapes. Rather than anchor to multi-year frameworks that quickly become outdated, the combination of AI and adaptive architecture practices helps organizations harness change with agility to sustain innovation and operational excellence over the long term.

Preparing for the Future of AI in Enterprise Architecture

As Enterprise Architecture Practitioners, preparing for the future of AI entails both an understanding of technological trends and a strategic approach to incorporate these advancements in the organizational fabric. To this end, architects must focus on several strategies that cater to a rapidly evolving technological landscape.

Continual Learning and Upskilling

When it comes to integrating AI capabilities into architectural design, the very first priority must be education. Architects simply cannot leverage the potential of AI to transform the built environment without committing themselves to constant learning. Sure, formal architecture training teaches core design principles and technical building skills. But to truly harness emerging technologies like AI, dedicated study of subjects like machine learning algorithms, neural network computing, predictive analytics—these advanced areas is essential.

Some architects may benefit from enrolling in specialized master's programs or certification courses from leading academic institutions to dive deep on AI. Others may choose to stick to self-directed education by reading widely—following relevant journals, publications, conferences around artificial intelligence advancements. Either way, the field evolves rapidly. What may be cutting-edge today could be obsolete tomorrow. Maintaining professional competency as an architect in the age of artificial intelligence demands lifelong learning... an ongoing dedication to understanding what's state-of-the-art in AI and how those innovations can create new possibilities in architectural design. Expertise in this area can't be static. Creative minds need to be open to where artificial intelligence breakthroughs can take them next.

The potential exists to transform not just buildings but cities, communities, the human experience itself through AI-powered design. But to reach this future, architects must first prioritize building knowledge. The foundations for progress remain education and an insatiable curiosity about how far emerging technology can stretch the boundaries of the built environment. This is where the focus must be.

Adaptive Framework Integration

Enterprise architecture frameworks provide blueprints for organizing and managing information across organizations. Traditionally, frameworks like TOGAF and Zachman have been relatively fixed. But in today's age of exponential technological change, these frameworks require more fluidity to adapt. Architectures that statically lock-in legacy systems struggle when novel capabilities like artificial intelligence emerge. Rather, a future-thinking, evolvable approach enables seamless integration of innovations over time.

What does that adaptable framework design involve in practice when it comes to leveraging AI? First, it means architecting with flexibility for where and how AI components layer into existing business processes and data flows. As machine learning shapes certain decisions and activities, the architecture needs malleability to slot those AI systems into the appropriate places within organizational workflows. Second, evolvable frameworks must holistically govern how data gets efficiently collected, stored, integrated, protected, and prepared for advanced analytics. As organizations depend more on AI insights, getting the data foundations right grows in importance. Finally, adaptable enterprise architectures should abstract away underlying IT infrastructure complexities so that where AI workloads run—on-premises servers, public cloud, edge devices—can shift as needed over time without disrupting the higher business processes.

Enabling architectural integration of emerging innovations is about designing for change rather than cementing rigidly for the present. Organizations that create more dynamic frameworks have an advantage in responsibly leveraging technologies like AI as they continue advancing. The enterprises that resist this evolution will likely struggle with legacy constraints. So modern enterprise architecture is all about building resilient foundations rather than static monuments.

Ethical and Regulatory Consideration

AI ethics and compliance are becoming increasingly crucial considerations when architecting AI solutions for enterprise use. Rather than treating them as afterthoughts, architects should bake ethical principles and regulatory awareness into their AI strategies from the initial planning stages.

A proactive approach here is advised. Taking the time upfront to develop guidelines and guardrails for ethical development, testing and deployment enables organizations to integrate core values like fairness, transparency and accountability into models from the ground up. It also prevents scrambling reactively when new regulations emerge that affect how AI can be responsibly leveraged across operations.

Architects play an important role in encouraging productive discourse on AI ethics within the broader enterprise. By providing pragmatic recommendations on governance frameworks, risk management procedures and monitoring methodologies, they can promote the safe, ethical application of AI amidst the breakneck pace of technological change.

And through continuous environmental scanning for shifts in public perception, government policy and industry best practices, architects can steer institutions toward sustainable AI adoption aligned with societal expectations. Rather than hampering innovation, integrating ethics and compliance helps build institutional trust and competitive differentiation for companies that get this balance right. The incentives are real for those architecting the AI future to take the high road.

Robust Disaster Recovery and Security

When we think about all the ways artificial intelligence is being integrated into various facets of organizations these days, it's understandable to just focus on the benefits—the efficiency gains, the improvements in products and services, the higher quality customer experiences made possible. But as helpful as these AI systems may be, we still need to keep in mind that they introduce new cybersecurity risks that our traditional measures aren't built to handle.

These AI applications have incredible complexity with so many interconnected systems working in tandem. That leaves a lot of potential vulnerabilities that hackers could exploit to steal data, take control, or even shut down operations. And because the technology is still so new, security experts are still playing catch up when it comes to penetration testing and identifying ways to keep these systems buttoned up tight.

It's not just about external threats either. We also have to consider what would happen if an AI system went down for any reason—a coding error that causes a cascade of failures, an insider threat situation, or just unavoidable hardware problems. With how ingrained AI already is in critical functions, a system outage could be catastrophic from a business continuity standpoint.

The smart approach is making sure our disaster recovery and business continuity plans get an upgrade at the same time we deploy new AI. That means running through scenarios specific to an AI outage and figuring out how we would recover if one of these tools is offline for any period of time. It also means our IT teams may need to revisit things like data backup strategies, redundancy protocols, and overall network resilience.

I know it's not the fun or exciting part of AI adoption—but making sure we avoid preventable crises down the road is just as essential.

Above all, Enterprise Architecture Practitioners must be proactive—anticipating where AI can offer strategic advantages or operational efficiencies and making appropriate recommendations. By addressing these strategic facets, architects can navigate the AI landscape with foresight and help their organizations leverage AI technologies effectively for competitive advantage.

Predictions From AI and TOGAF Experts

The intersection of artificial intelligence and The Open Group Architecture Framework is an intriguing subject among professionals concerned with enterprise architecture.

Here are the top most of the predictions about the future of enterprise architecture because of the inclusion of AI from the experts before we close off the book with a conclusion from me.

AI-Enhanced Architecture Development Method

The Open Group Architecture Framework provides proven methods for enterprise architects through its Architecture Development Method. As artificial intelligence capabilities continue advancing, we can expect AI to transform how the ADM gets applied.

Specifically, the rapid data processing and analytical capabilities of AI can automate aspects of the ADM. This would enable architects to input large volumes of organizational data into AI systems. In turn, these systems can analyze complex relationships and patterns within the data at speeds and depths not humanly possible. The AI models can detect insights that architects may miss or take much longer to derive manually.

Architects can then use these AI-generated insights to create more intelligent architecture designs finely tuned to the organization's landscape. For instance, AI could identify redundancies across systems or opportunities to consolidate applications. This data-driven approach allows architects to craft robust blueprints positioning the organization for the future versus just addressing immediate needs.

By handling time-intensive analytical tasks, AI systems integrated with the ADM can shorten architecture development and revision cycles. This enables architects to iterate blueprints faster while also devoting more time to high-value creative tasks. Together, this increases productivity and adaptability.

AI-Driven Decision-Making

Enterprise architecture design and transformation strategies aim to align business goals with technological capabilities. Historically, architects have relied heavily on experience and intuition when evaluating options and charting an organization's structural evolution. The inherent uncertainty in predicting the outcomes of strategic initiatives has inevitably led to oversights and diminished returns on investment.

Emerging techniques in artificial intelligence offer an intriguing path to more fully inform this deliberation by enhancing architects' capacity to model the future. Sophisticated predictive analytics, powered by self-improving neural networks, can rapidly process volumes of data to simulate scenarios—essentially peering into the years ahead to observe the potential ramifications of architecture decisions in their native context. Rather than view technology frameworks in static terms, machine learning allows them to be assessed as dynamic systems that interact with internal and external forces over time.

By continuously tuning predictive models against measurable results, architects can increase confidence in their application to new decisions. The ability to compress years of potential organizational development into fast-forwarding simulations grants an invaluable perspective. Technical risks, integration hurdles, and hidden costs that often undermine large-scale technology deployments could be anticipated and mitigated earlier in the planning life cycle. AI is positioned to amplify human expertise in recognizing multidimensional patterns and formulating high-impact strategies that keep complexity in check while ensuring initiatives remain targeted to serve overarching business goals.

Adoption of these AI capabilities promises to elevate enterprise architecture beyond disconnected documentation into an actively modeled discipline that guides organizations dexterously into the future by revealing the downstream effects of upstream decisions with greater clarity than ever before possible. Leaders who embrace this integration of human creativity and machine intelligence will drive more responsive and resilient transformations.

Enhanced Stakeholder Engagement

Stakeholder engagement is essential for the success of any major business initiative. Leveraging AI tools presents an opportunity to transform the way organizations interact with their stakeholders. By analyzing historical data and developing customized profiles for each stakeholder group, AI allows companies to tailor their communications and conceptual presentations specifically to the interests and priorities of their audience.

For example, when reaching out to engineering teams, proposals could highlight how new architectures could enable faster development cycles and easier maintenance. For leadership stakeholders, the focus could shift to how these changes would save costs or open new market opportunities. These specialized value propositions resonate more strongly than a one-size-fits-all pitch.

Additionally, AI helps process and integrate feedback from across an organization's diverse stakeholder ecosystem. Sentiment analysis tools can parse written and verbal comments to gauge alignment with the overarching vision. By aggregating these inputs and detecting potential points of divergence early on, businesses can proactively modify proposals and nip conflicts in the bud.

Rather than go back to the drawing board, the streamlined consensus-building enabled by AI means enterprises can push forward with agility. Architectural changes that once took months or years of delicate negotiations can now progress rapidly with stakeholder input integrated every step of the way.

With AI transforming stakeholder experiences from one-way communication to collaborative participation, companies can unlock greater commitment and enthusiasm for major initiatives like enterprise architecture overhauls. This paves the way for smoother implementations, faster value realization, and mutually beneficial relationships between organizations and their stakeholders.

Real-Time Architecture Governance

Ensuring good governance of an organization's technology landscape can be challenging, but artificial intelligence opens up new possibilities. Typically, governance in architectural frameworks like TOGAF refers to the methods and procedures organizations put in place to guarantee their technology blueprints remain comprehensive, accurate, and reliable over time. This has often relied on periodic reviews by teams of architects and technology leaders.

However, with artificial intelligence and machine learning, the vision is that continuous, real-time governance of enterprise architectures could become more feasible. Instead of periodic checks, AI systems could monitor configurations nonstop, instantly detecting any deviations from established architectural guidelines and triggering corrective actions without delay. This could allow organizations to achieve unprecedented consistency and integrity in the technology systems and processes that drive key areas of their business.

By enabling persistent supervision of things like security policies, integration touchpoints, data schemas and flows, and other critical architectural specifications, AI has the potential to automatically prevent gaps or issues before they have downstream impacts. Promising capabilities like natural language processing, pattern recognition, and predictive analytics could equip AI governance systems to not only identify compliance problems but also trace the root causes and prescribe targeted remediation plans.

With the complexity and rapid change inherent in today's technology landscapes, leveraging AI to strengthen governance could provide substantial benefits. Organizations stand to gain better mitigation of cybersecurity risks, fewer outages and errors stemming from change, and greater agility in deploying new innovations across the enterprise. By embedding intelligence and automation into the very fabric of technology oversight, the promise lies in elevated resilience, security, and responsiveness at a scale very difficult to achieve manually.

Conclusion: The AI-Driven Enterprise— Embracing the Future

W hen I reflect on the ground covered within this book, it traces an encouraging narrative arc about the continued integration of artificial intelligence into enterprise architecture. We started by recapping how the emergence of AI over recent decades has steadily strengthened its capabilities and applicability within the business sector. Focusing upon the transformative impact this has already had on revolutionizing everything from supply chains to customer interactions has been striking.

Enterprise architecture, specifically, is one area that has benefited tremendously from weaving AI more tightly into its fabric. As we saw through several detailed examples, AI has provided enterprise architecture teams with previously unthinkable tools to streamline and enhance nearly all aspects of their strategy, planning, and operations. Whether through enabling hyper-accurate simulations, providing razor-sharp analysis of interconnectivity, or automating routine reporting, AI has almost universally elevated enterprise architecture functions within organizations.

And the prospects for the future remain incredibly bright when it comes to leveraging AI across enterprise architecture. With cloud-based AI solutions becoming more robust and customizable for business needs by the day, there has never been a better time for enterprise architects to review where they can proactively build deeper AI integration into their existing tools. The actionable checklist provided in the book delivers a great starting point for any enterprise architecture team to start prioritizing quick wins vs longer-term objectives for deploying AI in their workflows.

While technological change can be intimidating, the personal narratives we explored showed how leading enterprise architects are embracing AI-driven transformation. By maintaining optimism about AI's possibilities and focusing on how it can enhance human creativity rather than replace it, they demonstrate a healthy perspective that we can all learn from. Because, ultimately, the melding of human and machine intelligence is what will propel enterprise architecture to unprecedented heights in the years ahead as AI assimilation accelerates.

I wish you all the best as an enterprise architect and I hope you use the skills and information learned from this book to improve your career further and help your organization achieve its goals.

References

A practical guide for TOGAF implementation. (n.d.). OrbusSoftware. https://www.orbussoftware.com/resources/blog/detail/a-practical-guide-for-togaf-implementation

Bosart, O., & Van der Wildt, N. (2021, July 27). *Evolving the enterprise architect role for a digital world*. McKinsey. https://www.mckinsey.com/capabilities/mckinsey-digital/our-insights/how-enterprise-architects-need-to-evolve-to-survive-in-a-digital-world

Brown, S. (2023, January 23). *Data literacy for leaders*. MIT Management Sloan School. https://mitsloan.mit.edu/ideas-made-to-matter/data-literacy-leaders

Case studies. (n.d.). The Open Group. https://pubs.opengroup.org/architecture/togaf8-doc/arch-redline/chap35.html

Crosley, N., Indrajit, R. E., & Dazki, E. (2023). TOGAF framework for an AI-enabled software house. *SinkrOn*, *8*(2), 1140–1152. https://doi.org/10.33395/sinkron.v8i2.12390

Cutieru, A. (2020, April 7). *Pioneers: 6 practices bringing AI into architecture*. ArchDaily. https://www.archdaily.com/936999/pioneers-6-practices-bringing-ai-into-architecture

Deloitte. (n.d.). *Challenges of using artificial intelligence*. Deloitte United States. https://www2.deloitte.com/us/en/pages/consulting/articles/challenges-of-using-artificial-intelligence.html

Faggella, D. (2019, April 8). *AI integration challenges - Pitfalls to AI adoption in the enterprise (Part 1 of 3).* Emerj Artificial Intelligence Research. https://emerj.com/ai-executive-guides/artificial-intelligence-integration-challenges/

50 AI terms every beginner should know. (2021, March 1). Telus International. https://www.telusinternational.com/insights/ai-data/article/50-beginner-ai-terms-you-should-know

McGinnis, D. (2019, April 1). *How the future of AI will impact business.* The 360 Blog from Salesforce. https://www.salesforce.com/blog/future-of-ai-artificial-intelligence-business-impact/

Overcoming the challenges of AI implementation. (2023, July 11). BCG Global. https://www.bcg.com/news/11june2023-overcoming-challenges-of-ai-implementation

Tung, T. (2023, June 5). *7 architecture considerations for generative AI.* Accenture. https://www.accenture.com/us-en/blogs/cloud-computing/7-generative-ai-architecture-considerations

Schmierer, R. (2023, July 13). *AI and enterprise architecture: Building the blueprint of tomorrow.* Sparx Systems North America. https://sparxsystems.us/enterprise-architecture/ai-and-enterprise-architecture-building-the-blueprint-of-tomorrow/

Strickrodt, D. (2023, October 27). *The future of enterprise architecture and AI integration.* Bizzdesign. https://bizzdesign.com/blog/the-future-of-enterprise-architecture-and-ai-integration/

West, D., & Allen, J. (2018, April 24). *How artificial intelligence is transforming the world.* Brookings. https://www.brookings.edu/articles/how-artificial-intelligence-is-transforming-the-world/

www.ingramcontent.com/pod-product-compliance
Lightning Source LLC
La Vergne TN
LVHW022333060326
832902LV00022B/4020